Praise for *Effective C#, Sec*

"Being an effective .NET developer requires one to have a deep understanding of the language of their choice. Wagner's book provides the reader with that knowledge via well-reasoned arguments and insight. Whether you're new to C# or you've been using it for years, you'll learn something new when you read this book."

—Jason Bock, Principal Consultant, Magenic

"If you're at all like me, you have collected a handful of C# language pearls that have immediately transformed your abilities as a professional developer. What you hold in your hands is quite possibly the best collection of these tips that have ever been assembled. Bill has managed to exceed my wildest expectations with the latest edition in his eponymous *Effective C#*."

—Bill Craun, Principal Consultant, Ambassador Solutions

"*Effective C#, Second Edition*, is a must-read for anyone building high performance and/or highly scalable applications. Bill has that rare and awesome ability to take an amazingly complex problem and break it down into human, digestible, and understandable chunks."

—Josh Holmes, Architect Evangelist, Microsoft

"Bill has done it again. This book is a concise collection of invaluable tips for any C# developer. Learn one tip every day, and you'll become a much better C# developer after fifty days!"

—Claudio Lassala, Lead Developer, EPS Software/CODE Magazine

"A fountain of knowledge and understanding of the C# language. Bill gives insight to what happens under the covers of the .NET runtime based on what you write in your code and teaches pragmatic practices that lead to cleaner, easier to write, and more understandable code. A great mix of tips, tricks, and deep understanding . . . that every C# developer should read."

—Brian Noyes, Chief Architect, IDesign Inc. (www.idesign.net)

"*Effective C#* is a must-have for every C# developer. Period. Its pragmatic advice on code design is invaluable."

—Shawn Wildermuth, Microsoft MVP (C#), Author, Trainer, and Speaker

"In this book Bill Wagner provides practical explanations of how to use the most important features in the C# language. His deep knowledge and sophisticated communication skills illuminate the new features in C# so that you can use them to write programs that are more concise and easier to maintain."

—Charlie Calvert, Microsoft C# Community Program Manager

Effective C#

Third Edition

Effective C#

50 Specific Ways to Improve Your C#

Third Edition

Bill Wagner

✦✦Addison-Wesley

Boston • Columbus • Indianapolis • New York • San Francisco • Amsterdam • Cape Town
Dubai • London • Madrid • Milan • Munich • Paris • Montreal • Toronto • Delhi • Mexico City
São Paulo • Sydney • Hong Kong • Seoul • Singapore • Taipei • Tokyo

For information about buying this title in bulk quantities, or for special sales opportunities (which may include electronic versions; custom cover designs; and content particular to your business, training goals, marketing focus, or branding interests), please contact our corporate sales department at corpsales@pearsoned.com or (800) 382-3419.

For government sales inquiries, please contact governmentsales@pearsoned.com.

For questions about sales outside the U.S., please contact intlcs@pearson.com.

Visit us on the Web: informit.com/aw

Library of Congress Control Number: 2016953545

ISBN-13: 978-0-672-33787-1
ISBN-10: 0-672-33787-8

1   16

To Marlene, who continues to provide inspiration and support for everything we do together.

Contents at a Glance

Contents

Introduction

The C# community is very different in 2016 from what it was in 2004 when the first edition of *Effective C#* was published. There are many more developers using C#. A large contingent of the C# community is now seeing C# as their first professional language. They aren't approaching C# with a set of ingrained habits formed using a different language. The community has a much broader range of experience. New graduates all the way to professionals with decades of experience are using C#. C# now runs on multiple platforms. You can build server applications, Web sites, desktop applications, and mobile applications for multiple platforms in the C# language.

I organized this third edition of *Effective C#* by taking into account both the changes in the language and the changes in the C# community. *Effective C#* does not take you on a historical journey through the changes in the language. Rather, I provide advice on how to use the current C# language. The items that have been removed from this edition are those that aren't as relevant in today's C# language, or to today's applications. The new items cover the new language and framework features, and those practices the community has learned from building several versions of software products using C#. Readers of earlier editions will note that content from the first edition of *More Effective C#* is included in this edition, and a larger number of items have been removed. With this edition, I'm reorganizing both books, and a new edition of *More Effective C#* will cover other concepts. Overall, these 50 items are a set of recommendations that will help you use C# more effectively as a professional developer.

This book assumes C# 6.0, but it is not an exhaustive treatment of the new language features. Like all books in the Effective Software Development Series, it offers practical advice on how to use these features to solve problems you're likely to encounter every day. I specifically cover C# 6.0 features where new language features introduce new and better ways to write common idioms. Internet searches may still point to earlier solutions that have years of history. I specifically point out older recommendations and why language enhancements enable better ways.

Many of the recommendations in this book can be validated by Roslyn-based Analyzers and Code Fixes. I maintain a repository of them here: https://github.com/BillWagner/EffectiveCSharpAnalyzers. If you have ideas or want to contribute, write an issue or send me a pull request.

Who Should Read This Book?

Effective C# was written for professional developers who use C# as part of their daily toolset. It assumes you are familiar with the C# syntax and the language's features. This book does not include tutorial instruction on language features. Instead, it discusses how you can integrate all the features of the current version of the C# language into your everyday development.

In addition to language features, I assume you have some knowledge of the Common Language Runtime (CLR) and Just-In-Time (JIT) compiler.

About The Content

There are language constructs you'll use every day in almost every C# program you write. Chapter 1, "C# Language Idioms," covers those language idioms you'll use so often they should feel like well-worn tools in your hands. These are the building blocks of every type you create and every algorithm you implement.

Working in a managed environment doesn't mean the environment absolves you of all your responsibilities. You still must work with the environment to create correct programs that satisfy the stated performance requirements. It's not just about performance testing and performance tuning. Chapter 2, ".NET Resource Management," teaches you the design idioms that enable you to work with the environment to achieve those goals before detailed optimization begins.

Generics are the enabling technology for everything else added to the C# language since C# 2.0. Chapter 3, "Working with Generics," covers generics as a replacement for `System.Object` and casts and then moves on to discuss advanced techniques such as constraints, generic specialization, method constraints, and backward compatibility. You'll learn several techniques in which generics will make it easier to express your design intent.

Chapter 4, "Working with LINQ," explains LINQ, query syntax, and related features. You'll see when to use extension methods to separate contracts from implementation, how to use C# closures effectively, and how to program with anonymous types. You'll learn how the compiler maps query keywords to method calls, how to distinguish between delegates and expression trees (and convert between them when needed), and how to escape queries when you're looking for scalar results.

Chapter 5, "Exception Practices," provides guidance on managing exceptions and errors in modern C# programs. You'll learn how to ensure that errors are reported properly and how to leave program state consistent and ideally unchanged when errors occur. You'll learn how to provide a better debugging experience for developers who use your code.

Code Conventions

Showing code in a book still requires making some compromises for space and clarity. I've tried to distill the samples down to illustrate the particular point of the sample. Often that means eliding other portions of a class or a method. Sometimes that will include eliding error recovery code for space. Public methods should validate their parameters and other inputs, but that code is usually elided for space. Similar space considerations remove validation of method calls and `try/finally` clauses that would often be included in complicated algorithms.

I also usually assume most developers can find the appropriate namespace when samples use one of the common ones. You can safely assume that every sample implicitly includes the following `using` statements:

```
using System;
using static System.Console;
using System.Collections.Generic;
using System.Linq;
using System.Text;
```

Providing Feedback

Despite my best efforts, and the efforts of the people who have reviewed the text, errors may have crept into the text or samples. If you believe you have found an error, please contact me at bill@thebillwagner.com, or on

Twitter @billwagner. Errata will be posted at http://thebillwagner.com/Resources/EffectiveCS. Many of the items in this book are the result of email and Twitter conversations with other C# developers. If you have questions or comments about the recommendations, please contact me. Discussions of general interest will be covered on my blog at http://thebillwagner.com/blog.

Register your copy of *Effective C#, Third Edition*, at informit.com for convenient access to downloads, updates, and corrections as they become available. To start the registration process, go to informit.com/register and log in or create an account. Enter the product ISBN (9780672337871) and click Submit. Once the process is complete, you will find any available bonus content under "Registered Products."

Acknowledgments

There are many people to whom I owe thanks for their contributions to this book. I've been privileged to be part of an amazing C# community over the years. Everyone on the C# Insiders mailing list (whether inside or outside Microsoft) has contributed ideas and conversations that made this a better book.

I must single out a few members of the C# community who directly helped me with ideas, and with turning ideas into concrete recommendations. Conversations with Jon Skeet, Dustin Campbell, Kevin Pilch-Bisson, Jared Parsons, Scott Allen, and, most importantly, Mads Torgersen are the basis for many new ideas in this edition.

I had a wonderful team of technical reviewers for this edition. Jason Bock, Mark Michaelis, and Eric Lippert pored over the text and the samples to ensure the quality of the book you now hold. Their reviews were thorough and complete, which is the best anyone can hope for. Beyond that, they added recommendations that helped me explain many of the topics better.

The team at Addison-Wesley is a dream to work with. Trina Macdonald is a fantastic editor, taskmaster, and the driving force behind anything that gets done. She leans on Mark Renfro and Olivia Basegio heavily, and so do I. Their contributions created the quality of the finished manuscript from the front cover to the back, and everything in between. Curt Johnson continues to do an incredible job marketing technical content. No matter what format of this book you chose, Curt has had something to do with its existence.

It's an honor, once again, to be part of Scott Meyers's series. He goes over every manuscript and offers suggestions and comments for improvement. He is incredibly thorough, and his experience in software, although not in C#, means he finds any areas where I haven't explained an item clearly or fully justified a recommendation. His feedback, as always, is invaluable.

My family gave up time with me so that I could finish this manuscript. My wife, Marlene, gave up countless hours while I went off to write or create samples. Without her support, I never would have finished this or any other book. Nor would it be as satisfying to finish.

About the Author

Bill Wagner is one of the world's foremost C# developers and a member of the ECMA C# Standards Committee. He is president of the Humanitarian Toolbox, has been awarded Microsoft Regional Director and .NET MVP for 11 years, and was recently appointed to the .NET Foundation Advisory Council. Wagner has worked with companies ranging from start-ups to enterprises improving the software development process and growing their software development teams. He is currently with Microsoft, working on the .NET Core content team. He creates learning materials for developers interested in the C# language and .NET Core. Bill earned a B.S. in computer science from the University of Illinois at Champaign-Urbana.

1 | C# Language Idioms

Why should you change what you are doing today if it works? The answer is that you can be better. You change tools or languages because you can be more productive. You don't realize the expected gains if you don't change your habits. This is harder when the new language, C#, has so much in common with a familiar language, such as C++ or Java. C# is another curly-braced language, making it easy to fall into the same idioms you used in other languages in the same family. That will prevent you from getting the most out of C#. The C# language has evolved since its first commercial release in 2001. It's now much farther removed from C++ or Java than it was in its original release. If you are approaching C# from another language, you need to learn the C# idioms so that the language works with you, rather than against you. This chapter discusses the habits that you should change—and what you should do instead.

Item 1: Prefer Implicitly Typed Local Variables

Implicitly typed local variables were added to the C# language to support anonymous types. A second reason for using implicitly typed locals is that some queries create results that are an `IQueryable<T>`, whereas others return `IEnumerable<T>`. If you coerce an `IQueryable<T>` collection into an `IEnumerable<T>` collection, you miss out on any enhancements provided by the `IQueryProvider` (see Item 42). Using `var` also improves a developer's comprehension of the code. `Dictionary<int, Queue<string>>` doesn't add much comprehension, but the variable name `jobsQueuedByRegion` does.

I prefer `var` and use it to declare many local variables because I find that it focuses the developer's attention on the important part (the semantic meaning) and not on the particulars of a variable's type. The compiler still warns me if I have created any construct that doesn't type-check. Variable type safety is not the same as developers writing full type names. In many cases, the differences between `IQueryable` and `IEnumerable` do not add any information to you as a developer. However, if you try to tell the compiler which type it is, you'll find that you can change the behavior by getting it wrong (see Item 42). There are times when it's better to use implicitly typed variables, because the compiler will pick a better type than you will. At other times, however, overusing var only decreases the readability of your code. Even worse, using implicitly typed variables can lead to subtle conversion bugs.

Local type inference doesn't have any real effect on the static typing used in C#. Why is that? First, you need to understand that local type inference is not the same thing as dynamic typing. Variables declared with var are not dynamic but instead are implicitly declared with the type of the right side of the assignment. With var, you are not telling the compiler which type you're creating; the compiler declares the type for you.

Let's begin with the problem of readability. Many times, the type of a local variable is clear from its initialization statement:

```
var foo = new MyType();
```

Any competent developer can tell the type of `foo` from the declaration. Similarly, most factory methods are clear:

```
var thing = AccountFactory.CreateSavingsAccount();
```

However, in some cases, the return type might not always be clear from the method name:

```
var result = someObject.DoSomeWork(anotherParameter);
```

Of course, that's a contrived example, and I hope that most of the methods in your codebase have names that give a better indication of what's returned. Even in this contrived example, a better variable name would give most developers a better indication of the meaning:

```
var HighestSellingProduct = someObject
    .DoSomeWork(anotherParameter);
```

Even without any type information, most developers would correctly assume the type of `Product`.

Depending on the actual signature of `DoSomeWork`, of course, `HighestSellingProduct` might not actually be a `Product`. It might be any class derived from `Product` or even any interface implemented by `Product`. The compiler believes that `HighestSellingProduct` is whatever type it has been told by the method signature for `DoSomeWork`.

It doesn't matter that the runtime type is actually `Product`. When the compile-time type is different from the runtime type, the compiler always wins. You don't get a say unless you use some kind of cast.

We've started to enter the realm where `var` introduces questions of readability. Introducing `var` as the variable type storing the returned value from a method is one of the ways that the use of `var` can confuse developers reading your code. A human reading the code will assume one type. At runtime, the human may be correct. But the compiler does not have the luxury of examining the runtime type of the object. The compiler examines the compile-time type and infers the type of the local variable based on those declarations. What's changed is that now the compiler determines the declared type of the variable. When you declare the type yourself, other developers can see the declared type. In contrast, when you use `var`, the compiler determines the type, but developers may not see the type written. Because of the way you've written your code, the human reader and the compiler come to different conclusions about the types involved. That will lead to maintenance errors and avoidable bugs.

Let's continue looking at problems caused by implicitly typed locals when you declare variables of built-in numeric types. There are numerous conversions between the built-in numeric types. Widening conversions, such as from `float` to `double`, are always safe. There are also narrowing conversions, such as from `long` to `int`, that involve a loss of precision. By explicitly declaring the types of all numeric variables, you retain some control over the types used, and you help the compiler warn you about possible dangerous conversions.

Examine this small bit of code:

```
var f = GetMagicNumber();
var total = 100 * f / 6;
Console.WriteLine(
    $"Declared Type: {total.GetType().Name}, Value: {total}");
```

What is `total`? It depends on the type returned from `GetMagicNumber`. Here are five outputs, all from different declarations of `GetMagicNumber`:

```
Declared Type: Double, Value: 166.666666666667
Declared Type: Single, Value: 166.6667
Declared Type: Decimal, Value: 166.6666666666666666666666667
Declared Type: Int32, Value: 166
Declared Type: Int64, Value: 166
```

The differences in the type are caused by the way the compiler infers the type of f, which modifies the inferred type of total. The compiler gives f the same type that it gives the declared return type of GetMagicNumber(). Because the constants used in the calculation of total are literals, the compiler converts those literals to the type of f, and the calculation is done using the rules appropriate for that type. The different rules of the different types create the different answers.

This isn't a problem with the language. The C# compiler is doing exactly what you requested. By using local type inference, you told the compiler that it knew more about your types than you did. It made the best decision it could based on the right side of the assignment. When you work with built-in numeric types, you need to be very careful. That's because many implicit conversions are available on numeric types. Furthermore, because the various numeric types have different degrees of precision, it's not only readability that suffers but also accuracy.

Of course, it's not the use of var that causes the problem. The cause is that it's not clear from reading the code which type is returned by GetMagicNumber() and which built-in conversions may be in play. The same problems occur when the variable declaration f is removed from the method:

```
var total = 100 * f / 6;
Console.WriteLine(
    $"Declared Type: {total.GetType().Name}, Value: {total}");
```

And it doesn't matter if you explicitly declare the type for total:

```
double total = 100 * GetMagicNumber() / 6;
Console.WriteLine(
    $"Declared Type: {total.GetType().Name}, Value: {total}");
```

The type for total is double, but the result may still be rounded if GetMagicNumber() returns an integer value.

The problem is that developers can't see the actual type of the return value from GetMagicNumber() and can't easily determine which numeric conversions have been performed.

Contrast that with the results of the same routine if you explicitly declare the expected return type of GetMagicNumber(). Now the compiler tells you whether your assumptions are wrong. If there is an implicit conversion from the return type of GetMagicNumber() to the declared type of f, it just works. That would be the case if f were declared as a decimal and `GetMagicNumber()` returned an `int`. However, if there is not an implicit conversion, you'll receive a compiler error. You must change your assumptions. That will give you the chance to look at the code and understand the conversions that should be in place.

That one example shows the scenarios when local variable type inference can make it harder for developers who are maintaining code. The compiler works in the same way, and it is the tool that performs the type checking. However, developers can't easily see which rules and conversions apply. In these situations, local type inference can hamper the view of the types involved.

Sometimes, though, the compiler may be smarter than you are in terms of picking the best type for a variable. Examine this simple routine, which retrieves customer names starting with some string from a database:

```
public IEnumerable<string> FindCustomersStartingWith1(
string start)
{
    IEnumerable<string> q =
        from c in db.Customers
        select c.ContactName;

    var q2 = q.Where(s => s.StartsWith(start));
    return q2;
}
```

This code has a serious performance problem. The original query, which defines the entire list of customer contact names, has been declared by the developer as `IEnumerable<string>`. Because the query is running against a database, it's actually in `IQueryable<string>`. However, by strongly declaring the return value, you've lost that information. `IQueryable<T>` derives from `IEnumerable<T>`, so the compiler does not even warn you about this assignment. Yet when the second portion of the query is compiled, `Enumerable.Where` will be used, rather than `Queryable.Where`. In this case, the compiler would have correctly determined a better type (`IQueryable<string>`) than the one you forced on it (`IEnumerable<string>`). If you were wrong in such a way that there was no implicit conversion from `IQueryable<string>`, then the compiler would give you an error. However, because `IQueryable<T>` derives from `IEnumerable<T>`, the compiler allows the conversion, letting you hurt yourself.

The second query does not call `Queryable.Where`; instead, it calls `Enumerable.Where`. That has a large negative implication for performance. In Item 42, you will learn that `IQueryable` composes multiple query expression trees into a single operation that can be executed at once, often at the remote server where the data is located. In this instance, the second portion of the query (the `where` clause) sees the source as an `IEnumerable<string>`. That change is significant, because only the first part of the query is built on the remote machine. The entire list of customer names will be returned from the source. The second statement (the `where` clause) locally examines the entire list of customer contact names and returns only those matching the search string.

Contrast that with this version:

```
public IEnumerable<string> FindCustomersStartingWith
    (string start)
{
    var q =
        from c in db.Customers
        select c.ContactName;

    var q2 = q.Where(s => s.StartsWith(start));
    return q2;
}
```

Now `q` is an `IQueryable<string>`. The compiler infers the return type because of the source of the query. The second statement composes the query, adding the `Where` clause to the query, and holds a new, more complete expression tree. The actual data is retrieved only when the caller executes the query by enumerating the results. The expression to filter the query gets passed to the data source, and the result sequence contains only those contact names that match the filter. Any network traffic is reduced, and the query is more efficient. This is a contrived example and you would likely create a single query, but real-life queries may be composed of multiple methods.

This miraculous change is that `q` is now declared (by the compiler) as `IQueryable<string>` instead of `IEnumerable<string>`. Extension methods cannot be virtual, and the dispatch does not depend on the runtime type of the object. Instead, extension methods are static methods, and the compiler decides which method is the best match based on the compile-time type and not the runtime type. There's no late binding mechanism going on here. Even if the runtime type contains instance members that would match the call, they're not visible to the compiler and therefore are not candidates.

It's important to note that any extension method can be written to examine the runtime type of its parameters. Extension methods could create a different implementation based on the runtime type. In fact, `Enumerable.Reverse()` does just that to get increased performance when the parameter implements either `IList<T>` or `ICollection<T>` (see Item 3 later in this chapter).

You, the developer, must decide whether letting the compiler silently declare the compile-time type of the variable harms readability. If not being able to immediately see the exact type of a local variable creates ambiguity when someone reads the code, it's best to declare that type explicitly. However, in many cases, the code clearly conveys the semantic information about the variable. In the examples you've seen, you know that `q` is a sequence of contact names (which happen to be strings). The semantic information is clear from the initialization statement. That is often the case when a variable is initialized from a query expression. Whenever the semantic information of the variable is clear, you can use `var`. Going back to my first point, you should avoid `var` when the initialization expression does not clearly show developers the semantic information about the variable but an explicit type declaration does convey that information.

In short, it's best to declare local variables using `var` unless developers (including you, in the future) need to see the declared type to understand the code. The title of this item says "prefer," not "always." I recommend explicitly declaring all numeric types (`int`, `float`, `double`, and others) rather than using a `var` declaration. For everything else, just use `var`. Merely typing more keystrokes—to explicitly declare the type—doesn't promote type safety or improve readability. You may also introduce inefficiencies that the compiler will avoid if you pick the wrong declared type.

Item 2: Prefer `readonly` to `const`

C# has two different versions of constants: **compile-time** constants and **runtime** constants. They have very different behaviors, and using the wrong one will cost you. You should prefer runtime constants to compile-time constants. Compile-time constants are slightly faster, but far less flexible, than runtime constants. Reserve the compile-time constants for when performance is critical and the value of the constant will never change between releases.

You declare runtime constants with the `readonly` keyword. Compile-time constants are declared with the `const` keyword:

```
// Compile-time constant:
public const int Millennium = 2000;


// Runtime constant:
public static readonly int ThisYear = 2004;
```

The code above shows both kinds of constants at the class or `struct` scope. Compile-time constants can also be declared inside methods. Read-only constants cannot be declared with method scope.

The differences in the behavior of compile-time and runtime constants follow from how they are accessed. A compile-time constant is replaced with the value of that constant in your object code. This construct:

```
if (myDateTime.Year == Millennium)
```

compiles to the same Microsoft Intermediate Language (MSIL, or IL) as if you had written this:

```
if (myDateTime.Year == 2000)
```

Runtime constants are evaluated at runtime. The IL generated when you reference a read-only constant references the `readonly` variable, not the value.

This distinction places several restrictions on when you are allowed to use either type of constant. Compile-time constants can be used only for the built-in integral and floating-point types, enums, or strings. These are the only types that enable you to assign meaningful constant values in initializers. These primitive types are the only ones that can be replaced with literal values in the compiler-generated IL. The following construct does not compile. You cannot initialize a compile-time constant using the `new` operator, even when the type being initialized is a value type:

```
// Does not compile, use readonly instead:
private const DateTime classCreation = new
    DateTime(2000, 1, 1, 0, 0, 0);
```

Compile-time constants are limited to numbers, strings, and null. Read-only values are also constants in that they cannot be modified after the constructor has executed. But read-only values are different in that they are assigned at runtime. You have much more flexibility when working with runtime constants. For one thing, runtime constants can be any type. You must initialize them in a constructor, or you can use an initializer. You can make readonly values of the DateTime structures; you cannot create DateTime values with const.

You can use readonly values for instance constants, storing different values for each instance of a class type. Compile-time constants are, by definition, static constants.

The most important distinction is that readonly values are resolved at runtime. The IL generated when you reference a readonly constant references the readonly variable, not the value. This difference has far-reaching implications for maintenance over time. Compile-time constants generate the same IL as though you used the numeric constants in your code, even across assemblies: A constant in one assembly is still replaced with the value when used in another assembly.

The way in which compile-time and runtime constants are evaluated affects runtime compatibility. Suppose you have defined both const and readonly fields in an assembly named Infrastructure:

```
public class UsefulValues
{
    public static readonly int StartValue = 5;
    public const int EndValue = 10;
}
```

In another assembly, you reference these values:

```
for (int i = UsefulValues.StartValue;
    i < UsefulValues.EndValue; i++)
    Console.WriteLine("value is {0}", i);
```

If you run your little test, you see the following obvious output:

```
Value is 5
Value is 6
...
Value is 9
```

Time passes, and you release a new version of the Infrastructure assembly with the following changes:

```
public class UsefulValues
{
    public static readonly int StartValue = 105;
    public const int EndValue = 120;
}
```

You distribute the Infrastructure assembly without rebuilding your Application assembly. You expect to get this:

```
Value is 105
Value is 106
...
Value is 119
```

In fact, you get no output at all. The loop now uses the value 105 for its start and 10 for its end condition. The C# compiler placed the `const` value of 10 into the Application assembly instead of a reference to the storage used by `EndValue`. Contrast that with the `StartValue` value. It was declared as `readonly`; it gets resolved at runtime. Therefore, the Application assembly makes use of the new value without even recompiling the Application assembly; simply installing an updated version of the Infrastructure assembly is enough to change the behavior of all clients using that value. Updating the value of a public constant should be viewed as an interface change. You must recompile all code that references that constant. Updating the value of a read-only constant is an implementation change; it is binary compatible with existing client code.

On the other hand, sometimes you really mean for a value to be fixed at compile time. For example, consider a program that performs tax calculations. Multiple assemblies may be involved in tax calculations, and the regulations that govern those calculations may change at any time. This leads to a situation where different assemblies have been updated in different cycles because regulations may have affected only some algorithms. You want each class to report on which regulation date it was last updated. By using a compile-time constant to track the appropriate regulation revision, you can make sure that each algorithm correctly reports when it was last updated.

One class would hold the master revisions:

```
public class RevisionInfo
{
    public const string RevisionString = "1.1.R9";
    public const string RevisionMessage = "Updated Fall 2015";
}
```

And any class that performs different calculations can report from this master revision information:

```
public class ComputationEngine
{
    public string Revision = RevisionInfo.RevisionString;
    public string RevisionMessage = RevisionInfo.
        RevisionMessage;


    // Other APIs elided
}
```

Any rebuild will update the revision numbers to the latest version. However, if individual assemblies are delivered as patches, the new patches would have new revisions, but any assembly that has not been updated would not be affected.

The final advantage of using const instead of readonly is performance: Known constant values can generate slightly more efficient code than the variable accesses necessary for readonly values. However, any gains are slight and should be weighed against the decreased flexibility. Be sure to profile performance differences before giving up the flexibility. (Try BenchmarkDotNet, available at https://github.com/PerfDotNet/ BenchmarkDotNet, if you don't already have a favorite tool.)

You'll encounter similar tradeoffs between runtime and compile-time processing of constant values when you use named and optional parameters. The default values for optional parameters are placed in the call site just like the default values for compile-time constants (those declared with const). Like working with readonly and const values, you'll want to be careful with changes to the values of optional parameters (see Item 10 later in this chapter).

const must be used when the value must be available at compile time: attribute parameters, switch case labels, and enum definitions, and those rare times when you mean to define a value that does not change from release to release. For everything else, prefer the increased flexibility of readonly constants.

Item 3: Prefer the `is` or `as` Operators to Casts

By embracing C#, you've embraced static typing. That is almost always a good thing. Strong typing means you expect the compiler to find type mismatches in your code. That also means your applications do not need to perform as much type checking at runtime. But sometimes runtime type checking is unavoidable. There will be times in C# when you write functions that take `object` parameters because the framework defines the method signature for you. You likely need to attempt to cast those objects to other types, either classes or interfaces. You have two choices: Use the `as` operator, or force the compiler to bend to your will using a cast. You also have a defensive variant: You can test a conversion with `is` and then use `as` or casts to convert it.

The correct choice is to use the `as` operator whenever you can because it is safer than blindly casting and is more efficient at runtime. The `as` and `is` operators do not perform any user-defined conversions. They succeed only if the runtime type matches the sought type; they rarely construct a new object to satisfy a request. (The `as` operator will create a new type when converting a boxed value type to an unboxed nullable value type.)

Take a look at an example. You write a piece of code that needs to convert an arbitrary object into an instance of `MyType`. You could write it this way:

```
object o = Factory.GetObject();

// Version one:
MyType t = o as MyType;

if (t != null)
{
    // work with t, it's a MyType.
}
else
{
    // report the failure.
}
```

Or you could write this:

```
object o = Factory.GetObject();

// Version two:
try
{
    MyType t;
    t = (MyType)o;
    // work with T, it's a MyType.
}
catch (InvalidCastException)
{
    // report the conversion failure.
}
```

You'll agree that the first version is simpler and easier to read. It does not have the `try`/`catch` clause, so you avoid both the overhead and the code. Notice that the cast version must check `null` in addition to catching exceptions. `null` can be converted to any reference type using a cast, but the `as` operator returns `null` when used on a `null` reference. So, with casts, you need to check `null` and catch exceptions. Using `as`, you simply check the returned reference against `null`.

The biggest difference between the `as` operator and the cast operator is how user-defined conversions are treated. The `as` and `is` operators examine the runtime type of the object being converted; they do not perform any other operations, except boxing when necessary. If a particular object is not the requested type or is derived from the requested type, they fail. Casts, on the other hand, can use conversion operators to convert an object to the requested type. This includes any built-in numeric conversions. Casting a `long` to a `short` can lose information.

The same problems are lurking when you cast user-defined types. Consider this type:

```
public class SecondType
{
    private MyType _value;

    // other details elided

    // Conversion operator.
    // This converts a SecondType to
```

```
// a MyType, see item 29.
public static implicit operator
MyType(SecondType t)
{
    return t._value;
}
}
```

Suppose an object of SecondType is returned by the Factory.GetObject() function in the first code snippet:

```
object o = Factory.GetObject();

// o is a SecondType:
MyType t = o as MyType; // Fails. o is not MyType

if (t != null)
{
    // work with t, it's a MyType.
}
else
{
    // report the failure.
}

// Version two:
try
{
    MyType t1;
    t1 = (MyType)o; // Fails. o is not MyType
    // work with t1, it's a MyType.
}
catch (InvalidCastException)
{
    // report the conversion failure.
}
```

Both versions fail. But I told you that casts will perform user-defined conversions. You'd think the cast would succeed. You're right—it should succeed if you think that way. But it fails because your compiler is generating code based on the compile-time type of the object, o. The compiler knows nothing about the runtime type of o; it views o as an instance of `object`. The compiler sees that there is no user-defined conversion from `object` to `MyType`. It checks the definitions of `object` and `MyType`. Lacking any user-defined conversion, the compiler generates the code to examine the runtime type of `o` and checks whether that type is a `MyType`. Because `o` is a `SecondType` object, that fails. The compiler does not check to see whether the actual runtime type of `o` can be converted to a `MyType` object.

You could make the conversion from `SecondType` to `MyType` succeed if you wrote the code snippet like this:

```
object o = Factory.GetObject();

// Version three:
SecondType st = o as SecondType;
try
{
    MyType t;
    t = (MyType)st;
    // work with T, it's a MyType.
}
catch (InvalidCastException)
{
    // report the failure.
}
```

You should never write this ugly code. It is a better programming practice to avoid catching exceptions that could be avoided by appropriate checks beforehand. It does illustrate a common problem. Although you would never write this, you can use an `object` parameter to a function that expects the proper conversions:

```
object o = Factory.GetObject();
DoStuffWithObject(o);

private static void DoStuffWithObject(object o)
{
    try
    {
        MyType t;
        t = (MyType)o; // Fails. o is not MyType
        // work with T, it's a MyType.
    }
```

```
    catch (InvalidCastException)
    {
        // report the conversion failure.
    }
}
```

Remember that user-defined conversion operators operate only on the compile-time type of an object, not on the runtime type. It does not matter that a conversion between the runtime type of o and MyType exists. The compiler just doesn't know or care. This statement has different behavior, depending on the declared type of st:

```
t = (MyType)st;
```

The next statement returns the same result, no matter what the declared type of st is. So, you should prefer as to casts—it's more consistent. In fact, if the types are not related by inheritance, but a user-defined conversion operator exists, the following statement will generate a compiler error:

```
t = st as MyType;
```

Now that you know to use as when possible, let's discuss when you can't use it. The following program fragment won't compile:

```
object o = Factory.GetValue();
int i = o as int; // Does not compile.
```

That's because ints are value types and can never be null. What value of int should be stored in i if o is not an integer? Any value you pick might also be a valid integer. Therefore, as can't be used. You might think you're stuck using exception-throwing cast operations. Instead, use the as operator to convert to a nullable type, and then check that nullable type against null:

```
object o = Factory.GetValue();
var i = o as int?;
if (i != null)
    Console.WriteLine(i.Value);
```

This technique works whenever the left operand of the as operator is a value type, or any nullable value type.

Now that you know the differences among is, as, and casts, which operator do you suppose the foreach loop uses? foreach loops can operate on nongeneric IEnumerable sequences and have the type coercion built into the iteration. (You should prefer the type-safe generic versions whenever possible. The nongeneric version exists for historical purposes, and to support some late binding scenarios.)

```
public void UseCollection(IEnumerable theCollection)
{
    foreach (MyType t in theCollection)
        t.DoStuff();
}
```

The `foreach` statement uses a cast operation to perform conversions from an object to the type used in the loop. The code generated by the `foreach` statement roughly equates to this hand-coded version:

```
public void UseCollectionV2(IEnumerable theCollection)
{
    IEnumerator it = theCollection.GetEnumerator();
    while (it.MoveNext())
    {
        MyType t = (MyType)it.Current;
        t.DoStuff();
    }
}
```

The `foreach` statement needs to use casts to support both value types and reference types. By choosing the cast operator, the `foreach` statement exhibits the same behavior, no matter what the destination type is. However, because a cast is used, `foreach` loops can cause an `InvalidCastException` to be thrown.

Because `IEnumerator.Current` returns a `System.Object`, which has no conversion operators, none is eligible for this test. A collection of `SecondType` objects cannot be used in the previous `UseCollection()` function because the conversion fails, as you already saw. The `foreach` statement (which uses a cast) does not examine the casts that are available in the runtime type of the objects in the collection. It examines only the conversions available in the `System.Object` class (the type returned by `IEnumerator.Current`) and the declared type of the loop variable (in this case, `MyType`).

Finally, sometimes you want to know the exact type of an object, not just whether the current type can be converted to a target type. The `is` operator follows the rules of polymorphism: `fido is Animal` returns `true` if `fido` is a `Dog` (which derives from `Animal`). The `GetType()` method gets the runtime type of an object. It is a stricter test than the `is` or `as` statement provides. `GetType()` returns the type of the object and can be compared to a specific type.

Consider this function again:

```
public void UseCollectionV3(IEnumerable theCollection)
{
    foreach (MyType t in theCollection)
        t.DoStuff();
}
```

If you made a `NewType` class derived from `MyType`, a collection of `NewType` objects would work just fine in the `UseCollection` function:

```
public class NewType : MyType
{
    // contents elided.
}
```

If you mean to write a function that works with all objects that are instances of `MyType`, that's fine. If you mean to write a function that works only with `MyType` objects exactly, you should use the exact type for comparison. Here, you would do that inside the `foreach` loop. The most common time when the exact runtime type is important is when doing equality tests. In most other comparisons, the `.isinst` comparisons provided by `as` and `is` are semantically correct.

The .NET Base Class Library (BCL) contains a method for converting elements in a sequence using the same type of operations: `Enumerable .Cast<T>()` converts each element in a sequence that supports the classic `IEnumerable` interface:

```
IEnumerable collection = new List<int>()
    { 1,2,3,4,5,6,7,8,9,10};

var small = from int item in collection
            where item < 5
            select item;

var small2 = collection.Cast<int>().Where(item => item < 5).
    Select(n => n);
```

The query generates the same method calls as the last line of code above. In both cases, the `Cast<T>` method converts each item in the sequence to the target type. The `Enumerable.Cast<T>` method uses an old-style cast rather than the as operator. Using the old-style cast means that `Cast<T>` does not need to have a class constraint. Using the as operator would be limiting, and rather than implement different `Cast<T>` methods, the BCL team chose to create a single method using the old-style cast operator. It's a tradeoff you should consider in your code as well. On those occasions when you need to convert an object that is one of the generic type parameters, you'll need to weigh the necessity of a class constraint against the different behavior of using the cast operator.

Also, note that casts with generics do not make use of any conversion operators. That means `Cast<double>()` on a sequence of integers will fail. In C# 4.0 and later, the type system can be circumvented even further by using dynamic and runtime type checking. There are quite a few ways to treat objects based on expectations of known behavior rather than knowing anything about a particular type or interface supplied.

Good object-oriented practice says that you should avoid converting types, but sometimes there are no alternatives. If you can't avoid the conversions, use the language's as and is operators to express your intent more clearly. Different ways of coercing types have different rules. The is and as operators are almost always the correct semantics, and they succeed only when the object being tested is the correct type. Prefer those statements to cast operators, which can have unintended side effects and succeed or fail when you least expect it.

Item 4: Replace `string.Format()` with Interpolated Strings

Developers have been converting information stored in computers to human-readable formats from the time they began writing programs. In C#, we've been doing that using APIs whose roots can be easily traced to those that were first introduced in the C language decades ago. It's time to move away from those techniques and embrace the new string interpolation feature that was introduced in C# 6.0.

The new syntax available in C# 6.0 provides several advantages over the classic string formatting syntax. It results in more readable code. It enables the compiler to provide better static type checking, which decreases the chances of mistakes. It also provides a richer syntax for the expressions that produce the string.

`String.Format()` works, but it has several weaknesses that can lead to mistakes that don't show up until the content of the generated strings has been tested and validated. All the substitutions are based on the numbers typed into the format string. The compiler does not validate that the number of arguments matches the numbers that you have typed into the string for argument replacement. When you get that wrong, you'll get an exception thrown when you run the code.

More insidiously, the separation between the numeric notation for parameters and the position in a `params` array means that it can be hard to verify that the correct arguments are in the correct order by inspection. You must run the code and carefully validate the contents of the generated string if you want to ensure the correct behavior.

All this can be done, of course, but it takes time. You can leverage language features to make it easier to write correct code. That's what the new interpolated strings feature of the language does.

Interpolated strings have a "`$`" as the prefix before the string. Then, instead of positional indices between the `{}` characters, you can place any C# expression. This greatly improves readability. It's easy to read the replacement expressions in place in the format strings. The result is easy verification. Also, because the expressions are inline in the format string instead of in a separate array, you can't have the wrong number of arguments in the replacement array. You can't easily put the wrong expression in the wrong spot in the string.

As a bit of syntactic sugar, this is nice to have. The power of string interpolation becomes more apparent as you look at how the language feature is integrated into normal programming practices.

First of all, let's explore the syntax and limitations for the expressions that can be used for replacement strings.

I've been very careful to use the term "expression" to describe the code that you can use for replacement strings. You cannot use control flow statements (such as `if`/`else` or `while`) as replacement strings. If you need that kind of control flow, you must put it inside a method and call the method as the replacement string.

String interpolation works by executing library code that's similar to what `string.Format()` does today (see Item 5 later in this chapter for a discussion of how it handles internationalization). That includes the necessity of converting a variable to a string when needed. For example, consider this interpolated string:

```
Console.WriteLine($"The value of pi is {Math.PI}");
```

The code generated by the string interpolation will call a formatting method whose argument is a `params` array of objects. The `Math.PI` property is a `double`, which is a value type. In order to coerce that `double` to be an `Object`, it will be boxed. In code that runs often, or in tight loops, that can have a significant impact on performance (see Item 9 later in this chapter). You should use your expressions to convert these arguments to strings. That avoids the necessity to box any value types that are used in the expressions:

```
Console.WriteLine(
$"The value of pi is {Math.PI.ToString()}");
```

The text that is returned by `ToString()` may not suit your needs, so you may want to do more work with your expression to create the exact text you want. That's easy: Just modify the expression to produce the exact text you want:

```
Console.WriteLine(
$"The value of pi is {Math.PI.ToString("F2")}");
```

Part of producing the exact string you want might include other string processing, or formatting the object returned by your expression. Let's start simply by applying standard format strings. That's a matter of using the built-in formatting strings to create the output you want. Inside the {} characters, place a ":" and then the format string.

```
Console.WriteLine($"The value of pi is {Math.PI:F2}");
```

Astute readers will notice that the ":" may be part of a conditional expression. That does cause a bit of a conflict: C# will find the ":" and assume it is the beginning of a format string. The following does not compile:

```
Console.WriteLine(
  $"The value of pi is {round ? Math.PI.ToString() :
Math.PI.ToString("F2")}");
```

The answer to getting this to compile is easy. You just have to force the compiler to believe that you want a conditional expression, not the beginning of a format string. Simply put the entire conditional expression inside parentheses, and you'll get the behavior you want:

```
Console.WriteLine($@"The value of pi is {(round ?
    Math.PI.ToString() : Math.PI.ToString("F2"))}");
```

Having string interpolation embedded into the language provides lots of power. The expression used in your string interpolation can be any valid C# expression. You've already seen variables and conditional expressions. But that's just the beginning. You can use the null coalescing or the null propagation operator to handle missing values clearly:

```
Console.WriteLine(
    $"The customer's name is {c?.Name ?? "Name is missing"}");
```

Yes, string nesting inside the interpolation expression is supported. Any construct you please between the "{" and the "}" characters will be treated as C# and parsed as part of the expression (with the one exception of the ":" character that would introduce a format string).

All this is good, and when you look at it in depth, it can become a trip down a rabbit hole. The expressions that form the arguments for an interpolated string can themselves contain interpolated strings. In limited form, this is very useful. Consider this example of how you might format a string to display information about a record, or the index for a missing record:

```
string result = default(string);
Console.WriteLine($@"Record is {(records.TryGetValue(index,out
result) ? result :
$"No record found at index {index}")}");
```

In the cases when a record is missing, the false clause of the conditional uses another interpolated string to return a message indicating what index was sought.

You can also use LINQ queries (see Chapter 4, "Working with LINQ") to create the values that are used in an interpolated string. Those queries may themselves use interpolated strings to format their output:

```
var output = $@"The First five items are: {src.Take(5).Select(
n => $@"Item: {n.ToString()}").Aggregate(
(c, a) => $@"{c}{Environment.NewLine}{a}")}";
```

That last example may be a bit beyond what you'd like to see in production code. However, it does illustrate how well integrated into the language interpolated strings are. This feature is even being incorporated into the Razor View engine for ASP.NET MVC. This can make it much easier to generate HTML output in a Web application. The default MVC applications now demonstrate how string interpolation works in Razor Views. Here's one example from the control that displays information about the currently logged-in user:

```
<a asp-controller="Manage" asp-action="Index"
   title="Manage">Hello@User.GetUserName()!</a>
```

You can follow the same technique when building any of the HTML pages that make up your application. It's a more concise way to express the output that you want.

These examples show how powerful the string interpolation feature is. It is much more convenient than using the classic string formatting options. However, remember that the result of string interpolation is a string. All the values have been substituted, and you are left with a single string. That's most important if you are creating a string for a SQL command. String interpolation *does not* create a parameterized SQL query. Rather, it creates a single string object in which all the parameter values have already been included. Using string interpolation to create a SQL command is very dangerous. In fact, anytime you are using string interpolation to create a string that represents data in a way that will be interpreted by a machine, you must be very careful about the risks.

Converting the internal representation that computers use to store information as text for humans to view has been part of the programming landscape for a long time. The previous methods that we've used, even in many modern languages, can be traced directly to methods that were introduced with the C language decades ago. Using these methods can cause many potential errors. The new string interpolation feature is easier to use correctly. It's more powerful, and it easily enables techniques that are more common in modern development.

Item 5: Prefer `FormattableString` for Culture-Specific Strings

In Item 4, you learned how the new string interpolation feature in C# provides a much easier way to build textual information that combines the value of variables with some formatting information. You'll need to dive a little deeper into how this feature works in order to get the same benefits when your tasks require more explicit control when programming for different cultures and languages.

The language design team gave this issue quite a bit of thought. The goal was to create a system that supports generating text for any culture, while making it easy to write code that always generates results for a single culture. Balancing those two goals means that diving into culture and how it works with string interpolation introduces new complexities.

All the work you've done with string interpolation would lead you to assume that using the "$" syntax to create a string results in a string being produced. In most cases, that simplification works. Actually, an interpolated string literal may be implicitly converted to either a string or a formattable string.

For example, this line of code uses string interpolation to construct a string:

```
string first =
$"It's the {DateTime.Now.Day} of the {DateTime.Now.Month} month";
```

This line of code uses string interpolation to construct an object of a type derived from `FormattableString`:

```
FormattableString second =
$"It's the {DateTime.Now.Day} of the {DateTime.Now.Month} month";
```

This line of code, using an implicitly typed local variable, assumes that `third` should be a string and generates code to create a string:

```
var third =
$"It's the {DateTime.Now.Day} of the {DateTime.Now.Month} month";
```

The compiler generates different code depending on the compile-time type of the output being requested. The code that generates a string will format that string based on the current culture on the machine where the code is executed. If you run the code in the United States, the decimal separator for a `double` value will be "."; if you ran the same code in most European countries, the decimal separator would be ",".

You can use the compiler's ability to generate either a string or a `Formattable-String` to use string interpolation to format strings for any culture. Consider these two methods that convert a `FormattableString` to a string, using a particular language and culture:

```
public static string ToGerman(FormattableString src)
{
    return string.Format(null,
        System.Globalization.CultureInfo.
            CreateSpecificCulture("de-de"),
```

```
        src.Format,
        src.GetArguments());
}


public static string ToFrenchCanada(FormattableString src)
{
    return string.Format(null,
        System.Globalization.CultureInfo.
            CreateSpecificCulture("de-CA"),
        src.Format,
        src.GetArguments());
}
```

These methods accept a `FormattableString` as the only argument. When these methods are called using a `FormattableString`, they will convert that `FormattableString` to a string using the specific culture (the German culture and language, or the Canadian culture for the French language). You can also call either of these methods directly on the result of a string interpolation.

First, it's important not to overload these methods with similar versions that would take a string as an argument. If overloads are available that could take both a string and a `FormattableString`, the compiler will generate code to create a string and then call the version with the string parameter.

You will also notice that I did not create extension methods for either of the methods above. That's because the logic in the compiler that determines whether it should create a string or a `FormattableString` would create a string instead of a `FormattableString` when the result is the left side of the "." operator. One goal for string interpolation was to make it easy to use with the existing string class. However, even with that goal, the team still wanted to enable all possible globalization scenarios. Those scenarios do require a little extra work of you but are easily handled.

The string interpolation feature does support everything you need for internationalization and specific localizations. Best of all, it does so in a way that enables you to ignore the complexity when all your code generates text for the current culture. When you need a specific culture, you must explicitly tell the string interpolation to create a `FormattableString`, and then you can convert that into a string using any specific culture you want.

Item 6: Avoid String-ly Typed APIs

As we move toward more distributed programs, we must transfer more and more data between different systems. We also use many different libraries that rely on names and string identifiers to work with our data. These are very convenient methods to work with data across different platforms and different languages. However, this convenience comes with a price. Working with these APIs and libraries means losing type safety. You lose tooling support. You lose many of the benefits of a statically typed language.

The C# language design team recognized this and added the `nameof()` expression in C# 6.0. This handy little keyword replaces a symbol with a string containing its name. The most common example of this is to implement the `INotifyPropertyChanged` interface:

```
public string Name
{
    get { return name;}
    set
    {
        if (value != name)
        {
            name = value;
            PropertyChanged?.Invoke(this,
                new PropertyChangedEventArgs(nameof(Name)));
        }
    }
}
private string name;
```

With the `nameof` operator, any changes to the property name are reflected correctly in the string used in the event arguments. These are the basics of using `nameof()`.

The `nameof()` operator evaluates to the name of the symbol. It works for types, variables, interfaces, and namespaces. It can be used with unqualified names, or with a fully qualified name. There are some limitations on generic type definitions: You need to have a closed generic type where all type parameters are specified.

The `nameof` operator must work with all these items but must also have consistent behavior. The string that is returned by the `nameof` operator always returns the local name. This provides consistent behavior: Even when a variable is declared using the fully qualified name (for example, `System.Int.MaxValue`), the name returned is the local name (`MaxValue`).

Many developers have seen this basic usage and do correctly use `nameof` in those simple cases where the name of a local variable must be used in some API. But many developers miss opportunities because they follow existing habits or don't realize that the `nameof` operator can be used in different locations.

Many exception types accept the name of an argument as one of their construction parameters. Replacing the hard-coded text with `nameof` ensures that the names match even after any rename operation:

```
public static void ExceptionMessage(object thisCantBeNull)
{
    if (thisCantBeNull == null)
        throw new
            ArgumentNullException(nameof(thisCantBeNull),
            "We told you this cant be null");
}
```

Static analysis tools can also ensure that the name of the argument is in the correct position in the `Exception` constructor. Both arguments are strings, so it is easy to get that wrong.

The `nameof` operator can be used to specify the string for an attribute argument (either a positional or a named argument). It can be used when defining routes for an MVC application or Web API application. This is an excellent time to consider using a namespace as the name of a route.

The payoff of using the `nameof` operator in all these locations is that any changes or updates in the name of the symbol will be correctly reflected in the name of the variable. Static analysis tools can also find mistakes and mismatches when the name of an argument is used in the wrong location. These tools can take many forms, from diagnostics that run in an editor or IDE, to build and Continuous Integration tools, refactoring tools, and more. By retaining as much symbolic information as possible, you enable those automated tools to find and potentially fix as many types of mistakes as possible. That leaves fewer mistakes that can be found only by automated tests or human examination. That leaves all of us more time to focus on the harder problems.

Item 7: Express Callbacks with Delegates

> Me: "Son, go mow the yard. I'm going to read for a while."
> Scott: "Dad, I cleaned up the yard."
> Scott: "Dad, I put gas in the mower."
> Scott: "Dad, the mower won't start."
> Me: "I'll start it."
> Scott: "Dad, I'm done."

This little exchange illustrates callbacks. I gave my son a task, and he (repeatedly) interrupted me with the status. I did not block my own progress while I waited for him to finish each part of the task. He was able to interrupt me periodically when he had an important (or even unimportant) status to report or needed my assistance. Callbacks are used to provide feedback from a server to a client asynchronously. They might involve multithreading, or they might simply provide an entry point for synchronous updates. Callbacks are expressed using delegates in the C# language.

Delegates provide type-safe callback definitions. Although the most common use of delegates is for events, that should not be the only time you use this language feature. Anytime you need to configure the communication between classes and you desire less coupling than you get from interfaces, a delegate is the right choice. Delegates let you configure the target at runtime and notify multiple clients. A delegate is an object that contains a reference to a method. That method can be either a static method or an instance method. Using the delegate, you can communicate with one or many client objects, configured at runtime.

Callbacks and delegates are such a common idiom that the C# language provides compact syntax in the form of lambda expressions to express delegates. In addition, the .NET Framework library defines many common delegate forms using `Predicate<T>`, `Action<>`, and `Func<>`. A predicate is a Boolean function that tests a condition. A `Func<>` takes a number of parameters and produces a single result. Yes, that means a `Func<T, bool>` has the same form as a `Predicate<T>`. The compiler will not view `Predicate<T>` and `Func<T, bool>` as the same, though. In general, different delegate type definitions with the same argument and return types are different types. The compiler will not allow conversions between them. Finally, `Action<>` takes any number of parameters and has the `void` return type.

LINQ was built using these concepts. The `List<T>` class also contains many methods that make use of callbacks. Examine this code snippet:

```
List<int> numbers = Enumerable.Range(1, 200).ToList();

var oddNumbers = numbers.Find(n => n % 2 == 1);
var test = numbers.TrueForAll(n => n < 50);

numbers.RemoveAll(n => n % 2 == 0);


numbers.ForEach(item => Console.WriteLine(item));
```

The `Find()` method takes a delegate, in the form of a `Predicate<int>`, to perform a test on each element in the list. It's a simple callback. The `Find()` method tests each item, using the callback, and returns the elements that pass the test embodied in the predicate. The compiler converts the lambda expression to a delegate and uses the delegate to express the callback.

`TrueForAll()` is similar in that it applies the test to each of the elements and determines if the predicate is true for all items. `RemoveAll()` modifies the list container by removing all items for which the predicate is true.

Finally, the `List.ForEach()` method performs the specified action on each of the elements in the list. As before, the compiler converts the lambda expression into a method and creates a delegate referring to that method.

You'll find numerous examples of this concept in the .NET Framework. All of LINQ is built on delegates. Callbacks are used to handle cross-thread marshalling in Windows Presentation Foundation (WPF) and Windows Forms. Everywhere that the .NET Framework needs a single method, it will use a delegate that callers can express in the form of a lambda expression. You should follow the same example when you need a callback idiom in any of your APIs.

For historical reasons, all delegates are multicast delegates. Multicast delegates wrap all the target functions that have been added to the delegate in a single call. Two caveats apply to this construct: It is not safe in the face of exceptions, and the return value will be the return value of the last target function invoked by the multicast delegate.

Inside a multicast delegate invocation, each target is called in succession. The delegate does not catch any exceptions. Therefore, any exception that the target throws ends the delegate invocation chain.

A similar problem exists with return values. You can define delegates that have return types other than `void`. You could write a callback to check for user aborts:

```
public void LengthyOperation(Func<bool> pred)
{
    foreach (ComplicatedClass cl in container)
    {
        cl.DoLengthyOperation();
        // Check for user abort:
        if (false == pred())
            return;
    }
}
```

It works as a single delegate, but using it as a multicast is problematic:

```
Func<bool> cp = () => CheckWithUser();
cp += () => CheckWithSystem();
c.LengthyOperation(cp);
```

The value returned from invoking the delegate is the return value from the last function in the multicast chain. All other return values are ignored. The return from the `CheckWithUser()` predicate is ignored.

You address both issues by invoking each delegate target yourself. Each delegate you create contains a list of delegates. To examine the chain yourself and call each one, iterate the invocation list:

```
public void LengthyOperation2(Func<bool> pred)
{
    bool bContinue = true;
    foreach (ComplicatedClass cl in container)
    {
        cl.DoLengthyOperation();
        foreach (Func<bool> pr in pred.GetInvocationList())
            bContinue &= pr();

        if (!bContinue)
            return;
    }
}
```

In this case, I've defined the semantics so that each delegate must be true for the iteration to continue.

Delegates provide the best way to use callbacks at runtime, with simpler requirements on client classes. You can configure delegate targets at runtime. You can support multiple client targets. Client callbacks should be implemented using delegates in .NET.

Item 8: Use the Null Conditional Operator for Event Invocations

Raising events seems like such a simple task when you first approach it. You define an event and, when necessary, simply invoke any event handlers that were attached to that event. The underlying multicast delegate object would manage the complexity of invoking all attached handlers in succession. In practice, there are many pitfalls around invoking events in such a naïve manner. What if there are no handlers attached to an event? There could even be race conditions involving the code that checks for an attached event handler and the code that invokes it. The new null conditional operator, introduced in C# 6.0, provides a much cleaner syntax for this idiom. You should change your existing habits to use the new syntax as soon as you can.

Let's look at the older syntax and what had to be done to write safe event invocation code. The simplest example of event invocation would look like this:

```
public class EventSource
{
    private EventHandler<int> Updated;

    public void RaiseUpdates()
    {
        counter++;
        Updated(this, counter);
    }

    private int counter;
}
```

This code has an obvious issue. If this object runs when no event handlers have been attached to the `Updated` event, the code will throw a `NullReferenceException`. Event handlers in C# have the `null` value when no handlers have been added to an event.

Therefore, developers needed to wrap any event invocation in a check to determine if the event handler is `null`:

```
public void RaiseUpdates()
{
    counter++;
    if (Updated != null)
        Updated(this, counter);
}
```

This code would work in almost all instances, but there's a possible bug lurking there. It's possible that it will execute the first line, where it checks the event handler against null, and find that the event handler is not null. Then, between the check and the invocation of the event, it's possible that another thread will execute and unsubscribe the single event handler. When the first thread continues execution and invokes the event handler, the handler is null. You'll still get that `NullReferenceException`. However, you'll get it more rarely, and not in easy-to-reproduce scenarios.

This bug is much harder to diagnose and fix. The code looks correct. In order to see the error, you need to have threads execute code in exactly the right order. Experienced developers have learned from harsh experience that this idiom is dangerous and have replaced it with this code:

```
public void RaiseUpdates()
{
    counter++;
    var handler = Updated;
    if (handler != null)
        handler(this, counter);
}
```

This code has been the recommended practice for raising events in .NET and C#. It works, and it's thread safe. But it has several issues in terms of readability. It's not at all obvious how this change makes the previous code thread safe.

Let's understand why this works and is thread safe.

The first line assigns the current event handler to a new local variable. That new local variable now contains a multicast delegate that refers to all the original handlers from the member variable event.

The event assignment creates a shallow copy of the right-hand side of the assignment. That shallow copy contains new copies of references to each attached event handler. In the case of an event field with no attached handlers, the right-hand side is null, and the `null` value is stored in the left side of the assignment.

If code in another thread unsubscribes from the event, the unsubscribe code modifies the event field of the class, but it does not remove the event handler from the local variable. The local variable still has all the event subscribers that were present at the time of the copy.

Therefore, when this code checks for `null`, it's viewing a snapshot of the event subscribers at the time the copy was made. Then the event is conditionally invoked, and all event handlers that were subscribed at the time of the copy will be invoked.

It works, but it's not easy for new .NET developers to see and understand. Also, it must be replicated everywhere the event is raised. Alternatively, you can create a private method to raise the event and wrap this idiom in a private method.

That's a lot of code and a lot of cognitive overhead for a feature that should be very easy to use: event invocation.

The null conditional operator restores this action to a much simpler code construct:

```
public void RaiseUpdates()
{
    counter++;
    Updated?.Invoke(this, counter);
}
```

This code uses the null conditional operator ("?.") to safely invoke the event handlers. The "?." operator evaluates the left-hand side of the operator. If that evaluates to a non-null value, the expression on the right-hand side of the operator is executed. If the expression is null, it short-circuits and execution continues at the next statement.

It's semantically similar to the earlier construct using `if` statements. The only exception is that the left-hand side of the "?." operator is evaluated exactly once.

You must use the `Invoke` method when you use the "?." operator because the language does not allow parentheses immediately following the "?." operator. The compiler generates a type-safe `Invoke()` method for every delegate or event definition. That means the `Invoke()` is exactly the same code as raising the event directly as shown in the earlier examples.

This code is thread safe. It's also more concise. Because it's one line of code, there's no motivation to create another helper method that clutters the class design. One line of code to raise an event—that's the clarity we want.

Old habits can die hard, though, and if you've been using .NET for years, you'll need to build new habits. You'll also have a body of existing code that uses the previous idiom. Building new habits may also be harder for your team. There's more than a decade of recommendations online showing the earlier practices. Developers who search for help when they first encounter `NullReferenceExceptions` in code that raises events will find many resources that point to the earlier practices.

The new idiom is better for its simplicity and its clarity. Adopt its usage. Every time.

Item 9: Minimize Boxing and Unboxing

Value types are containers for data. They are not polymorphic types. On the other hand, the .NET Framework was designed with a single reference type, `System.Object`, at the root of the entire object hierarchy. These two goals are at odds. The .NET Framework uses boxing and unboxing to bridge the gap between them. Boxing places a value type in an untyped reference object to allow the value type to be used where a reference type is expected. Unboxing extracts a copy of that value type from the box. Boxing and unboxing are necessary for you to use value types where the `System.Object` type or an interface type is expected. But boxing and unboxing are always performance-robbing operations. Sometimes, when boxing and unboxing also create temporary copies of objects, they can lead to subtle bugs in your programs. Avoid boxing and unboxing when possible.

Boxing converts a value type to a reference type. A new reference object, the box, is allocated on the heap, and a copy of the value type is stored inside that reference object. See Figure 1.1 for an illustration of how the boxed object is stored and accessed. The box contains the copy of the value type object and duplicates the interfaces implemented by the boxed value type. When you need to retrieve anything from the box, a copy of the value type is created and returned. That's the key concept of boxing and unboxing: A copy of the value goes in the box, and another is created whenever you access what's in the box.

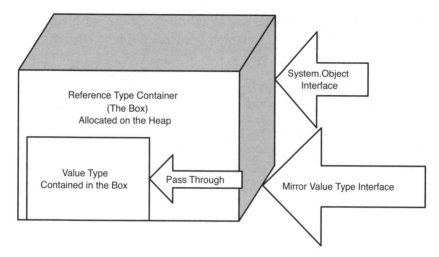

Figure 1.1   Value type in a box. To convert a value type into a `System.Object` reference, an unnamed reference type is created. The value type is stored inline inside the unnamed reference type. All methods that access the value type are passed through the box to the stored value type.

In many ways, the addition of generics in .NET 2.0 means that you can avoid boxing and unboxing simply by using generic classes and generic methods. That is certainly the most powerful way to create code that uses value types without unnecessary boxing operations. However, there are many locations in the .NET Framework where methods have parameters typed as `System.Object`. Those APIs still produce boxing and unboxing operations. It happens automatically. The compiler generates the boxing and unboxing instructions whenever you use a value type where a reference type, such as `System.Object`, is expected. In addition, the boxing and unboxing operations occur when you use a value type through an interface pointer. You get no warnings—boxing just happens. Even a simple statement such as this performs boxing:

```
Console.WriteLine($"A few numbers:{firstNumber},
{secondNumber}, {thirdNumber}");
```

The work done to create the interpolated string uses an array of `System .Object` references. Integers are value types and must be boxed so that they can be passed to the compiler-generated method that creates the string from the values. The only way to coerce the three integer arguments into `System.Object` is to box them. In addition, inside this method, code reaches inside the box to call the ToString() method of the object in the box. In a sense, you have generated this construct:

```
int i = 25;
object o = i; // box
Console.WriteLine(o.ToString());
```

The boxing and unboxing are repeated for each object. Inside the method that creates the string from the arguments, code like the following executes:

```
object firstParm = 5;

object o = firstParm;
int i = (int)o; // unbox
string output = i.ToString();
```

You would never write this code yourself. However, by letting the compiler automatically convert from a specific value type to System.Object, you did let it happen. The compiler was just trying to help you. It wants you to succeed. It happily generates the boxing and unboxing statements necessary to convert any value type into an instance of System.Object. To avoid this particular penalty, you should convert your types to string instances yourself before you send them to WriteLine:

```
Console.WriteLine($@"A few numbers:{firstNumber.ToString()},
{secondNumber.ToString()}, {thirdNumber.ToString()}");
```

This code uses the known type of integer, and value types (integers) are never implicitly converted to System.Object. This common example illustrates the first rule to avoid boxing: Watch for implicit conversions to System.Object. Value types should not be substituted for System.Object if you can avoid it.

Another common case when you might inadvertently substitute a value type for System.Object is when you place value types in .NET 1.x collections. You should use the generic collections added in the 2.0 version of the .NET BCL over the 1.x object-based collections. However, some components in the .NET BCL still use 1.x-style collections. You should understand the issues and how to avoid them.

The first incarnation of the .NET Framework collections stored references to System.Object instances. Anytime you add a value type to a collection, it goes in a box. Anytime you remove an object from a collection, it gets copied from the box. Taking an object out of the box always makes a copy. That introduces some subtle bugs into your application. Those bugs are the result of the rules that define boxing. Start with a simple structure that lets you modify one of its fields, and put some of those objects in a collection:

```
public struct Person
{
    public string Name { get; set; }

    public override string ToString()
    {
        return Name;
    }
}

// Using the Person in a collection:
var attendees = new List<Person>();
Person p = new Person { Name = "Old Name" };
attendees.Add(p);

// Try to change the name:
// Would work if Person was a reference type.
Person p2 = attendees[0];
p2.Name = "New Name";

// Writes "Old Name":
Console.WriteLine(attendees[0].ToString( ));

int i = 25;
object o = i; // box
Console.WriteLine(o.ToString());
```

Person is a value type. The JIT compiler creates a specific closed generic type for List<Person> so that Person objects are not boxed, because they are stored in the attendees collection. Another copy gets made when you remove the Person object to access the Name property to change. All you did was change the copy. In fact, a third copy was made to call the ToString() function through the attendees[0] object. For this and many other reasons, you should create immutable value types.

Yes, value types can be converted to System.Object or any interface reference. Those conversions happen implicitly, complicating the task of finding them. Those are the rules of the environment and the language. The boxing and unboxing operations make copies where you might not expect. That causes bugs. There is also a performance cost to treating value types polymorphically. Be on the lookout for any constructs that convert value types to either `System.Object` or interface types: placing values in collections, calling methods defined in `System.Object`, and casts to `System.Object`. Avoid these whenever you can.

Item 10: Use the `new` Modifier Only to React to Base Class Updates

You can use the `new` modifier on a class member to redefine a nonvirtual member inherited from a base class. Just because you can do something doesn't mean you should, though. Redefining nonvirtual methods creates ambiguous behavior. Most developers would look at these two blocks of code and immediately assume that they do exactly the same thing, if the two classes are related by inheritance:

```
object c = MakeObject();

// Call through MyClass reference:
MyClass cl = c as MyClass;
cl.MagicMethod();

// Call through MyOtherClass reference:
MyOtherClass cl2 = c as MyOtherClass;
cl2.MagicMethod();
```

When the new modifier is involved, that just isn't the case:

```
public class MyClass
{
    public void MagicMethod()
    {
        Console.WriteLine("MyClass");
        // details elided.
    }
}

public class MyOtherClass : MyClass
{
```

```
    // Redefine MagicMethod for this class.
    public new void MagicMethod()
    {
        Console.WriteLine("MyOTherClass");
        // details elided
    }
}
```

This kind of practice leads to a lot of developer confusion. If you call the same function on the same object, you expect the same code to execute. The fact that changing the reference or label that you use to call the function changes the behavior feels very wrong. It's inconsistent. A MyOtherClass object behaves differently in response to how you refer to it. The new modifier does not make a nonvirtual method into a virtual method after the fact. Instead, it lets you add a different method in your class's naming scope.

Nonvirtual methods are statically bound. Any source code anywhere that references MyClass.MagicMethod() calls exactly that function. Nothing in the runtime looks for a different version defined in any derived classes. Virtual functions, on the other hand, are dynamically bound. The runtime invokes the proper function based on the runtime type of the object.

The recommendation to avoid using the new modifier to redefine non-virtual functions should not be interpreted as a recommendation to make everything virtual when you define base classes. A library designer makes a contract when making a function virtual. You indicate that any derived class is expected to change the implementation of virtual functions. The set of virtual functions defines all behaviors that derived classes are expected to change. The "virtual by default" design says that derived classes can modify all the behavior of your class. It really says that you didn't think through all the ramifications of which behaviors derived classes might want to modify. Instead, spend the time to think through what methods and properties are intended as polymorphic. Make those—and only those—virtual. Don't think of it as restricting the users of your class. Instead, think of it as providing guidance for the entry points you provided for customizing the behavior of your types.

There is one time, and one time only, when you want to use the new modifier. You add the new modifier to incorporate a new version of a base class that contains a method name that you already use. You've already got code that depends on the name of the method in your class. You might already have other assemblies in the field that use this method. You've created the following class in your library, using `BaseWidget` which is defined in another library:

```csharp
public class MyWidget : BaseWidget
{
    public new void NormalizeValues()
    {
        // details elided.
    }
}
```

You finish your widget, and customers are using it. Then you find that the BaseWidget company has released a new version. Eagerly awaiting new features, you immediately purchase it and try to build your `MyWidget` class. It fails because the BaseWidget folks have added their own `NormalizeValues` method:

```csharp
public class BaseWidget
{
    public void Normalizevalues()
    {
        // details elided.
    }
}
```

This is a problem. Your base class snuck a method underneath your class's naming scope. There are two ways to fix this. You could change the name of your `NormalizeValues` method. Note that I've implied that `BaseWidget.NormalizeValues()` is semantically the same operation as `MyWidget.NormalizeAllValues`. If not, you should not call the base class implementation.

```csharp
public class MyWidget : BaseWidget
{
    public void NormalizeAllValues()
    {
        // details elided.
        // Call the base class only if (by luck)
        // the new method does the same operation.
        base.Normalizevalues();
    }
}
```

Or, you could use the new modifier:

```
public class MyWidget : BaseWidget
{
    public new void NormalizeValues()
    {
        // details elided.
        // Call the base class only if (by luck)
        // the new method does the same operation.
        base.Normalizevalues();
    }
}
```

If you have access to the source for all clients of the MyWidget class, you should change the method name because it's easier in the long run. However, if you have released your MyWidget class to the world, that would force all your users to make numerous changes. That's where the new modifier comes in handy. Your clients will continue to use your NormalizeValues() method without changing. None of them would be calling BaseWidget.NormalizeValues() because it does not exist. The new modifier handles the case where an upgrade to a base class collides with a member that you previously declared in your class.

Of course, over time, your users might begin wanting to use the BaseWidget .NormalizeValues() method. Then you are back to the original problem: two methods that look the same but are different. Think through all the long-term ramifications of the new modifier. Sometimes the short-term inconvenience of changing your method is still better.

The new modifier must be used with caution. If you apply it indiscriminately, you create ambiguous method calls in your objects. It's for the special case in which upgrades in your base class cause collisions in your class. Even in that situation, think carefully before using it. Most importantly, don't use it in any other situations.

2 | .NET Resource Management

The simple fact that .NET programs run in a managed environment has a big impact on the kinds of designs that create effective C#. Taking advantage of that environment requires changing your thinking from other environments to the .NET Common Language Runtime (CLR). It means understanding the .NET garbage collector (GC). It means understanding object lifetimes. It means understanding how to control unmanaged resources. This chapter covers the practices that help you create software that makes the best use of the environment and its features.

Item 11: Understand .NET Resource Management

You can't be an effective developer without understanding how the environment handles memory and other important resources. In .NET, that means understanding memory management and the garbage collector.

The GC controls managed memory for you. Unlike in native environments, you are not responsible for most memory leaks, dangling pointers, uninitialized pointers, or a host of other memory-management issues. But the garbage collector works better when you need to clean up after yourself. You are responsible for unmanaged resources such as database connections, GDI+ objects, COM objects, and other system objects. In addition, you can cause objects to stay in memory longer than you'd like because you've created links between them using event handlers or delegates. Queries, which execute when results are requested, can also cause objects to remain referenced longer than you would expect (see Item 41).

Here's the good news: Because the GC controls memory, certain design idioms are much easier to implement than when you must manage all memory yourself. Circular references, both simple relationships and complex webs of objects, are much easier to implement correctly than in environments where you must manage memory. The GC's Mark and Compact algorithm efficiently detects these relationships and removes unreachable webs of objects in their entirety. The GC determines whether an object is reachable by walking the object tree from the application's root object instead of forcing each object to keep track of references to it, as in COM. The EntitySet class provides an example of how this algorithm simplifies object ownership decisions. An entity is a collection of objects loaded from a database. Each entity may contain references to other entity objects. Any of these entities may also contain links to other entities. Just like the relational database entity sets model, these links and references may be circular.

There are references all through the web of objects represented by different entity sets. Releasing memory is the GC's responsibility. Because the .NET Framework designers did not need to free these objects, the complicated web of object references did not pose a problem. No decision needed to be made regarding the proper sequence of freeing this web of objects; it's the GC's job. The GC's design simplifies the problem of identifying this kind of web of objects as garbage. The application can stop referencing any entity when it's done. The garbage collector will know if the entity is still reachable from live objects in the application. Any objects that cannot be reached from the application are garbage.

The garbage collector compacts the managed heap each time it runs. Compacting the heap moves each live object in the managed heap so that the free space is located in one contiguous block of memory. Figure 2.1 shows two snapshots of the heap before and after a garbage collection. All free memory is placed in one contiguous block after each GC operation.

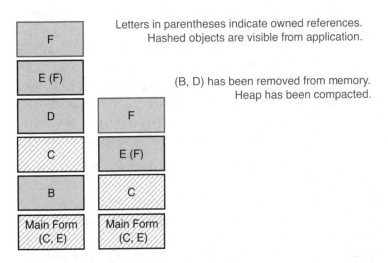

Figure 2.1 The garbage collector not only removes unused memory, but it also moves other objects in memory to compact used memory and maximize free space.

As you've just learned, memory management (for the managed heap) is completely the responsibility of the garbage collector. Other system resources must be managed by developers: you and the users of your classes. Two mechanisms help developers control the lifetimes of unmanaged resources: finalizers and the IDisposable interface. A finalizer is a defensive mechanism that ensures that your objects always have a way to release unmanaged resources. Finalizers have many drawbacks, so you also have the IDisposable interface that provides a less intrusive way to return resources to the system in a timely manner.

Finalizers are called by the garbage collector at some time after an object becomes garbage. You don't know when that happens. All you know is that in most environments it happens sometime after your object cannot be reached. That is a big change from C++, and it has important ramifications for your designs. Experienced C++ programmers wrote classes that allocated a critical resource in its constructor and released it in its destructor:

```
// Good C++, bad C#:
class CriticalSection
{
    // Constructor acquires the system resource.
    public CriticalSection()
    {
        EnterCriticalSection();
    }

    // Destructor releases system resource.
    ~CriticalSection()
    {
        ExitCriticalSection();
    }

    private void ExitCriticalSection()
    {
    }
    private void EnterCriticalSection()
    {
    }
}

// usage:
void Func()
```

```
{
    // The lifetime of s controls access to
    // the system resource.
    CriticalSection s = new CriticalSection();
    // Do work.

    //...

    // compiler generates call to destructor.
    // code exits critical section.
}
```

This common C++ idiom ensures that resource deallocation is exception proof. This doesn't work in C#, however—at least not in the same way. Deterministic finalization is not part of the .NET environment or the C# language. Trying to force the C++ idiom of deterministic finalization into the C# language won't work well. In C#, the finalizer eventually executes in most environments, but it doesn't execute in a timely fashion. In the previous example, the code eventually exits the critical section, but in C# it doesn't exit the critical section when the function exits. That happens at some unknown time later. You don't know when. You can't know when. Finalizers are the only way to guarantee that unmanaged resources allocated by an object of a given type are eventually released. But finalizers execute at nondeterministic times, so your design and coding practices should minimize the need for creating finalizers, and also minimize the need for executing the finalizers that do exist. Throughout this chapter you'll learn techniques to avoid creating your own finalizer, and how to minimize the negative impact of having one when it must be present.

Relying on finalizers also introduces performance penalties. Objects that require finalization put a performance drag on the garbage collector. When the GC finds that an object is garbage but also requires finalization, it cannot remove that item from memory just yet. First, it calls the finalizer. Finalizers are not executed by the same thread that collects garbage. Instead, the GC places each object that is ready for finalization in a queue and executes all the finalizers for those objects. It continues with its business, removing other garbage from memory. On the next GC cycle, those objects that have been finalized are removed from memory. Figure 2.2 shows three different GC operations and the difference in memory usage. Notice that the objects that require finalizers stay in memory for extra cycles.

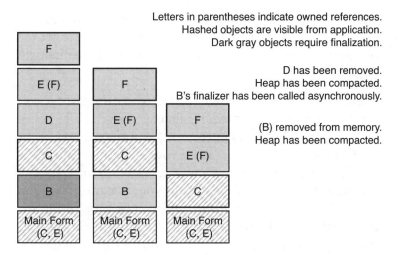

Letters in parentheses indicate owned references.
Hashed objects are visible from application.
Dark gray objects require finalization.

D has been removed.
Heap has been compacted.
B's finalizer has been called asynchronously.

(B) removed from memory.
Heap has been compacted.

Figure 2.2 This sequence shows the effect of finalizers on the garbage collector. Objects stay in memory longer, and an extra thread needs to be spawned to run the garbage collector.

This might lead you to believe that an object that requires finalization lives in memory for one GC cycle more than necessary. But I simplified things. It's more complicated than that because of another GC design decision. The .NET garbage collector defines generations to optimize its work. Generations help the GC identify the likeliest garbage candidates more quickly. Any object created since the last garbage collection operation is a generation 0 object. Any object that has survived one GC operation is a generation 1 object. Any object that has survived two or more GC operations is a generation 2 object. The purpose of generations is to separate short-lived objects from objects that stay around for the life of the application. Generation 0 objects are mostly those short-lived object variables. Member variables and global variables quickly enter generation 1 and eventually enter generation 2.

The GC optimizes its work by limiting how often it examines first- and second-generation objects. Every GC cycle examines generation 0 objects. Roughly one GC out of ten examines the generation 0 and 1 objects. Roughly one GC cycle out of 100 examines all objects. Think about finalization and its cost again: An object that requires finalization might stay in memory for nine GC cycles more than it would if it did not require finalization. If it still has not been finalized, it moves to generation 2. In generation 2, an object lives for an extra 100 GC cycles until the next generation 2 collection.

I've spent some time explaining why finalizers are not a good solution. Yet you still need to free resources. You address these issues using the IDisposable interface and the standard dispose pattern (see Item 17 later in this chapter).

To close, remember that a managed environment, where the garbage collector takes the responsibility for memory management, is a big plus: Memory leaks and a host of other pointer-related problems are no longer your problem. Nonmemory resources force you to create finalizers to ensure proper cleanup of those nonmemory resources. Finalizers can have a serious impact on the performance of your program, but you must write them to avoid resource leaks. Implementing and using the IDisposable interface avoids the performance drain on the garbage collector that finalizers introduce. The next item describes the specific techniques that will help you create programs that use this environment more effectively.

Item 12: Prefer Member Initializers to Assignment Statements

Classes often have more than one constructor. Over time, it's easy for the member variables and the constructors to get out of sync. The best way to make sure this doesn't happen is to initialize variables where you declare them instead of in the body of every constructor. You should use the initializer syntax for both static and instance variables.

Constructing a member variable when you declare that variable is natural in C#. Just initialize the variable when you declare it:

```
public class MyClass
{
    // declare the collection, and initialize it.
    private List<string> labels = new List<string>();


}
```

Regardless of the number of constructors you eventually add to the MyClass type, labels will be initialized properly. The compiler generates code at the beginning of each constructor to execute all the initializers you have defined for your instance member variables. When you add a new constructor, labels get initialized. Similarly, if you add a new member variable, you do not need to add initialization code to every constructor; initializing the variable where you define it is sufficient. Equally important, the initializers are added to the compiler-generated default constructor. The C# compiler creates a default constructor for your types whenever you don't explicitly define any constructors.

Initializers are more than a convenient shortcut for statements in a constructor body. The statements generated by initializers are placed in object code before the body of your constructors. Initializers execute before the base class constructor for your type executes, and they are executed in the order in which the variables are declared in your class.

Using initializers is the simplest way to avoid uninitialized variables in your types, but it's not perfect. In three cases, you should not use the initializer syntax. The first is when you are initializing the object to 0, or `null`. The default system initialization sets everything to 0 for you before any of your code executes. The system-generated 0 initialization is done at a very low level using the CPU instructions to set the entire block of memory to 0. Any extra 0 initialization on your part is superfluous. The C# compiler dutifully adds the extra instructions to set memory to 0 again. It's not wrong—but it can create brittle code.

```
public struct MyValType
{
    // elided
}


MyValType myVal1;  // initialized to 0
MyValType myVal2 = new MyValType(); // also 0
```

Both statements initialize the variable to all 0s. The first does so by setting the memory containing `myVal1` to 0. The second uses the IL instruction `initobj`, which causes both a box and an unbox operation on the `myVal2` variable. This takes quite a bit of extra time (see Item 9).

The second inefficiency comes when you create multiple initializations for the same object. You should use the initializer syntax only for variables that receive the same initialization in all constructors. This version of `MyClass` has a path that creates two different `List` objects as part of its construction:

```
public class MyClass2
 {
    // declare the collection, and initialize it.
    private List<string> labels = new List<string>();
```

```
    MyClass2()
    {
    }

    MyClass2(int size)
    {
        labels = new List<string>(size);
    }
}
```

When you create a new `MyClass2`, specifying the size of the collection, you create two array lists. One is immediately garbage. The variable initializer executes before every constructor. The constructor body creates the second array list. The compiler creates this version of `MyClass2`, which you would never code by hand. (For the proper way to handle this situation, see Item 14 later in this chapter.)

```
public class MyClass2
{
    // declare the collection, and initialize it.
    private List<string> labels;

    MyClass2()
    {
        labels = new List<string>();
    }

    MyClass2(int size)
    {
        labels = new List<string>();
        labels = new List<string>(size);
    }
}
```

You can run into the same situation whenever you use implicit properties. For those data elements where implicit properties are the right choice, Item 14 shows how to minimize any duplication when you initialize data held in implicit properties.

The final reason to move initialization into the body of a constructor is to facilitate exception handling. You cannot wrap the initializers in a `try` block. Any exceptions that might be generated during the construction of your member variables get propagated outside your object. You cannot attempt any recovery inside your class. You should move that initialization code into the body of your constructors so that you implement the proper recovery code to create your type and gracefully handle the exception (see Item 47).

Member initializers are the simplest way to ensure that the member variables in your type are initialized regardless of which constructor is called. The initializers are executed before each constructor you make for your type. Using this syntax means that you cannot forget to add the proper initialization when you add new constructors for a future release. Use initializers when all constructors create the member variable the same way; it's simpler to read and easier to maintain.

Item 13: Use Proper Initialization for Static Class Members

You know that you should initialize static member variables in a type before you create any instances of that type. C# lets you use static initializers and a static constructor for this purpose. A static constructor is a special function that executes before any other methods, variables, or properties defined in that class are accessed for the first time. You use this function to initialize static variables, enforce the singleton pattern, or perform any other necessary work before a class is usable. You should not use your instance constructors, some special private function, or any other idiom to initialize static variables. For static fields that require complex or expensive initialization, consider using `Lazy<T>` to execute the initialization when a field is first accessed.

As with instance initialization, you can use the initializer syntax as an alternative to the static constructor. If you simply need to allocate a static member, use the initializer syntax. When you have more complicated logic to initialize static member variables, create a static constructor.

Implementing the singleton pattern in C# is the most frequent use of a static constructor. Make your instance constructor private, and add an initializer:

```
public class MySingleton
{
    private static readonly MySingleton theOneAndOnly =
    new MySingleton();
```

```
    public static MySingleton TheOnly
    {
        get { return theOneAndOnly; }
    }

    private MySingleton()
    {
    }

    // remainder elided
}
```

The singleton pattern can just as easily be written this way, in case you have more complicated logic to initialize the singleton:

```
public class MySingleton2
{
    private static readonly MySingleton2 theOneAndOnly;

    static MySingleton2()
    {
        theOneAndOnly = new MySingleton2();
    }
    public static MySingleton2 TheOnly
    {
        get { return theOneAndOnly; }
    }

    private MySingleton2()
    {
    }

    // remainder elided
}
```

Like instance initializers, the static initializers are executed before any static constructors are called. And, yes, your static initializers may execute before the base class's static constructor.

The CLR calls your static constructor automatically before your type is first accessed in an application space (an `AppDomain`). You can define only one static constructor, and it must not take any arguments. Because static constructors are called by the CLR, you must be careful about exceptions generated in them. If you let an exception escape a static constructor, the CLR will terminate your program by throwing a `TypeInitializationException`. The situation where the caller catches the exception is even more insidious. Code that tries to create the type will fail until that `AppDomain` is unloaded. The CLR could not initialize the type by executing the static constructor. It won't try again, and yet the type did not get initialized correctly. An object of that type (or any type derived from it) would not be well defined. Therefore, it is not allowed.

Exceptions are the most common reason to use the static constructor instead of static initializers. If you use static initializers, you cannot catch the exceptions yourself. With a static constructor, you can (see Item 47):

```
static MySingleton2()
{
    try
    {
        theOneAndOnly = new MySingleton2();
    }
    catch
    {
        // Attempt recovery here.
    }
}
```

Static initializers and static constructors provide the cleanest, clearest way to initialize static members of your class. They are easy to read and easy to get correct. They were added to the language to specifically address the difficulties involved with initializing static members in other languages.

Item 14: Minimize Duplicate Initialization Logic

Writing constructors is often a repetitive task. Many developers write the first constructor and then copy and paste the code into other constructors to satisfy the multiple overrides defined in the class interface. Ideally, you're not one of those. If you are, stop it. Veteran C++ programmers would factor the common algorithms into a private helper method. Stop that, too. When you find that multiple constructors contain the same logic, factor that logic into a common constructor instead. You'll get the benefits of avoiding code duplication, and constructor initializers generate much more efficient object code. The C# compiler recognizes the constructor initializer as special syntax and removes the duplicated variable initializers and the duplicated base class constructor calls. The result is that your final object executes the minimum amount of code to properly initialize the object. You also write the least amount of code by delegating responsibilities to a common constructor.

Constructor initializers allow one constructor to call another constructor. This example shows a simple usage:

```
public class MyClass
{
    // collection of data
    private List<ImportantData> coll;
    // Name of the instance:
    private string name;

    public MyClass() :
        this(0, "")
    {
    }

    public MyClass(int initialCount) :
        this(initialCount, string.Empty)
    {
    }

    public MyClass(int initialCount, string name)
    {
        coll = (initialCount > 0) ?
        new List<ImportantData>(initialCount) :
        new List<ImportantData>();
        this.name = name;
    }
}
```

C# 4.0 added default parameters, which you can use to minimize the duplicated code in constructors. You could replace all the different constructors for MyClass with one constructor that specifies default values for all or many of the values:

```
public class MyClass
{
    // collection of data
    private List<ImportantData> coll;
```

```
    // Name of the instance:
    private string name;

    // Needed to satisfy the new() constraint.
    public MyClass() :
        this(0, string.Empty)
    {
    }

    public MyClass(int initialCount = 0, string name = "")
    {
        coll = (initialCount > 0) ?
        new List<ImportantData>(initialCount) :
        new List<ImportantData>();
        this.name = name;
    }
}
```

There are tradeoffs in choosing default parameters over using multiple overloads. Default parameters create more options for your users. This version of MyClass specifies the default value for both parameters. Users could specify different values for either or both parameters. Producing all the permutations using overloaded constructors would require four different constructor overloads: a parameterless constructor, one that asks for the initial count, one that asks for the name, and one that asks for both parameters. Add more members to your class, and the number of potential overloads grows as the number of permutations of all the parameters grows. That complexity makes default parameters a very powerful mechanism to minimize the number of potential overloads that you need to create.

Defining default values for all parameters to your type's constructor means that user code will be valid when you call the new MyClass(). When you intend to support this concept, you should create an explicit parameterless constructor in that type, as shown in the example code above. While most code would default all parameters, generic classes that use the new() constraint will not accept a constructor with parameters that have default values. To satisfy the new() constraint, a class must have an explicit parameterless constructor. Therefore, you should create one so that clients can use your type in generic classes or methods that enforce the new() constraint. That's not to say that every type needs a parameterless constructor. However, if you support one, make sure to add the code so that the parameterless constructor works in all cases, even when called from a generic class with a new() constraint.

You'll note that the second constructor specifies "" for the default value on the name parameter, rather than the more customary string.Empty. That's because string.Empty is not a compile-time constant. It is a static property defined in the string class. Because it is not a compile-time constant, you cannot use it for the default value for a parameter.

However, using default parameters instead of overloads creates tighter coupling between your class and all the clients that use it. In particular, the formal parameter name becomes part of the public interface, as does the current default value. Changing parameter values requires a recompile of all client code in order to pick up those changes. That makes overloaded constructors more resilient in the face of potential future changes. You can add new constructors, or change the default behavior for those constructors that don't specify values, without breaking client code.

Default parameters are the preferred solution to this problem. However, some APIs use reflection to create objects and rely on a parameterless constructor. A constructor with defaults supplied for all arguments is not the same as a parameterless constructor. You may need to write separate constructors that you support as a separate function. With constructors, that can mean a lot of duplicated code. Use constructor chaining, by having one constructor invoke another constructor declared in the same class, instead of creating a common utility routine. Several inefficiencies are present in this alternative method of factoring out common constructor logic:

```
public class MyClass
{
    private List<ImportantData> coll;
    private string name;

    public MyClass()
    {
        commonConstructor(0, "");
    }
```

```
    public MyClass(int initialCount)
    {
        commonConstructor(initialCount, "");
    }

    public MyClass(int initialCount, string Name)
    {
        commonConstructor(initialCount, Name);
    }

    private void commonConstructor(int count,
    string name)
    {
        coll = (count > 0) ?
        new List<ImportantData>(count) :
        new List<ImportantData>();
        this.name = name;
    }
}
```

That version looks the same, but it generates far-less-efficient object code. The compiler adds code to perform several functions on your behalf in constructors. It adds statements for all variable initializers (see Item 12 earlier in this chapter). It calls the base class constructor. When you write your own common utility function, the compiler cannot factor out this duplicated code. The IL for the second version is the same as if you'd written this:

```
public class MyClass
{
    private List<ImportantData> coll;
    private string name;

    public MyClass()
    {
        // Instance Initializers would go here.
        object(); // Not legal, illustrative only.
        commonConstructor(0, "");
    }
```

```
    public MyClass(int initialCount)
    {
        // Instance Initializers would go here.
        object(); // Not legal, illustrative only.
        commonConstructor(initialCount, "");
    }

    public MyClass(int initialCount, string Name)
    {
        // Instance Initializers would go here.
        object(); // Not legal, illustrative only.
        commonConstructor(initialCount, Name);
    }

    private void commonConstructor(int count,
    string name)
    {
        coll = (count > 0) ?
        new List<ImportantData>(count) :
        new List<ImportantData>();
        this.name = name;
    }
}
```

If you could write the construction code for the first version the way the compiler sees it, you'd write this:

```
// Not legal, illustrates IL generated:
public class MyClass
{
    private List<ImportantData> coll;
    private string name;

    public MyClass()
    {
        //. No variable initializers here.
        // Call the third constructor, shown below.
        this(0, ""); // Not legal, illustrative only.
    }
```

```
public MyClass(int initialCount)
{
    // No variable initializers here.
    // Call the third constructor, shown below.
    this(initialCount, "");
}

public MyClass(int initialCount, string Name)
{
    // Instance Initializers would go here.
    //object(); // Not legal, illustrative only.
    coll = (initialCount > 0) ?
    new List<ImportantData>(initialCount) :
    new List<ImportantData>();
    name = Name;
}
}
```

The difference is that the compiler does not generate multiple calls to the base class constructor, nor does it copy the instance variable initializers into each constructor body. The fact that the base class constructor is called only from the last constructor is also significant: You cannot include more than one constructor initializer in a constructor definition. You can delegate to another constructor in this class using this(), or you can call a base class constructor using base(). You cannot do both.

Still don't buy the case for constructor initializers? Then think about read-only constants. In this example, the name of the object should not change during its lifetime. This means that you should make it read-only. That causes the common utility function to generate compiler errors:

```
public class MyClass
{
    // collection of data
    private List<ImportantData> coll;
    // Number for this instance
    private int counter;
    // Name of the instance:
    private readonly string name;
```

```
public MyClass()
{
    commonConstructor(0, string.Empty);
}

public MyClass(int initialCount)
{
    commonConstructor(initialCount, string.Empty);
}

public MyClass(int initialCount, string Name)
{
    commonConstructor(initialCount, Name);
}

private void commonConstructor(int count,
string name)
{
    coll = (count > 0) ?
    new List<ImportantData>(count) :
    new List<ImportantData>();
    // ERROR changing the name outside of a constructor.
    //this.name = name;
}
}
```

The compiler enforces the read-only nature of this.name and will not allow any code not in a constructor to modify it. C#'s constructor initializers provide the alternative. All but the most trivial classes contain more than one constructor. Their job is to initialize all the members of an object. By their very nature, these functions have similar or, ideally, shared logic. Use the C# constructor initializer to factor out those common algorithms so that you write them once and they execute once.

Both default parameters and overloads have their place. In general, you should prefer default values to overloaded constructors. After all, if you are letting client developers specify parameter values at all, your constructor must be capable of handling any values that users specify. Your original default values should always be reasonable and shouldn't generate exceptions. Therefore, even though changing the default parameter values is technically a breaking change, it shouldn't be observable to your clients. Their code will still use the original values, and those original values should still produce reasonable behavior. That minimizes the potential hazards of using default values.

This is the last item about object initialization in C#. That makes it a good time to review the entire sequence of events for constructing an instance of a type. You should understand both the order of operations and the default initialization of an object. You should strive to initialize every member variable exactly once during construction. The best way for you to accomplish this is to initialize values as early as possible. Here is the order of operations for constructing the first instance of a type:

1. Static variable storage is set to 0.
2. Static variable initializers execute.
3. Static constructors for the base class execute.
4. The static constructor executes.
5. Instance variable storage is set to 0.
6. Instance variable initializers execute.
7. The appropriate base class instance constructor executes.
8. The instance constructor executes.

Subsequent instances of the same type start at step 5 because the class initializers execute only once. Also, steps 6 and 7 are optimized so that constructor initializers cause the compiler to remove duplicate instructions.

The C# language compiler guarantees that everything gets initialized in some way when an object is created. At a minimum, you are guaranteed that all memory your object uses has been set to 0 when an instance is created. This is true for both static members and instance members. Your goal is to make sure that you initialize all the values the way you want and execute that initialization code only once. Use initializers to initialize simple resources. Use constructors to initialize members that require more sophisticated logic. Also factor calls to other constructors to minimize duplication.

Item 15: Avoid Creating Unnecessary Objects

The garbage collector does an excellent job of managing memory for you, and it removes unused objects in a very efficient manner. But no matter how you look at it, allocating and destroying a heap-based object takes more processor time than not allocating and not destroying a heap-based object. You can introduce serious performance drains on your program by creating an excessive number of reference objects that are local to your methods.

So don't overwork the garbage collector. You can follow some simple techniques to minimize the amount of work that the GC needs to do on your program's behalf. All reference types, even local variables, create memory allocations. These objects become garbage when no root is keeping them alive. For local variables, that is typically when the method in which they are declared is no longer active. One very common bad practice is to allocate GDI objects in a Windows paint handler:

```
protected override void OnPaint(PaintEventArgs e)
{
    // Bad. Created the same font every paint event.
    using (Font MyFont = new Font("Arial", 10.0f))
    {
        e.Graphics.DrawString(DateTime.Now.ToString(),
            MyFont, Brushes.Black, new PointF(0, 0));
    }
    base.OnPaint(e);
}
```

OnPaint() gets called frequently. Every time it gets called, you create another Font object that contains the exact same settings. The garbage collector needs to clean those up for you. Among the conditions that the GC uses to determine when to run are the amount of memory allocated and the frequency of memory allocations. More allocations mean more pressure on the GC, causing it to run more often. That's incredibly inefficient.

Instead, promote the Font object from a local variable to a member variable. Reuse the same font each time you paint the window:

```
private readonly Font myFont =
    new Font("Arial", 10.0f);

protected override void OnPaint(PaintEventArgs e)
{
    e.Graphics.DrawString(DateTime.Now.ToString(),
        myFont, Brushes.Black, new PointF(0, 0));
    base.OnPaint(e);
}
```

Your program no longer creates garbage with every paint event. The garbage collector does less work. Your program runs just a little faster. When you elevate a local variable that implements IDisposable to a member variable, such as the font in this example, you need to implement `IDisposable` in your class. Item 17 explains how to properly do just that.

You should promote local variables to member variables when they are reference types (value types don't matter) and they will be used in routines that are called frequently. The font in the paint routine is an excellent example. Only local variables in routines that are frequently accessed are good candidates. Infrequently called routines are not. You're trying to avoid creating the same objects repeatedly, not turn every local variable into a member variable.

The static property `Brushes.Black` used earlier illustrates another technique that you should use to avoid repeatedly allocating similar objects. Create static member variables for commonly used instances of the reference types you need. Consider the black brush used earlier as an example. Every time you need to draw something in your window using the color black, you need a black brush. If you allocate a new one every time you draw anything, you create and destroy a huge number of black brushes during the course of a program. The first approach of creating a black brush as a member of each of your types helps, but it doesn't go far enough. Programs might create dozens of windows and controls and would create dozens of black brushes. The .NET Framework designers anticipated this and created a single black brush for you to reuse whenever you need it. The `Brushes` class contains a number of static `Brush` objects, each with a different common color. Internally, the `Brushes` class uses a lazy evaluation algorithm to create only those brushes you request. A simplified implementation looks like this:

```
private static Brush blackBrush;
public static Brush Black
{
    get
    {
        if (blackBrush == null)
            blackBrush = new SolidBrush(Color.Black);
        return blackBrush;
    }
}
```

The first time you request a black brush, the `Brushes` class creates it. The `Brushes` class keeps a reference to the single black brush and returns that same handle whenever you request it again. The end result is that you create one black brush and reuse it forever. Furthermore, if your application does not need a particular resource—say, the lime green brush—it never gets created. The framework provides a way to limit the objects created to the minimum set you need to accomplish your goals. Consider that technique in your programs. On the positive side, you create fewer objects. On the minus side, this may cause objects to be in memory for longer than necessary. It can even mean not being able to dispose of unmanaged resources because you can't know when to call the `Dispose()` method.

You've learned two techniques to minimize the number of allocations your program performs as it goes about its business. You can promote often-used local variables to member variables. You can use dependency injection to create and reuse objects that represent common instances of a given type. The last technique involves building the final value for immutable types. The `System.String` class is immutable: After you construct a string, the contents of that string cannot be modified. Whenever you write code that appears to modify the contents of a string, you are actually creating a new string object and leaving the old string object as garbage. This seemingly innocent practice:

```
string msg = "Hello, ";
msg += thisUser.Name;
msg += ". Today is ";
msg += System.DateTime.Now.ToString();
```

is just as inefficient as if you had written this:

```
string msg = "Hello, ";
// Not legal, for illustration only:
string tmp1 = new String(msg + thisUser.Name);
msg = tmp1; // "Hello " is garbage.
string tmp2 = new String(msg + ". Today is ");
msg = tmp2; // "Hello <user>" is garbage.
string tmp3 = new String(msg + DateTime.Now.ToString());
msg = tmp3; // "Hello <user>. Today is " is garbage.
```

The strings `tmp1`, `tmp2`, and `tmp3` and the originally constructed `msg` ("Hello") are all garbage. The += operator on the `string` class creates a new string object and returns that string. It does not modify the existing string by concatenating the characters to the original storage. For simple constructs such as the previous one, you should use interpolated strings:

```
string msg = string.Format("Hello, {0}. Today is {1}",
        thisUser.Name, DateTime.Now.ToString());
```

For more complicated string operations, you can use the `StringBuilder` class:

```
StringBuilder msg = new StringBuilder("Hello, ");
msg.Append(thisUser.Name);
msg.Append(". Today is ");
msg.Append(DateTime.Now.ToString());
string finalMsg = msg.ToString();
```

The example above is simple enough that you'd use string interpolation (see Item 4). Use `StringBuilder` when the logic needed to build the final string is too complex for string interpolation. `StringBuilder` is the mutable string class used to build an immutable string object. It provides facilities for mutable strings that let you create and modify text data before you construct an immutable string object. Use `StringBuilder` to create the final version of a string object. More importantly, learn from that design idiom. When your designs call for immutable types, consider creating builder objects to facilitate the multiphase construction of the final object. That provides a way for users of your class to construct an object in steps, yet maintain the immutability of your type.

The garbage collector does an efficient job of managing the memory that your application uses. But remember that creating and destroying heap objects still takes time. Avoid creating excessive objects; don't create what you don't need. Also avoid creating multiple objects of reference types in local functions. Instead, consider promoting local variables to member variables, or create static objects of the most common instances of your types. Finally, consider creating mutable builder classes for immutable types.

Item 16: Never Call Virtual Functions in Constructors

Virtual functions exhibit strange behaviors during the construction of an object. An object is not completely created until all constructors have executed. In the meantime, virtual functions may not behave the way you'd like or expect. Examine the following simple program:

```
class B
{
    protected B()
    {
        VFunc();
    }
```

```
    protected virtual void VFunc()
    {
        Console.WriteLine("VFunc in B");
    }
}


class Derived : B
{
    private readonly string msg = "Set by initializer";

    public Derived(string msg)
    {
        this.msg = msg;
    }

    protected override void VFunc()
    {
        Console.WriteLine(msg);
    }

    public static void Main()
    {
        var d = new Derived("Constructed in main");
    }
}
```

What do you suppose gets printed—"Constructed in main," "VFunc in B," or "Set by initializer"? Experienced C++ programmers would say, "VFunc in B." Some C# programmers would say, "Constructed in main." But the correct answer is "Set by initializer."

The base class constructor calls a virtual function that is defined in its class but overridden in the derived class. At runtime, the derived class version gets called. After all, the object's runtime type is `Derived`. The C# language definition considers the derived object completely available, because all the member variables have been initialized by the time any constructor body is entered. After all, all the variable initializers have executed. You had your chance to initialize all variables. But this doesn't mean that you have necessarily initialized all your member variables to the value you want. Only the variable initializers have executed; none of the code in any derived class constructor body has had the chance to do its work.

No matter what, some inconsistency occurs when you call virtual functions while constructing an object. The C++ language designers decided that virtual functions should resolve to the runtime type of the object being constructed. They decided that an object's runtime type should be determined as soon as the object is created.

There is logic behind this. For one thing, the object being created is a Derived object; every function should call the correct override for a Derived object. The rules for C++ are different here: The runtime type of an object changes as each class's constructor begins execution. Second, this C# language feature avoids the problem of having a null method pointer in the underlying implementation of virtual methods when the current type is an abstract base class. Consider this variant base class:

```
abstract class B
{
    protected B()
    {
        VFunc();
    }


    protected abstract void VFunc();
}


class Derived : B
{
    private readonly string msg = "Set by initializer";

    public Derived(string msg)
    {
        this.msg = msg;
    }


    protected override void VFunc()
    {
        Console.WriteLine(msg);
    }
    public static void Main()
    {
        var d = new Derived("Constructed in main");
    }
}
```

The sample compiles, because B objects aren't created, and any concrete derived object must supply an implementation for VFunc(). The C# strategy of calling the version of VFunc() matching the actual runtime type is the only possibility of getting anything except a runtime exception when an abstract function is called in a constructor. Experienced C++ programmers will recognize the potential runtime error if you use the same construct in that language. In C++, the call to VFunc() in the B constructor would crash.

Still, this simple example shows the pitfalls of the C# strategy. The msg variable is immutable. It should have the same value for the entire life of the object. Because of the small window of opportunity when the constructor has not yet finished its work, you can have different values for this variable: one set in the initializer, and one set in the body of the constructor. In the general case, any number of derived class variables may remain in the default state, as set by the initializer or by the system. They certainly don't have the values you thought, because your derived class's constructor has not executed.

Calling virtual functions in constructors makes your code extremely sensitive to the implementation details in derived classes. You can't control what derived classes do. Code that calls virtual functions in constructors is very brittle. The derived class must initialize all instance variables properly in variable initializers. That rules out quite a few objects: Most constructors take some parameters that are used to set the internal state properly. So you could say that calling a virtual function in a constructor mandates that all derived classes define a default constructor, and no other constructor. But that's a heavy burden to place on all derived classes. Do you really expect everyone who ever uses your code to play by those rules? I didn't think so. There is very little gain, and lots of possible future pain, from playing this game. In fact, this situation will work so rarely that it's included in the FxCop and Static Code Analyzer tools bundled with Visual Studio.

Item 17: Implement the Standard Dispose Pattern

We've discussed the importance of disposing of objects that hold unmanaged resources. Now it's time to cover how to write your own resource management code when you create types that contain resources other than memory. A standard pattern is used throughout the .NET Framework for disposing of unmanaged resources. The users of your type will expect you to follow this standard pattern. The standard dispose idiom frees your unmanaged resources using the IDisposable interface when clients remember, and it uses the finalizer defensively when clients forget. It works with the garbage collector to ensure that your objects pay the performance penalty associated with finalizers only when necessary. This is the right way to handle unmanaged resources, so it pays to understand it thoroughly. In practice, unmanaged resources in .NET can be accessed through a class derived from System.Runtime.Interop.SafeHandle, which implements the pattern described here correctly.

The root base class in the class hierarchy should do the following:

- It should implement the IDisposable interface to free resources.
- It should add a finalizer as a defensive mechanism if and only if your class directly contains an unmanaged resource.
- Both Dispose and the finalizer (if present) delegate the work of freeing resources to a virtual method that derived classes can override for their own resource management needs.

The derived classes need to

- Override the virtual method only when the derived class must free its own resources
- Implement a finalizer if and only if one of its direct member fields is an unmanaged resource
- Remember to call the base class version of the function

To begin, your class must have a finalizer if and only if it directly contains unmanaged resources. You should not rely on clients to always call the Dispose() method. You'll leak resources when they forget. It's their fault for not calling Dispose, but you'll get the blame. The only way you can guarantee that unmanaged resources get freed properly is to create a finalizer. So if and only if your type contains an unmanaged resource, create a finalizer.

When the garbage collector runs, it immediately removes from memory any garbage objects that do not have finalizers. All objects that have finalizers remain in memory. These objects are added to a finalization queue, and the GC runs the finalizers on those objects. After the finalizer thread has finished its work, the garbage objects can usually be removed from memory. They are bumped up a generation because they survived collection. They are also marked as not needing finalization because the finalizers have run. They will be removed from memory on the next collection of that higher generation. Objects that need finalization stay in memory for far longer than objects without a finalizer. But you have no choice. If you're going to be defensive, you must write a finalizer when your type holds unmanaged resources. But don't worry about performance just yet. The next steps ensure that it's easier for clients to avoid the performance penalty associated with finalization.

Implementing IDisposable is the standard way to inform users and the runtime system that your objects hold resources that must be released in a timely manner. The IDisposable interface contains just one method:

```
public interface IDisposable
{
    void Dispose();
}
```

The implementation of your IDisposable.Dispose() method is responsible for four tasks:

1. Freeing all unmanaged resources.
2. Freeing all managed resources (this includes unhooking events).
3. Setting a state flag to indicate that the object has been disposed of. You need to check this state and throw ObjectDisposed exceptions in your public members if any get called after disposing of an object.
4. Suppressing finalization. You call GC.SuppressFinalize(this) to accomplish this task.

You accomplish two things by implementing IDisposable: You provide the mechanism for clients to release all managed resources that you hold in a timely fashion, and you give clients a standard way to release all unmanaged resources. That's quite an improvement. After you've implemented IDisposable in your type, clients can avoid the finalization cost. Your class is a reasonably well-behaved member of the .NET community.

But there are still holes in the mechanism you've created. How does a derived class clean up its resources and still let a base class clean up as well? If derived classes override finalize or add their own implementation of IDisposable, those methods must call the base class; otherwise, the base class doesn't clean up properly. Also, finalize and Dispose share some of the same responsibilities; you have almost certainly duplicated code between the finalize method and the Dispose method. Overriding interface functions does not always work the way you'd expect. Interface functions are not virtual by default. We need to do a little more work to address these concerns. The third method in the standard dispose pattern, a protected virtual helper function, factors out these common tasks and adds a hook for derived classes to free resources they allocate. The base class contains the code for the core interface. The virtual function provides the hook for derived classes to clean up resources in response to `Dispose()` or finalization:

```
protected virtual void Dispose(bool isDisposing)
```

This overloaded method does the work necessary to support both finalize and `Dispose`, and because it is virtual, it provides an entry point for all derived classes. Derived classes can override this method, provide the proper implementation to clean up their resources, and call the base class version. You clean up managed and unmanaged resources when `isDisposing` is `true`, and you clean up only unmanaged resources when `isDisposing` is `false`. In both cases, call the base class's `Dispose(bool)` method to let it clean up its own resources.

Here is a short sample that shows the framework of code you supply when you implement this pattern. The `MyResourceHog` class shows the code to implement `IDisposable` and create the virtual `Dispose` method:

```
public class MyResourceHog : IDisposable
{
    // Flag for already disposed
    private bool alreadyDisposed = false;

    // Implementation of IDisposable.
    // Call the virtual Dispose method.
    // Suppress Finalization.
    public void Dispose()
    {
        Dispose(true);
        GC.SuppressFinalize(this);
    }

    // Virtual Dispose method
    protected virtual void Dispose(bool isDisposing)
    {
        // Don't dispose more than once.
        if (alreadyDisposed)
            return;
        if (isDisposing)
        {
            // elided: free managed resources here.
        }
```

```
        // elided: free unmanaged resources here.
        // Set disposed flag:
        alreadyDisposed = true;
    }


    public void ExampleMethod()
    {
        if (alreadyDisposed)
            throw new
                ObjectDisposedException("MyResourceHog",
                "Called Example Method on Disposed object");
        // remainder elided.
    }
}
```

If a derived class needs to perform additional cleanup, it implements the protected Dispose method:

```
public class DerivedResourceHog : MyResourceHog
{
    // Have its own disposed flag.
    private bool disposed = false;

    protected override void Dispose(bool isDisposing)
    {
        // Don't dispose more than once.
        if (disposed)
            return;
        if (isDisposing)
        {
            // TODO: free managed resources here.
        }
        // TODO: free unmanaged resources here.

        // Let the base class free its resources.
        // Base class is responsible for calling
        // GC.SuppressFinalize( )
        base.Dispose(isDisposing);

        // Set derived class disposed flag:
        disposed = true;
    }
}
```

Notice that both the base class and the derived class contain a flag for the disposed state of the object. This is purely defensive. Duplicating the flag encapsulates any possible mistakes made while disposing of an object to only the one type, not all types that make up an object.

You need to write `Dispose` and finalizers defensively. They must be idempotent. `Dispose()` may be called more than once, and the effect should be the same as calling them exactly once. Disposing of objects can happen in any order. You will encounter cases in which one of the member objects in your type is already disposed of before your `Dispose()` method gets called. You should not view that as a problem because the `Dispose()` method can be called multiple times. Note that `Dispose()` is the exception to the rule of throwing an `ObjectDisposedException` when public methods are called on an object that has been disposed of. If it's called on an object that has already been disposed of, it does nothing. Finalizers may run when references have been disposed of, or have never been initialized. Any object that you reference is still in memory, so you don't need to check null references. However, any object that you reference might be disposed of. It might also have already been finalized.

You'll notice that neither `MyResourceHog` nor `DerivedResourceHog` contains a finalizer. The example code I wrote does not directly contain any unmanaged resources. Therefore, a finalizer is not needed. That means the example code never calls `Dispose(false)`. That's the correct pattern. Unless your class directly contains unmanaged resources, you should not implement a finalizer. Only those classes that directly contain an unmanaged resource should implement the finalizer and add that overhead. Even if it's never called, the presence of a finalizer does introduce a rather large performance penalty for your types. Unless your type needs the finalizer, don't add it. However, you should still implement the pattern correctly so that if any derived classes do add unmanaged resources, they can add the finalizer and implement `Dispose(bool)` in such a way that unmanaged resources are handled correctly.

This brings me to the most important recommendation for any method associated with disposal or cleanup: You should be releasing resources only. Do not perform any other processing during a dispose method. You can introduce serious complications to object lifetimes by performing other processing in your `Dispose` or finalize methods. Objects are born when you construct them, and they die when the garbage collector reclaims them. You can consider them comatose when your program can no longer access them. If you can't reach an object, you can't call any of its methods. For all intents and purposes, it is dead. But objects that have finalizers get to breathe a last breath before they are declared dead. Finalizers should do nothing but clean up unmanaged resources. If a finalizer somehow makes an object reachable again, it has been resurrected. It's alive and not well, even though it has awoken from a comatose state. Here's an obvious example:

```
public class BadClass
{
    // Store a reference to a global object:
    private static readonly List<BadClass> finalizedList =
        new List<BadClass>();
    private string msg;

    public BadClass(string msg)
    {
        // cache the reference:
        msg = (string)msg.Clone();
    }

    ~BadClass()
    {
        // Add this object to the list.
        // This object is reachable, no
        // longer garbage. It's Back!
        finalizedList.Add(this);
    }
}
```

When a `BadClass` object executes its finalizer, it puts a reference to itself on a global list. It has just made itself reachable. It's alive again! The number of problems you've just introduced would make anyone cringe. The object has been finalized, so the garbage collector now believes there is no need to call its finalizer again. If you actually need to finalize a resurrected object, it won't happen. Second, some of your resources might not be available. The GC will not remove from memory any objects that are reachable only by objects in the finalizer queue, but it might have already finalized them. If so, they are almost certainly no longer usable. Although the members that `BadClass` owns are still in memory, they will have likely been disposed of or finalized. There is no way in the language that you can control the order of finalization. You cannot make this kind of construct work reliably. Don't try.

I've never seen code that has resurrected objects in such an obvious fashion, except as an academic exercise. But I have seen code in which the finalizer attempts to do some real work and ends up bringing itself back to life when some function that the finalizer calls saves a reference to the object. The moral is to look very carefully at any code in a finalizer and, by extension, both `Dispose` methods. If that code is doing anything other than releasing resources, look again. Those actions likely will cause bugs in your program in the future. Remove those actions, and make sure that finalizers and `Dispose()` methods release resources and do nothing else.

In a managed environment, you do not need to write a finalizer for every type you create; you do it only for types that store unmanaged types or when your type contains members that implement `IDisposable`. Even if you need only the `IDisposable` interface, not a finalizer, implement the entire pattern. Otherwise, you limit your derived classes by complicating their implementation of the standard dispose idiom. Follow the standard dispose idiom I've described. That will make life easier for you, for the users of your class, and for those who create derived classes from your types.

3 | Working with Generics

Some articles and papers might lead you to believe that generics are useful only in the context of collections. That's not true. There are many other ways to use generics. You can use them to create interfaces, event handlers, common algorithms, and more.

Many other discussions compare C# generics to C++ templates, usually to advocate one as being better than the other. Comparing C# generics to C++ templates is useful to help you understand the syntax, but that's where the comparison should end. Certain idioms are more natural to C++ templates, and others are more natural to C# generics. But, as you'll see in Item 19 a bit later in this chapter, trying to decide which is "better" will only hurt your understanding of both of them. Adding generics required changes to the C# compiler, the Just-In-Time (JIT) compiler, and the Common Language Runtime (CLR). The C# compiler takes your C# code and creates the Microsoft Intermediate Language (MSIL, or IL) definition for the generic type. In contrast, the JIT compiler combines a generic type definition with a set of type parameters to create a closed generic type. The CLR supports both concepts at runtime.

There are costs and benefits associated with generic type definitions. Sometimes, replacing specific code with a generic equivalent makes your program smaller. At other times, it makes it larger. Whether or not you encounter this generic code bloat depends on the specific type parameters you use and the number of closed generic types you create.

Generic class definitions are fully compiled MSIL types. The code they contain must be completely valid for any type parameters that may be used. The generic definition is called a **generic type definition**. A specific instance of a generic type, in which all the type parameters have been specified, is called a **closed generic type**. (If only some of the parameters are specified, it's called an **open generic type**.)

Generics in IL are a partial definition of a real type. The IL contains the placeholder for an instantiation of a specific completed generic type.

The JIT compiler completes that definition when it creates the machine code to instantiate a closed generic type at runtime. This practice introduces a tradeoff between paying the increased code cost for multiple closed generic types and gaining the decreased time and space required in order to store data.

This process happens for every type you create, generic or not. With nongeneric types, there is a 1:1 correspondence between the IL for a class and the machine code created. Generics introduce some new wrinkles to that translation. When a generic class is JIT-compiled, the JIT compiler examines the type parameters and emits specific instructions depending on the type parameters. The JIT compiler performs a number of optimizations to fold different type parameters into the same machine code. First and foremost, the JIT compiler creates one machine version of a generic class for all reference types.

All these instantiations share the same code at runtime:

```
List<string> stringList = new List<string>();
List<Stream> OpenFiles = new List<Stream>();
List<MyClassType> anotherList = new List<MyClassType>();
```

The C# compiler enforces type safety at compile time, and the JIT compiler can produce a more optimized version of the machine code by assuming that the types are correct.

Different rules apply to closed generic types that have at least one value type used as a type parameter. The JIT compiler creates a different set of machine instructions for different type parameters. Therefore, the following three closed generic types have different machine code pages:

```
List<double> doubleList = new List<double>();
List<int> markers = new List<int>();
List<MyStruct> values = new List<MyStruct>();
```

This may be interesting, but why should you care? Generic types that will be used with multiple different reference types do not affect the memory footprint. All JIT-compiled code is shared. However, when closed generic types contain value types as parameters, that JIT-compiled code is not shared. Let's dig a little deeper into that process to see how it will be affected.

When the runtime needs to JIT-compile a generic definition (either a method or a class) and at least one of the type parameters is a value type, it goes through a two-step process. First, it creates a new IL class that represents the closed generic type. I'm simplifying, but essentially the runtime replaces T with int, or the appropriate value type, in all locations in the generic definition. After that replacement, it JIT-compiles the necessary code into x86 instructions. This two-step process is necessary because the JIT compiler does not create the x86 code for an entire class when loaded; instead, each method is JIT-compiled only when first called. Therefore, it makes sense to do a block substitution in the IL and then JIT-compile the resulting IL on demand, as is done with normal class definitions.

This means that the runtime costs of memory footprint add up in this way: one extra copy of the IL definition for each closed generic type that uses a value type, and a second extra copy of machine code for each method called in each different value type parameter used in a closed generic type.

There is, however, a plus side to using generics with value type parameters: You avoid the boxing and unboxing of value types, thereby reducing the size of both code and data for value types. Furthermore, type safety is ensured by the compiler; thus, fewer runtime checks are needed, and that reduces the size of the codebase and improves performance. Furthermore, as discussed in Item 25 later in this chapter, creating generic methods instead of generic classes can limit the amount of extra IL code created for each separate instantiation. Only those methods actually referenced will be instantiated. Generic methods defined in a nongeneric class are not JIT-compiled.

This chapter discusses many of the ways you can use generics and explains how to create generic types and methods that will save you time and help you create usable components.

Item 18: Always Define Constraints That Are Minimal and Sufficient

The constraints you declare on your type parameters specify the must-have behaviors your class needs from any type used as a type argument in order to accomplish its work. A type that doesn't satisfy all your constraints simply won't work. Balance that against the fact that every constraint you impose could mean more work for developers who want to use your type. The right choice varies from task to task, but either extreme is wrong. If you don't specify any constraints, you must perform more checks at runtime; you'll perform more casts, possibly using reflection and generating more runtime errors if developers misuse your type. Specifying unneeded constraints means making too much work for the developers using your class. Your goal is to find the middle ground, where you specify what you need but not everything you want.

Constraints enable the compiler to expect capabilities in a type parameter beyond those in the public interface defined in System.Object. When you create a generic type, the C# compiler must generate valid IL for the generic type definition. While doing so, the compiler must create a valid assembly even though it has only limited knowledge of the actual type that may be used to substitute for any type parameters. Without any guidance from you, the compiler can only assume the most basic capabilities about those types: the methods exposed by System.Object. The compiler cannot enforce any assumptions you have made about your types. All the compiler knows is that your types must derive from System .Object. (This means that you cannot create unsafe generics using pointers as type parameters.) Assuming only the capabilities of System.Object is very limiting. The compiler will emit errors on anything not defined in System.Object. This includes even such fundamental operations as new T(), which is hidden if you define a constructor that has parameters.

You use constraints to communicate (to both the compiler and developers) any assumptions you've made about the generic types. Constraints communicate to the compiler that your generic type expects functionality beyond System.Object's public interface. This communication helps the compiler in two ways. First, it helps when you create your generic type: The compiler asserts that any generic type parameter contains the capabilities you specified in your constraints. Second, the compiler ensures that anyone using your generic type defines type parameters that meet your specifications. You may specify that a type parameter must be a struct, or that it must be a class. You may specify any number of interfaces that a type must implement. You may also specify a base class, which implies the class constraint.

The alternative is for you to perform a lot of casting and runtime testing. For example, the following generic method does not declare any constraints on T, so therefore it must check for the presence of the IComparable<T> interface before using those methods:

```
public static bool AreEqual<T>(T left, T right)
{
    if (left == null)
        return right == null;
```

```
    if (left is IComparable<T>)
    {
        IComparable<T> lval = left as IComparable<T>;
        if (right is IComparable<T>)
            return lval.CompareTo(right) == 0;
        else
            throw new ArgumentException(
"Type does not implement IComparable<T>",
            nameof(right));
    }
    else // failure
    {
        throw new ArgumentException(
"Type does not implement IComparable<T>",
            nameof(left));
    }
}
```

The equivalent method is much simpler if you specify that T must implement IComparable<T>:

```
public static bool AreEqual2<T>(T left, T right)
    where T : IComparable<T> =>
        left.CompareTo(right) == 0;
```

This second version trades runtime errors for compile-time errors. You write less code, and the compiler prevents those runtime errors that you must code against in the first version. Without the constraint, you don't have good options for reporting an obvious programmer error. You need to specify the necessary constraints on your generic types. Not doing so would mean that your class could easily be misused, producing exceptions or other runtime errors when developers guess wrong. They'll guess wrong often, because the only way client developers can determine how to use your class is to read your documentation. Being a developer yourself, you know how likely that is. Using constraints helps the compiler enforce the assumptions you've already made. It minimizes the number of runtime errors and the likelihood of misuse.

But it's easy to go too far in defining constraints. The more constraints you place on the generic type parameters, the less often your generic class can be used by the client developers you're trying to help. Although you need to specify the necessary constraints, you also need to minimize the number of constraints you place on your generic parameters.

There are a number of ways that you can minimize the constraints you specify. One of the most common ways is to ensure that your generic types don't require functionality that they can do without. For example, let's look at `IEquatable<T>`. It's a common interface, and certainly one that many developers would implement when creating new types. You could rewrite the `AreEqual` method using `Equals`:

```
public static bool AreEqual<T>(T left, T right) =>
    left.Equals(right);
```

What's interesting about this version of `AreEqual` is that if `AreEqual<T>()` is defined in a generic class declaring the `IEquatable<T>` constraint, it will call `IEquatable<T>.Equals`. Otherwise, the C# compiler cannot assume that `IEquatable<T>` is present. The only `Equals()` method in scope is `System.Object.Equals()`.

This example illustrates the major difference between C# generics and C++ templates. In C#, the compiler must generate IL using only the information specified in constraints. Even if the type specified for a specific instantiation has a better method, it won't be used unless it was specified when the generic type was compiled.

`IEquatable<T>` is certainly a more efficient way to test equality when it is implemented on the type. You avoid the runtime tests necessary to implement a proper override of `System.Object.Equals()`. You avoid the boxing and unboxing that would be necessary if the type used as your generic type were a value type. If you are highly performance conscious, `IEquatable<T>` also avoids the small overhead of a virtual method call.

So asking your client developers to support `IEquatable<T>` is a good thing. But does it rise to the level of a constraint? Must everyone using your class implement `IEquatable<T>` when there is a perfectly good `System.Object.Equals` method that works correctly, if somewhat less efficiently? I recommend that you use the preferred method (`IEquatable<T>`) if available but transparently downgrade to the less preferred API method (`Equals()`) if the preferred method is not available. You can do that by creating your own internal methods that are overloaded based on the capabilities you support. Essentially, this is the original `AreEqual()` method I showed at the beginning of this item. This approach takes more work, but we'll look at how to query a type for capabilities and use the best interface available in the type parameter, without mandating extra work on the part of client developers.

Sometimes mandating a constraint is too limiting for the use of a class, and you should instead view the presence or absence of a particular interface or base class as an upside rather than a mandate. In those cases, you should code your methods to consider the case when the type parameter may provide extra benefits, but those enhanced functions may not always be available. This is the design implemented in `Equatable<T>` and `Comparable<T>`.

You can extend this technique to other constraints when there are generic and nongeneric interfaces—for example, `IEnumerable` and `IEnumerable<T>`.

The other location you need to carefully consider is the default constructor constraint. Some of the time, you can replace the `new()` constraint by replacing `new` calls with a call to `default()`. The latter is an operator in C# that produces the default value for a type. This operator creates the default 0 bit pattern for value types and produces `null` for reference types. So replacing `new()` with `default()` may often mean introducing either the class or value constraints. Notice that the semantics of `default()` are very different from the semantics of `new()` when you're working with reference types.

You'll often see code that uses `default()` in generic classes that need default values for objects of the type parameters. Following is a method that searches for the first occurrence of an object that satisfies a predicate. If the sought object exists, it is returned. Otherwise, a default value is returned.

```
public static T FirstOrDefault<T>(this IEnumerable<T> sequence,
    Predicate<T> test)
{
    foreach (T value in sequence)
        if (test(value))
            return value;
    return default(T);
}
```

Contrast that with the following method. It wraps a factory method to create an object of type `T`. If the factory method returns `null`, the method returns the value returned by the default constructor.

```
public delegate T FactoryFunc<T>();
public static T Factory<T>(FactoryFunc<T> makeANewT)
where T : new()
{
    T rVal = makeANewT();
    if (rVal == null)
        return new T();
    else
        return rVal;
}
```

The method that uses `default()` needs no constraints. The method that calls `new T()` must specify the `new()` constraint. Also, because of the test for null, the behavior is very different for value types, as compared with reference types. Value types cannot be null. Therefore, the clause under the `if` statement will never be executed. `Factory<T>` can still be used with value types, even though it checks for a `null` value internally. The JIT compiler (which replaces `T` with the specific type) will remove the null test if `T` is a value type.

You should pay careful attention to constraints for `new()`, `struct`, and `class`. The foregoing example shows that adding any of those constraints creates assumptions about how an object will be constructed, whether or not the default value for an object is all zeros or a null reference, and whether or not instances of your generic type parameter can be constructed inside the generic class. Ideally, you should avoid any of these three constraints whenever you can. Think carefully about whether you must have those assumptions for your generic types. Often, you've merely created an assumption in your own mind ("Of course I can call `new T()`") when there is a suitable alternative (such as `default(T)`). Pay careful attention to the assumptions you've implicitly made. Remove those that aren't truly necessary.

To communicate your assumptions to your client programmers, you need to specify constraints. However, the more constraints you specify, the less often your class can be used. The whole point of creating a generic type is to create a type definition that can be used efficiently in as many scenarios as possible. You need to balance the safety of specifying constraints against the extra work required by client programmers to deal with every extra constraint. Strive for the minimal set of assumptions you need, but specify all the assumptions you make as constraints.

Item 19: Specialize Generic Algorithms Using Runtime Type Checking

You can easily reuse generics by simply specifying new type parameters. A new instantiation with new type parameters means a new type having similar functionality.

All this is great, because you write less code. However, sometimes being more generic means not taking advantage of a more specific, but clearly superior, algorithm. The C# language rules take this into account. All it takes is for you to recognize that your algorithm can be more efficient when the type parameters have greater capabilities, and then to write that specific code. Furthermore, creating a second generic type that specifies different constraints doesn't always work. Generic instantiations are based on the compile-time type of an object, and not the runtime type. If you fail to take that into account, you can miss possible efficiencies.

For example, suppose you write a class that provides a reverse-order enumeration on a sequence of items:

```csharp
public sealed class ReverseEnumerable<T> : IEnumerable<T>
{
    private class ReverseEnumerator : IEnumerator<T>
    {
        int currentIndex;
        IList<T> collection;

        public ReverseEnumerator(IList<T> srcCollection)
        {
            collection = srcCollection;
            currentIndex = collection.Count;
        }

        // IEnumerator<T> Members
        public T Current => collection[currentIndex];

        // IDisposable Members
        public void Dispose()
        {
            // no implementation but necessary
            // because IEnumerator<T> implements IDisposable
```

```
            // No protected Dispose() needed
            // because this class is sealed.
        }


        //   IEnumerator Members
        object System.Collections.IEnumerator.Current
            => this.Current;

        public bool MoveNext() => --currentIndex >= 0;

        public void Reset() => currentIndex = collection.Count;
    }

    IEnumerable<T> sourceSequence;
    IList<T> originalSequence;

    public ReverseEnumerable(IEnumerable<T> sequence)
    {
        sourceSequence = sequence;
    }

    // IEnumerable<T> Members
    public IEnumerator<T> GetEnumerator()
    {
        // Create a copy of the original sequence,
        // so it can be reversed.
        if (originalSequence == null)
        {
            originalSequence = new List<T>();
            foreach (T item in sourceSequence)
                originalSequence.Add(item);
        }
        return new ReverseEnumerator(originalSequence);
    }

    // IEnumerable Members
    System.Collections.IEnumerator
        System.Collections.IEnumerable.GetEnumerator() =>
            this.GetEnumerator();
}
```

This implementation assumes the least amount of information from its arguments. The `ReverseEnumerable` constructor assumes that its input parameter supports `IEnumerable<T>`, and that's it. `IEnumerable<T>` does not provide any random access to its elements. Therefore, the only way to reverse the list is shown in the body of `ReverseEnumerator<T>` `.GetEnumerator()`. Here, if the constructor is being called for the first time, it walks the entire input sequence and creates a copy. Then the nested class can walk the list of items backward.

It works, and when the actual input collection does not support random access of the sequence, that's the only way to create a reverse enumeration of a sequence. Many collections you work with support random access, and this code is highly inefficient in those cases. When the input sequence supports `IList<T>`, you've created an extra copy of the entire sequence for no good reason. Let's make use of the fact that many of the types that implement `IEnumerable<T>` also implement `IList<T>` and improve the efficiency of this code.

The only change is in the constructor of the `ReverseEnumerable<T>` class:

```
public ReverseEnumerable(IEnumerable<T> sequence)
{
    sourceSequence = sequence;
    // If sequence doesn't implement IList<T>,
    // originalSequence is null, so this works
    // fine
    originalSequence = sequence as IList<T>;
}
```

Why don't we simply create a second constructor using `IList<T>`? That helps when the compile-time type of the parameter is `IList<T>`. But it doesn't work in some cases—for example, when the compile-time type of a parameter is `IEnumerable<T>` but the runtime type implements `IList<T>`. To catch those cases, you should provide both the runtime check and the compile-time overload.

```
public ReverseEnumerable(IEnumerable<T> sequence)
{
    sourceSequence = sequence;
    // If sequence doesn't implement IList<T>,
    // originalSequence is null, so this works
```

```
    // fine
    originalSequence = sequence as IList<T>;
}

public ReverseEnumerable(IList<T> sequence)
{
    sourceSequence = sequence;
    originalSequence = sequence;
}
```

IList<T> enables a more efficient algorithm than does IEnumerable<T>. You haven't forced consumers of this class to provide more functionality, but you have made use of greater capabilities when they have provided it.

That change handles the vast majority of cases, but there are collections that implement ICollection<T> without implementing IList<T>. In those cases, there are still inefficiencies. Look again at the Reverse-Enumerable<T>.GetEnumerator() method:

```
public IEnumerator<T> GetEnumerator()
{
    // Create a copy of the original sequence,
    // so it can be reversed.
    if (originalSequence == null)
    {
        originalSequence = new List<T>();
        foreach (T item in sourceSequence)
            originalSequence.Add(item);
    }
    return new ReverseEnumerator(originalSequence);
}
```

The code that creates the copy of the input sequence will execute more slowly than needed if the source collection implements ICollection<T>. The following method adds a Count property that you can use to initialize the final storage:

```
public IEnumerator<T> GetEnumerator()
{
    // String is a special case:
    if (sourceSequence is string)
```

```
    {
        // Note the cast because T may not be a char at
        // compile time
        return new
            ReverseStringEnumerator(sourceSequence as string)
            as IEnumerator<T>;
    }
    // Create a copy of the original sequence,
    // so it can be reversed.
    if (originalSequence == null)
    {
        if (sourceSequence is ICollection<T>)
        {
            ICollection<T> source =
                sourceSequence as ICollection<T>;
            originalSequence = new List<T>(source.Count);
        }
        else
            originalSequence = new List<T>();
        foreach (T item in sourceSequence)
            originalSequence.Add(item);
    }
    return new ReverseEnumerator(originalSequence);
}
```

The code I've shown here is similar to the code in the List<T> constructor that creates a list from an input sequence:

```
List<T>(IEnumerable<T> inputSequence);
```

There's one side point I want to cover before we leave this item. You'll notice that all the tests I make in the ReverseEnumerable<T> are run-time tests on the runtime parameter. This means that you assume a run-time cost to query for the extra capabilities. In almost all cases, the cost of the runtime test is much less than the cost of copying the elements.

You may be thinking that we've looked at all the possible uses of the ReverseEnumerable<T> class. But there is still one variation: the string class. string provides methods that have random access to the characters, such as IList<char>, but string does not implement IList<char>. Using the more specific methods requires writing more specific code inside your generic class. The ReverseStringEnumerator class (shown next), which is nested inside the ReverseEnumerable<T>, is straightforward. Notice that the constructor uses the string's Length parameter, and the other methods are almost the same as in the ReverseEnumerator<T> class.

```
private sealed class ReverseStringEnumerator :
    IEnumerator<char>
{
    private string sourceSequence;
    private int currentIndex;

    public ReverseStringEnumerator(string source)
    {
        sourceSequence = source;
        currentIndex = source.Length;
    }

    // IEnumerator<char> Members
    public char Current => sourceSequence[currentIndex];

    //  IDisposable Members
    public void Dispose()
    {
        // no implementation but necessary
        // because IEnumerator<T> implements IDisposable
    }

    // IEnumerator Members
    object System.Collections.IEnumerator.Current
        => sourceSequence[currentIndex];

    public bool MoveNext() => --currentIndex >= 0;

    public void Reset() => currentIndex = sourceSequence.
    Length;
}
```

To complete the specific implementation, the ReverseEnumerable<T>.GetEnumerator() needs to look at the proper type and create the right enumerator type:

```
public IEnumerator<T> GetEnumerator()
{
    // String is a special case:
    if (sourceSequence is string)
    {
        // Note the cast because T may not be a char at
        // compile time
        return new ReverseStringEnumerator(sourceSequence as
string)
            as IEnumerator<T>;
    }
    // Create a copy of the original sequence,
    // so it can be reversed.
    if (originalSequence == null)
    {
        if (sourceSequence is ICollection<T>)
        {
            ICollection<T> source = sourceSequence as
            ICollection<T>;
            originalSequence = new List<T>(source.Count);
        }
        else
            originalSequence = new List<T>();
        foreach (T item in sourceSequence)
            originalSequence.Add(item);
    }
    return new ReverseEnumerator(originalSequence);
}
```

As before, the goal is to hide any specialized implementations inside the generic class. This is a bit more work, because the string class specialization requires a completely separate implementation of the inner class.

You'll also note that the implementation of GetEnumerator() requires a cast when the ReverseStringEnumerator is used. At compile time, T could be anything, and therefore it might not be a char. The cast is safe; the only path through the code ensures that T is a char, because the sequence is a string. That's OK, because it is safely hidden inside the class and won't pollute the public interface. As you can see, the existence of generics does not completely remove the need to occasionally convince the compiler that you know more than it does.

This small sample shows how you can create generic classes that work with the fewest formal constraints and still use specific constraints that will provide a better implementation when the type parameter supports enhanced functionality. That provides the best compromise between maximum reuse and the best implementation you can write for a particular algorithm.

Item 20: Implement Ordering Relations with `IComparable<T>` and `IComparer<T>`

Your types need ordering relationships to describe how collections should be sorted and searched. The .NET Framework defines two interfaces that describe ordering relationships in your types: `IComparable<T>` and `IComparer<T>`. `IComparable<T>` defines the natural order for your types. A type implements `IComparer` to describe alternative orderings. You can define your own implementations of the relational operators (<, >, <=, >=) to provide type-specific comparisons to avoid some runtime inefficiencies in the interface implementations. This item discusses how to implement ordering relations so that the core .NET Framework orders your types through the defined interfaces and so that other users get the best performance from these operations.

The `IComparable` interface contains one method: `CompareTo()`. This method follows the long-standing tradition started with the C library function `strcmp`: Its return value is less than 0 if the current object is less than the comparison object, 0 if they are equal, and greater than 0 if the current object is greater than the comparison object. `IComparable<T>` is used by most newer APIs in the .NET landscape. However, some older APIs use the classic `IComparable` interface. Therefore, when you implement `IComparable<T>`, you should also implement `IComparable`. `IComparable` takes parameters of type `System.Object`. You need to perform runtime type checking on the argument to this function. Every time comparisons are performed, you must reinterpret the type of the argument:

```
public struct Customer : IComparable<Customer>, IComparable
{
    private readonly string name;

    public Customer(string name)
    {
```

```
        this.name = name;
    }


    // IComparable<Customer> Members
    public int CompareTo(Customer other) =>
        name.CompareTo(other.name);


    // IComparable Members
    int IComparable.CompareTo(object obj)
    {
        if (!(obj is Customer))
            throw new ArgumentException(
                "Argument is not a Customer", "obj");
        Customer otherCustomer = (Customer)obj;
        return this.CompareTo(otherCustomer);
    }
}
```

Notice that `IComparable` is explicitly implemented in this structure. That ensures that the only code that will call the object-typed version of `CompareTo()` is code that was written for the previous interface. There's just too much to dislike about the classic version of `IComparable`. You've got to check the runtime type of the argument. Incorrect code could legally call this method with anything as the argument to the `CompareTo` method. More so, proper arguments must be boxed and unboxed to provide the actual comparison. That's an extra runtime expense for each compare. Sorting a collection will make, on average, $n \log(n)$ comparisons of your object using the `IComparable.Compare` method. Each of those will cause three boxing and unboxing operations. For an array with 1,000 points, that is more than 20,000 boxing and unboxing operations, on average: $n \log(n)$ is almost 7,000, and there are three box and unbox operations per comparison.

You may be wondering why you should implement the nongeneric `IComparable` interface at all. There are two reasons. First, there's simple backward compatibility. Your types will interact with code created before .NET 2.0, even though that is several versions old. Some of the Base Class Library classes (consider WinForms or ASP.NET Web Forms) require backward compatibility with 1.0 implementations. That means supporting the nongeneric interface.

Because the classic `IComparable.CompareTo()` is now an explicit interface implementation, it can be called only through an `IComparable` reference. Users of your `Customer struct` will get the type-safe comparison, and the unsafe comparison is inaccessible. The following innocent mistake no longer compiles:

```
Customer c1;
Employee e1;
if (c1.CompareTo(e1) > 0)
    Console.WriteLine("Customer one is greater");
```

It does not compile because the arguments are wrong for the public `Customer.CompareTo(Customer right)` method. The `IComparable.CompareTo(object right)` method is not accessible. You can access the `IComparable` method only by explicitly casting the reference:

```
Customer c1;
Employee e1;
if (c1.CompareTo(e1) > 0)
    Console.WriteLine("Customer one is greater");
```

When you implement `IComparable`, use explicit interface implementation and provide a strongly typed public overload. The strongly typed overload improves performance and decreases the likelihood that someone will misuse the `CompareTo` method. You won't see all the benefits in the `Sort` function that the .NET Framework uses because it will still access `CompareTo()` through the interface pointer, but code that knows the type of both objects being compared will get better performance.

We'll make one last small change to the `Customer struct`. The C# language lets you overload the standard relational operators. Those should make use of the type-safe `CompareTo()` method:

```
public struct Customer : IComparable<Customer>, IComparable
{
    private readonly string name;

    public Customer(string name)
    {
        this.name = name;
    }
```

```
    // IComparable<Customer> Members
    public int CompareTo(Customer other) =>
        name.CompareTo(other.name);

    // IComparable Members
    int IComparable.CompareTo(object obj)
    {
        if (!(obj is Customer))
            throw new ArgumentException(
                "Argument is not a Customer", "obj");
        Customer otherCustomer = (Customer)obj;
        return this.CompareTo(otherCustomer);
    }

    // Relational Operators.
    public static bool operator <(Customer left,
        Customer right) =>
            left.CompareTo(right) < 0;
    public static bool operator <=(Customer left,
        Customer right) =>
            left.CompareTo(right) <= 0;
    public static bool operator >(Customer left,
        Customer right) =>
            left.CompareTo(right) > 0;
    public static bool operator >=(Customer left,
        Customer right) =>
            left.CompareTo(right) >= 0;
}
```

That's all for the standard order of customers: by name. Later, you must create a report sorting all customers by revenue. You still need the normal comparison functionality defined by the `Customer` `struct`, sorting them by name. Most APIs developed after generics became part of the .NET Framework will ask for a `Comparison<T>` delegate to perform some other sort. It's simple to create static properties in the `Customer` type that provide other comparison orders. For example, this delegate compares the revenue generated by two customers:

```
public static Comparison<Customer> CompareByRevenue =>
    (left,right) => left.revenue.CompareTo(right.revenue);
```

Older libraries will ask for this kind of functionality using the ICompar er interface. IComparer provides the standard way to provide alternative orders for a type without using generics. Any of the methods delivered in the 1.x .NET Framework class library that work on IComparable types provide overloads that order objects through IComparer. Because you authored the Customer struct, you can create this new class (RevenueComparer) as a private nested class inside the Customer struct. It gets exposed through a static property in the Customer struct:

```csharp
public struct Customer : IComparable<Customer>, IComparable
{
    private readonly string name;
    private double revenue;

    public Customer(string name, double revenue)
    {
        this.name = name;
        this.revenue = revenue;
    }

    // IComparable<Customer> Members
    public int CompareTo(Customer other)
    {
        return name.CompareTo(other.name);
    }

    // IComparable Members
    int IComparable.CompareTo(object obj)
    {
        if (!(obj is Customer))
            throw new ArgumentException(
                "Argument is not a Customer", "obj");
        Customer otherCustomer = (Customer)obj;
        return this.CompareTo(otherCustomer);
    }

    // Relational Operators.
    public static bool operator <(Customer left,
    Customer right)
    {
        return left.CompareTo(right) < 0;
    }
```

```
public static bool operator <=(Customer left,
Customer right)
{
    return left.CompareTo(right) <= 0;
}
public static bool operator >(Customer left,
Customer right)
{
    return left.CompareTo(right) > 0;
}
public static bool operator >=(Customer left,
Customer right)
{
    return left.CompareTo(right) >= 0;
}

private static Lazy<RevenueComparer> revComp =
    new Lazy<RevenueComparer>(() => new RevenueComparer());
public static IComparer<Customer> RevenueCompare
    =>   revComp.Value;

public static Comparison<Customer> CompareByRevenue =>
    (left,right) => left.revenue.CompareTo(right.revenue);

// Class to compare customers by revenue.
// This is always used via the interface pointer,
// so only provide the interface override.
private class RevenueComparer : IComparer<Customer>
{
    //   IComparer<Customer> Members
    int IComparer<Customer>.Compare(Customer left,
        Customer right) =>
        left.revenue.CompareTo(right.revenue);
}
}
```

The last version of the `Customer` struct, with the embedded
`RevenueComparer`, lets you order a collection of customers by name,
the natural order for customers, and provides an alternative order by
exposing a class that implements the `IComparer` interface to order customers by revenue. If you don't have access to the source for the `Customer`

class, you can still provide an `IComparer` that orders customers using any of its public properties. You should use that idiom only when you do not have access to the source for the class, such as when you need a different ordering for one of the classes in the .NET Framework.

Nowhere in this item did I mention `Equals()` or the `==` operator. Ordering relations and equality are distinct operations. You do not need to implement an equality comparison to have an ordering relation. In fact, reference types commonly implement ordering based on the object contents, yet implement equality based on object identity. `CompareTo()` returns 0, even though `Equals()` returns `false`. That's perfectly legal. Equality and ordering relations are not necessarily the same.

`IComparable` and `IComparer` are the standard mechanisms for providing ordering relations for your types. `IComparable` should be used for the most natural ordering. When you implement `IComparable`, you should overload the comparison operators (`<`, `>`, `<=`, `>=`) consistently with our `IComparable` ordering. `IComparable.CompareTo()` uses `System.Object` parameters, so you should also provide a type-specific overload of the `CompareTo()` method. `IComparer` can be used to provide alternative orderings or can be used when you need to provide ordering for a type that does not provide it for you.

Item 21: Always Create Generic Classes That Support Disposable Type Parameters

Constraints do two things for you and users of your class. First, using constraints transforms runtime errors into compile-time errors. Second, constraints provide a clear set of documentation for users of your class as to what is expected when they create an instantiation of your parameterized type. But you can't use constraints to specify what a type parameter *can't* do. In almost all cases, you don't care what capabilities a type parameter has beyond those your type expects and uses. But in the special case of a type parameter that implements `IDisposable`, you have some extra work on your hands.

Real-world examples that demonstrate this issue become complicated rather quickly, so I've fabricated a simple example to show how this issue occurs and how to rectify it in your code. The problem occurs when you have a generic method that needs to create and use an instance of the type parameter in one of its methods:

```
public interface IEngine
{
    void DoWork();
}


public class EngineDriverOne<T> where T : IEngine, new()
{
    public void GetThingsDone()
    {
        T driver = new T();
        driver.DoWork();
    }
}
```

You may have introduced a resource leak if T implements IDisposable. In every case where you create a local variable of type T, you need to check whether T implements IDisposable and, if so, dispose of it correctly:

```
public void GetThingsDone()
{
    T driver = new T();
    using (driver as IDisposable)
    {
        driver.DoWork();
    }
}
```

This may look a bit confusing if you've never seen that sort of cast in a using statement, but it works. The compiler creates a hidden local variable that stores a reference to the driver cast as an IDisposable. If T does not implement IDisposable, then the value of this local variable is null. In those cases, the compiler does not call Dispose(), because it checks against null before doing this extra work. However, in all cases where T implements IDisposable, the compiler generates a call to the Dispose() method upon exiting the using block.

That's a fairly simple idiom: Wrap local instances of type parameters in a using statement. You need to use the cast I've shown here, because T may or may not implement IDisposable.

Your life gets more complicated when your generic class needs to create and use an instance of the type parameters as member variables. Your generic class now owns a reference to a type that may implement IDisposable.

This means that your generic class must implement IDisposable. You need to have your class check whether the resource implements IDisposable, and, if so, it must dispose of that resource:

```
public sealed class EngineDriver2<T> : IDisposable
    where T : IEngine, new()
{
    // It's expensive to create, so initialize to null
    private Lazy<T> driver = new Lazy<T>(() => new T());
    public void GetThingsDone() =>
        driver.Value.DoWork();

    // IDisposable Members
    public void Dispose()
    {
        if (driver.IsValueCreated)
        {
            var resource = driver.Value as IDisposable;
            resource?.Dispose();
        }
    }
}
```

Your class picked up quite a bit of baggage on this round. You have the added work of implementing IDisposable. Second, you've added the sealed keyword to the class. It's either that or implement the full IDisposable pattern to allow derived classes to also use your Dispose() method. (See Krzysztof Cwalina and Brad Abrams, *Framework Design Guidelines* [Addison-Wesley, 2009], pp. 248–261, or Item 17.) Sealing the class means that you don't need that extra work. However, it does limit the users of your class, who can no longer derive a new type from your class.

Finally, notice that this class, as coded, can't guarantee that you don't call Dispose() on the driver more than once. That's allowed, and any type that implements IDisposable must support multiple calls to Dispose(). That's because there isn't a class constraint on T, so you can't set driver to null before exiting the Dispose method. (Remember that value types cannot be set to null.)

In practice, you often can avoid this design by changing the interface of the generic class somewhat. You can move the Dispose responsibility outside the generic class and remove the new() constraint by moving the ownership outside this generic class:

```
public sealed class EngineDriver<T> where T : IEngine
{
    // It's expensive to create, so initialize to null
    private T driver;
    public EngineDriver(T driver)
    {
        this.driver = driver;
    }

    public void GetThingsDone()
    {
        driver.DoWork();
    }
}
```

Of course, the comment in the earlier listing implies that creating a T object might be very expensive. This latest version ignores that concern. In the end, how you solve this problem depends on many other factors in your application design. But one thing is certain: If you create instances of any of the types described by your generic class's type parameters, you must consider that those types may implement IDisposable. You must code defensively and ensure that you don't leak resources when those objects go out of scope.

Sometimes you can do that by refactoring the code so that it does not create those instances. At other times the best design is to create and use local variables, writing the code to dispose of them if needed. Finally, the design may call for lazy creation of instances of the type parameters and implementing IDisposable in the generic class. It's a bit more work, but it is necessary work if you want to create a class that is useful.

Item 22: Support Generic Covariance and Contravariance

Type variance, and specifically covariance and contravariance, defines the conditions under which a value of one type can be converted to a value of another type. Whenever possible, you should decorate generic interfaces and delegate definitions to support generic covariance and contravariance. Doing so will enable your APIs to be used in more different ways, and safely. If you cannot substitute one type for another, it is called **invariant**.

Type variance is one of those topics that many developers have encountered but not really understood. Covariance and contravariance are the ability to deduce the compatibility of two generic types from a fact about the compatibility of their type arguments. A generic type C<T> is covariant in T if we can deduce that C<X> is convertible to C<Y> by knowing that X is convertible to Y. C<T> is contravariant in T if we can deduce that C<X> is convertible to C<Y> by knowing that Y is convertible to X.

Most developers think you should be able to use an IEnumerable<My-DerivedType> with a method that has a parameter of IEnumerable <Object>. You would expect that if a method returns an IEnumerable-<MyDerivedType>, you could assign that to a variable of type IEnumerable<object>. Not so. Prior to C# 4.0, all generic types were invariant. That meant there were many times when you would reasonably expect covariance or contravariance with generics only to be told by the compiler that your code was invalid. Arrays were treated covariantly. However, arrays do not support safe covariance. From C# 4.0 and later, new keywords are available to enable you to use generics covariantly and contravariantly. That makes generics much more useful, especially if you remember to include the in and out parameters where possible on generic interfaces and delegates.

Let's begin by understanding the problems with array covariance. Consider this small class hierarchy:

```
abstract public class CelestialBody :
    IComparable<CelestialBody>
{
    public double Mass { get; set; }
    public string Name { get; set; }
    // elided
}


public class Planet : CelestialBody
{
    // elided
}


public class Moon : CelestialBody
{
    // elided
}
```

```
public class Asteroid : CelestialBody
{
    // elided
}
```

This method treats arrays of `CelestialBody` objects covariantly and does so safely:

```
public static void CoVariantArray(CelestialBody[] baseItems)
{
    foreach (var thing in baseItems)
        Console.WriteLine("{0} has a mass of {1} Kg",
            thing.Name, thing.Mass);
}
```

This method also treats arrays of `CelestialBody` objects covariantly, but it is not safe. The assignment statement will throw an exception.

```
public static void UnsafeVariantArray(CelestialBody[] baseItems)
{
    baseItems[0] = new Asteroid
        { Name = "Hygiea", Mass = 8.85e19 };
}
```

You can have the same problem simply by assigning an array of a derived class to a variable that is an array of a base type:

```
CelestialBody[] spaceJunk = new Asteroid[5];
spaceJunk[0] = new Planet();
```

Treating collections as covariant means that when there is an inheritance relationship between two types, you can imagine there is a similar inheritance relationship between arrays of those two types. This isn't a strict definition, but it's a useful picture to keep in your mind. A `Planet` can be passed to any method that expects `CelestialBody`. That's because `Planet` is derived from `CelestialBody`. Similarly, you can pass a `Planet[]` to any method that expects a `CelestialBody[]`. But, as the example above shows, that doesn't always work the way you'd expect.

When generics were first introduced, this issue was dealt with in a rather draconian fashion. Generics were always treated invariantly by the C# compiler. Generic types had to have an exact match. However, in C# 4.0 and newer, you can decorate generic interfaces so that they can be treated covariantly, or contravariantly. Let's discuss generic covariance first, and then we'll move on to contravariance.

This method can be called with a `List<Planet>`:

```
public static void CovariantGeneric
    (IEnumerable<CelestialBody> baseItems)
{
    foreach (var thing in baseItems)
        Console.WriteLine("{0} has a mass of {1} Kg",
            thing.Name, thing.Mass);
}
```

That's because `IEnumerable<T>` has been augmented to limit `T` to only output positions in its interface:

```
public interface IEnumerable<out T> : IEnumerable
{
    new IEnumerator<T> GetEnumerator();
}
public interface IEnumerator<out T> :
    IDisposable, IEnumerator
{
    new T Current { get; }
    // MoveNext(), Reset() inherited from IEnumerator
}
```

I included both the `IEnumerable<T>` and `IEnumerator<T>` definitions here because the `IEnumerator<T>` has the important restrictions. Notice that `IEnumerator<T>` now decorates the type parameter `T` with the `out` modifier. That forces the compiler to limit `T` to output positions. Output positions are limited to function return values, property get accessors, and certain delegate positions.

Therefore, using `IEnumerable<out T>`, the compiler knows that you will look at every `T` in the sequence but never modify the contents of the source sequence. Treating every `Planet` as a `CelestialBody` in this case works.

`IEnumerable<T>` can be covariant only because `IEnumerator<T>` is also covariant. If `IEnumerable<T>` returned an interface that was not declared as covariant, the compiler would generate an error.

However, the method that replaces the first item in the list will be invariant when using generics:

```
public static void InvariantGeneric(
    IList<CelestialBody> baseItems)
```

```
{
    baseItems[0] = new Asteroid
        { Name = "Hygiea", Mass = 8.85e19 };
}
```

Because ILis̄t<T> is decorated with neither the in nor out modifier on T, you must use the exact type match.

Of course, you can create contravariant generic interfaces and delegates as well. Substitute the in modifier for the out modifier. That instructs the compiler that the type parameter may appear only in input positions. The .NET Framework has added the in modifier to the IComparable<T> interface:

```
public interface IComparable<in T>
{
    int CompareTo(T other);
}
```

That means you could make CelestialBody implement IComparable<T>, using an object's mass. It would compare two Planets, a Planet and a Moon, a Moon and an Asteroid, or any other combination. By comparing the mass of the objects, that's a valid comparison.

You'll notice that IEquatable<T> is invariant. By definition, a Planet cannot be equal to a Moon. They are different types, so it makes no sense. It is necessary, if not sufficient, for two objects to be of the same type if they are equal.

Type parameters that are contravariant can only appear as method parameters, and in some locations in delegate parameters.

Let's finish by discussing covariant and contravariant delegate arguments. Delegate definitions can be covariant or contravariant as well. It's usually pretty simple: Method parameters are contravariant (in), and method return types are covariant (out). The .NET Base Class Library (BCL) updated many of their delegate definitions to include variance:

```
public delegate TResult Func<out TResult>();
public delegate TResult Func<in T, out TResult>(T arg);
public delegate TResult Func<in T1, T2, out TResult>(T1 arg1,
    T2 arg2);
public delegate void Action<in T>(T arg);
public delegate void Action<in T1, in T2>(T1 arg1, T2 arg2);
public delegate void Action<in T1, in T2, T3>(T1 arg1,
    T2 arg2, T3 arg3);
```

Again, this probably isn't too hard. But when you mix them, things start to be mind-bending. You already saw that you cannot return invariant interfaces from covariant interfaces. You can't use delegates to get around the covariant and contravariant restrictions, either.

Delegates have a tendency to "flip" the covariance and contravariance in an interface if you're not careful. Here are a couple of examples:

```
public interface ICovariantDelegates<out T>
{
    T GetAnItem();
    Func<T> GetAnItemLater();
    void GiveAnItemLater(Action<T> whatToDo);
}


public interface IContravariantDelegates<in T>
{
    void ActOnAnItem(T item);
    void GetAnItemLater(Func<T> item);
    Action<T> ActOnAnItemLater();
}
```

I've named the methods in these interfaces specifically to show why covariance and contravariance for delegates work the way they do. Look closely at the `ICovariantDelegate` interface definition. `GetAnItemLater()` is just a way to retrieve an item lazily. The caller can invoke the `Func<T>` returned by the method later to retrieve a value. `T` still exists in the output position. That probably still makes sense. The `GiveAnItemLater()` method probably is a bit more confusing. Here, `GiveAnItemLater()` takes a delegate that will accept a `T` object whenever you call it. So, even though `Action<in T>` is covariant, its position in the `ICovariantDelegate` interface means that it is actually a means by which `T` objects are returned from an `ICovariantDelegate<T>` implementing object. It may look like it should be contravariant, but it is covariant with respect to the interface.

`IContravariantDelegate<T>` is similar but shows how you can use delegates in a contravariant interface. Again, the `ActOnAnItem` method should be obvious. The `ActOnAnItemLater()` method is just a little more complicated. You're returning a method that will accept a `T` object sometime later. That last method, once again, may cause some confusion. It's the same concept as with the other interface. The `GetAnItemLater()`

method accepts a method that will return a T object sometime later. Even though Func<out T> is declared covariant, its use is to bring an input to the object implementing IContravariantDelegate. Its use is contra-variant with respect to the IContravariantDelegate.

It certainly can get complicated describing exactly how covariance and contravariance work. Thankfully, now the language supports decorating generic interfaces and delegates with in (contravariant) and out (covariant) modifiers. You should decorate any interfaces and delegates you define with the in or out modifier wherever possible. Then the compiler can correct any possible misuses of the variance you've defined. The compiler will catch it in both your interface and delegate definitions, and it will detect any misuse of the types you've created.

Item 23: Use Delegates to Define Method Constraints on Type Parameters

At first glance, the constraint mechanism in C# seems too restrictive: You can specify only a single base class, interfaces, class or struct, and a parameterless constructor. That leaves a lot out. You can't specify static methods (which include any operators), and you can't specify any other constructors. From one perspective, the constraints defined by the language can satisfy every contract. You can use parameters to define an IFactory<T> interface that creates T objects. You can define IAdd<T> to add T objects and use the static operator "+" defined on T (or use some other method that adds T objects). But that's not a good way to solve this problem. It's a lot of extra work, and it obscures your basic design.

Let's consider the Add() example. If your generic class needed an Add() method on T, you'd need to perform several tasks: You would create an IAdd<T> interface. You'd code against that interface. So far, that's not too bad. But all developers who want to use your generic class would need to do even more work. They'd need to create a class that implements IAdd<T>, define the methods needed for IAdd<T>, and then specify the closed generic class for your generic class definition. To call one method, you've made developers create a class simply to match an API signature. That introduces quite a bit of friction and confusion for developers who want to use your class.

But it doesn't have to be that way. You can specify a delegate signature that matches the method your generic class needs to call. It doesn't mean any more work for you, the author of the generic class. But it saves a great deal of work for the developers who are using your generic class.

Here's how you would define a generic class that needs some method that adds two objects of type T. You don't even need to define your own delegate definition; the System.Func<T1, T2, TOutput> delegate matches the signature you need. Here is a generic method that adds two objects, using a supplied method that implements Add:

```
public static class Example
{
    public static T Add<T>(T left, T right,
        Func<T, T, T> AddFunc) =>
    AddFunc(left, right);
}
```

Developers using your class can use type inference and lambda expressions to define the method that should be called when your generic class needs to call AddFunc(). You would call the Add generic method using a lambda expression like this:

```
int a = 6;
int b = 7;
int sum = Example.Add(a, b, (x, y) => x + y);
```

The C# compiler infers the types and return values from the lambda expression. The C# compiler creates a private static method that returns the sum of the two integers. The name of the method is generated by the compiler. The compiler also creates a Func<T,T,T> delegate object and assigns the method pointer to that compiler-generated method. Finally, the compiler passes that delegate to the generic Example.Add() method.

I've used the lambda syntax to specify the method that defines the delegate to show why you should create delegate-based interface contracts. The code is a contrived example, but the concept is what's important. When it's unwieldy to use an interface to define a constraint, you can define a method signature and a delegate type that suit your needs. Then you add an instance of that delegate to the list of the parameters of the generic method. The developers using your class can use a lambda expression to define that method, writing much less code, in a much clearer fashion. Developers using your class need to create the lambda expression that defines the method functionality they need. There's no extra code to support the syntax of interface-based constraints.

More often, you'll want to use delegate-based contracts to create algorithms that operate on sequences. Imagine you need to write code that combines samples taken from various mechanical probes and turns these two sequences into a single sequence of points.

Your `Point` class might look like this:

```
public class Point
{
    public double X { get; }
    public double Y { get; }
    public Point(double x, double y)
    {
        this.X = x;
        this.Y = y;
    }
}
```

The values you've read from your device are `List<double>` sequences. You need a way to create a sequence by repeatedly calling the `Point(double,double)` constructor with each successive (X,Y) pair. `Point` is an immutable type. You can't call the default constructor and then set the X and Y properties. But neither can you create a constraint that specifies parameters on a constructor. The solution is to define a delegate that takes two parameters and returns a point. Again, it's already in the .NET Framework 3.5:

```
delegate TOutput Func<T1, T2, TOutput>(T1 arg1, T2 arg2);
```

In this example, T1 and T2 are the same type: `double`. A generic method in the Base Class Library that creates an output sequence looks similar to this:

```
public static IEnumerable<TOutput> Zip<T1, T2, TOutput>
    (IEnumerable<T1> left, IEnumerable<T2> right,
    Func<T1, T2, TOutput> generator)
{
    IEnumerator<T1> leftSequence = left.GetEnumerator();
    IEnumerator<T2> rightSequence = right.GetEnumerator();
    while (leftSequence.MoveNext() && rightSequence.MoveNext())
    {
        yield return generator(leftSequence.Current,
            rightSequence.Current);
    }
```

```
        leftSequence.Dispose();
        rightSequence.Dispose();
}
```

`Zip` enumerates both input sequences, and for each pair of items in the input sequence, it calls the generator delegate, returning the newly constructed `Point` object (see Items 29 and 33). The delegate contract specifies that you need a method that constructs the output type from two different inputs. Notice that `Zip` is defined so that the two input types don't need to be the same type. You could create key/value pairs of disparate types using this same method. You'd just need a different delegate.

You would call `Zip` this way:

```
double[] xValues = { 0, 1, 2, 3, 4, 5, 6, 7, 8, 9,
    0, 1, 2, 3, 4, 5, 6, 7, 8, 9 };
double[] yValues = { 0, 1, 2, 3, 4, 5, 6, 7, 8, 9,
    0, 1, 2, 3, 4, 5, 6, 7, 8, 9 };

List<Point> values = new List<Point>(
    Utilities.Zip(xValues, yValues, (x, y) =>
    new Point(x, y)));
```

As before, the compiler generates a private static method, instantiates a delegate object using a reference to that method, and passes that delegate object to the `Merge()` method.

In the general case, any method your generic class needs to call can be replaced by a specific delegate. These first two examples contain a delegate that is called for a generic method. This practice works even if your type needs the delegate method in many locations. You can create a generic class in which one of the class type parameters is a delegate. Then, when you create an instance of the class, you assign a member of the class to a delegate of that type.

The following simple example caches a delegate that reads a point from a stream and calls that delegate to convert the text input to a `Point`. The first step is to add a constructor to the `Point` class that reads a point from a file:

```
public Point(System.IO.TextReader reader)
{
    string line = reader.ReadLine();
    string[] fields = line.Split(',');
```

```
if (fields.Length != 2)
    throw new InvalidOperationException(
        "Input format incorrect");
double value;
if (!double.TryParse(fields[0], out value))
    throw new InvalidOperationException(
        "Could not parse X value");
else
    X = value;

if (!double.TryParse(fields[1], out value))
    throw new InvalidOperationException(
        "Could not parse Y value");
else
    Y = value;
}
```

Creating the collection class requires some indirection. You can't enforce a constraint that your generic type includes a constructor that takes parameters. However, you can mandate a method that does what you want. You define a delegate type that constructs a T from a file:

```
public delegate T CreateFromStream<T>(TextReader reader);
```

Next, you create the container class, and the constructor of that container takes an instance of the delegate type as a parameter:

```
public class InputCollection<T>
{
    private List<T> thingsRead = new List<T>();
    private readonly CreateFromStream<T> readFunc;

    public InputCollection(CreateFromStream<T> readFunc)
    {
        this.readFunc = readFunc;
    }

    public void ReadFromStream(TextReader reader) =>
        thingsRead.Add(readFunc(reader));

    public IEnumerable<T> Values => thingsRead;
}
```

When you instantiate an `InputCollection`, you supply the delegate:

```
var readValues = new InputCollection<Point>(
    (inputStream) => new Point(inputStream));
```

This sample is simple enough that you'd probably create the nongeneric class instead. However, this technique will help you build generic types that rely on behavior that cannot be specified by a normal constraint.

Often, the best way to express your design is to use class constraints or interface constraints to specify your constraints. The .NET BCL does that in many places, expecting your types to implement `IComparable<T>`, or `IEquatable<T>`, or `IEnumerable<T>`. That's the right design choice, because those interfaces are common and are used by many algorithms. Also, they are clearly expressed as interfaces: A type implementing `IComparable<T>` declares that it supports an ordering relation. A type implementing `IEquatable<T>` declares that it supports equality.

However, if you need to create a custom interface contract to support only a particular generic method or class, you may find that it's much easier for your users to use delegates to specify that contract as a method constraint. Your generic type will be easy to use, and the code calling it will be easy to understand. Whether it's the presence of an operator, another static method, a delegate type, or some other construction idiom, you can define some generic interfaces for the constraint, and you can create a helper type that implements that interface so that you can satisfy the constraints. Don't let a semantic contract that's not directly compatible with constraints stop you from enforcing your design.

Item 24: Do Not Create Generic Specialization on Base Classes or Interfaces

Introducing generic methods can make it highly complicated for the compiler to resolve method overloads. Each generic method can match any possible substitute for each type parameter. Depending on how careful you are (or aren't), your application will behave very strangely. When you create generic classes or methods, you are responsible for creating a set of methods that will enable developers using that class to safely use your code with minimal confusion. This means that you must pay careful attention to overload resolution, and you must determine when generic methods will create better matches than the methods developers might reasonably expect.

Examine this code, and try to guess the output:

```
using static System.Console;

public class MyBase
{
}

public interface IMessageWriter
{
    void WriteMessage();
}

public class MyDerived : MyBase, IMessageWriter
{
    void IMessageWriter.WriteMessage() =>
        WriteLine("Inside MyDerived.WriteMessage");
}

public class AnotherType : IMessageWriter
{
    public void WriteMessage() =>
        WriteLine("Inside AnotherType.WriteMessage");
}

class Program
{
    static void WriteMessage(MyBase b)
    {
        WriteLine("Inside WriteMessage(MyBase)");
    }

    static void WriteMessage<T>(T obj)
    {
        Write("Inside WriteMessage<T>(T):   ");
        WriteLine(obj.ToString());
    }

    static void WriteMessage(IMessageWriter obj)
    {
        Write("Inside WriteMessage(IMessageWriter):   ");
```

```
        obj.WriteMessage();
    }

    static void Main(string[] args)
    {
        MyDerived d = new MyDerived();
        WriteLine("Calling Program.WriteMessage");
        WriteMessage(d);
        WriteLine();

        WriteLine("Calling through IMessageWriter interface");
        WriteMessage((IMessageWriter)d);
        WriteLine();

        WriteLine("Cast to base object");
        WriteMessage((MyBase)d);
        WriteLine();

        WriteLine("Another Type test:");
        AnotherType anObject = new AnotherType();
        WriteMessage(anObject);
        WriteLine();

        WriteLine("Cast to IMessageWriter:");
        WriteMessage((IMessageWriter)anObject);
    }
}
```

Some of the comments might give it away, but make your best guess before looking at the output. It's important to understand how the existence of generic methods affects the method resolution rules. Generics are almost always a good match, and they wreak havoc with our assumptions about which methods get called. Here's the output:

```
Calling Program.WriteMessage
Inside WriteMessage<T>(T):  Item14.MyDerived

Calling through IMessageWriter interface
Inside WriteMessage(IMessageWriter):
    Inside MyDerived.WriteMessage

Cast to base object
Inside WriteMessage(MyBase)
```

```
Another Type test:
Inside WriteMessage<T>(T):  Item14.AnotherType

Cast to IMessageWriter:
Inside WriteMessage(IMessageWriter):
    Inside AnotherType.WriteMessage
```

The first test shows one of the more important concepts to remember: `WriteMessage<T>(T obj)` is a better match than `WriteMessage(MyBase b)` for an expression whose type is derived from `MyBase`. That's because the compiler can make an exact match by substituting `MyDerived` for `T` in that message, and `WriteMessage(MyBase)` requires an implicit conversion. The generic method is better. This concept will become even more important when you see the extension methods defined in the `Queryable` and `Enumerable` classes. Generic methods are always perfect matches, so they win over base class methods.

The next two tests show how you can control this behavior by explicitly invoking the conversion (either to `MyBase` or to an `IMessageWriter` type). And the last two tests show that the same type of behavior is present for interface implementations even without class inheritance.

Name resolution rules are interesting, and you can show off your arcane knowledge about them at geek cocktail parties. But what you really need is a strategy to create code that ensures that your concept of "best match" agrees with the compiler's concept. After all, the compiler always wins this battle.

It's not a good idea to create generic specializations for base classes when you intend to support the class and all its descendants. It's equally error prone to create generic specializations for interfaces. But numeric types do not present those pitfalls. There is no inheritance chain between integral and floating-point numeric types. As Item 18 earlier in this chapter explains, often there are good reasons to provide specific versions of a method for different value types. Specifically, the .NET Framework includes specialization on all numeric types for `Enumerable.Max<T>`, `Enumerable.Min<T>`, and similar methods. But it's best to use the compiler instead of adding runtime checks to determine the type. That's what you're trying to avoid by using generics in the first place, right?

```
// Not the best solution
// this uses runtime type checking
static void WriteMessage<T>(T obj)
```

```
{
    if (obj is MyBase)
        WriteMessage(obj as MyBase);
    else if (obj is IMessageWriter)
        WriteMessage((IMessageWriter)obj);
    else
    {
        Write("Inside WriteMessage<T>(T):  ");
        WriteLine(obj.ToString());
    }
}
```

This code might be fine, but only if there are only a few conditions to check. It does hide all the ugly behavior from developers who use your class, but notice that it introduces some runtime overhead. Your generic method is now checking specific types to determine whether they are (in your mind) a better match than the one the compiler would choose if left to its own devices. Use this technique only when it's clear that a better match is quite a bit better, and measure the performance to see whether there are better ways to write your library to avoid the problem altogether.

Of course, this is not to say that you should never create more specific methods for a given implementation. Item 19 earlier in this chapter shows how to create a better implementation when advanced capabilities are available. The code in Item 33 creates a reverse iterator that adapts itself correctly when advanced capabilities are created. Notice that the Item 33 code does not rely on generic types for any name resolution. Each constructor expresses the various capabilities correctly to ensure that the proper method can be called at each location. However, if you want to create a specific instantiation of a generic method for a given type, you need to create that instantiation for that type and all its descendants. If you want to create a generic specialization for an interface, you need to create a version for all types that implement that interface.

Item 25: Prefer Generic Methods Unless Type Parameters Are Instance Fields

It's easy to fall into the habit of limiting yourself to generic class definitions. But often you can more clearly express utility classes by using a nongeneric class that contains numerous generic methods. The reason, again, is that the C# compiler must generate valid IL for an entire generic class based on the constraints specified. One set of constraints must be valid for the entire class. A utility class that contains generic methods can specify different constraints for each method. Those different constraints can make it much easier for the compiler to find the best match and therefore much easier for your clients to use your algorithms.

Also, each type parameter needs to satisfy the constraints only for the methods in which it is used. With generic classes, in contrast, the type parameters must satisfy all the constraints defined for the complete class. As you expand a class over time, it becomes much more constraining if the type parameters are specified on the class level rather than at the method level. After two releases you'll wish you'd specified your generic methods at the method level. Here's one simple guideline: If a type needs type-level data members, especially data members involving the type parameter, make it a generic class. Otherwise, use generic methods.

Let's consider a simple example that contains generic `Min` and `Max` methods:

```
public static class Utils<T>
{
    public static T Max(T left, T right) =>
        Comparer<T>.Default.Compare(left, right) < 0 ?
            right : left;

    public static T Min(T left, T right) =>
        Comparer<T>.Default.Compare(left, right) < 0 ?
            left : right;
}
```

At first review, it seems to work perfectly. You can compare numbers:

```
double d1 = 4;
double d2 = 5;
double max = Utils<double>.Max(d1, d2);
```

You can compare strings:

```
string foo = "foo";
string bar = "bar";
string sMax = Utils<string>.Max(foo, bar);
```

You're happy, and you head home. But folks who are using your class aren't so happy. You'll notice that every call in the preceding code snippets needs to explicitly specify the type parameter. That's because you've created a generic class instead of a set of generic methods. The extra work is an annoyance, but there are deeper problems here. Many of the built-in types already have accessible `Max` and `Min` methods defined. `Math.Max()` and `Math.Min()` are defined for all the numeric types. Instead of using those, your generic class always picks up the version you've created using `Comparer<T>`. That works, but it forces extra runtime checks to determine whether a type implements `IComparer<T>`, followed by a call to the correct method.

Naturally, you'd like to have your users automatically pick up the best method possible. That's much easier if you create generic methods in a nongeneric class:

```
public static class Utils
{
    public static T Max<T>(T left, T right) =>
        Comparer<T>.Default.Compare(left, right) < 0 ? right :
        left;

    public static double Max(double left, double right) =>
        Math.Max(left, right);
    // versions for other numeric types elided

    public static T Min<T>(T left, T right) =>
        Comparer<T>.Default.Compare(left, right) < 0 ? left :
        right;

    public static double Min(double left, double right) =>
        Math.Min(left, right);
    // versions for other numeric types elided
}
```

This `Utils` class is no longer a generic class. Instead, it has several overloads of both `Min` and `Max`. Those specific methods are more efficient than the generic version (see Item 3). Better still, users no longer need to specify which version they call:

```
double d1 = 4;
double d2 = 5;
double max = Utils.Max(d1, d2);

string foo = "foo";
string bar = "bar";
string sMax = Utils.Max(foo, bar);
```

```
double? d3 = 12;
double? d4 = null;
double? Max2 = Utils.Max(d3, d4).Value;
```

If there is a specific version of the parameter type, the compiler calls that version. If there isn't a specific version, the compiler calls the generic version. Furthermore, if you later extend the `Utils` class with more versions for different specific types, the compiler will immediately pick them up.

It's not only static utility classes that should use generic methods instead of a generic class. Consider this simple class, which builds a comma-separated list of items:

```
public class CommaSeparatedListBuilder
{
    private StringBuilder storage = new StringBuilder();

    public void Add<T>(IEnumerable<T> items)
    {
        foreach (T item in items)
        {
            if (storage.Length > 0)
                storage.Append(", ");
            storage.Append("\"");
            storage.Append(item.ToString());
            storage.Append("\"");
        }
    }

    public override string ToString() =>
        storage.ToString();
}
```

As coded, this lets you create any number of disparate types in the list. Whenever you use a new type, the compiler generates a new version of `Add<T>`. If you had instead applied the type parameter to the class declaration, every `CommaSeparatedListBuilder` would be forced to hold only one type. Either approach is valid, but the semantics are very different.

This sample is simple enough that you could replace the type parameter with `System.Object`. But the concept is one you can apply often. You can use a catchall generic method in a nongeneric class to create different specialized methods in the class. This class does not use T in its fields but uses it only as a parameter to methods in the public API. Using different types in place of the parameters to that method doesn't mean that you need a different instantiation.

Obviously, not every generic algorithm is suited for generic methods instead of a generic class. Some simple guidelines can help you determine which to use. In two cases you must make a generic class: The first occurs when your class stores a value of one of the type parameters as part of its internal state. (Collections are an obvious example.) The second occurs when your class implements a generic interface. Except for those two cases, you can usually create a nongeneric class and use generic methods. You'll end up with more granularity in your options for updating the algorithms in the future.

Look again at the code for the preceding sample. You'll see that the second Utils class does not force the callers to explicitly declare each type in each call to one of the generic methods. When possible, the second version is a better API solution, for a number of reasons. First, it's simpler for callers. When you don't specify the type parameter, the compiler picks the best possible method. That practice gives you, the library developer, many options moving forward. If you find that a specific implementation is better, your callers automatically get the specific method you created. If, on the other hand, your methods force callers to specify all the type parameters, they will continue to use the generic methods even though you have provided a better alternative.

Item 26: Implement Classic Interfaces in Addition to Generic Interfaces

So far, the items in this chapter have explored all the wonderful benefits of generics. It would be great if we could just ignore everything that predated generics support in .NET and C#. But a developer's life isn't that simple, for a variety of reasons. Your classes will be much more useful if you support the classic nongeneric interfaces in addition to the generic interfaces you'll want to support in new libraries. This recommendation applies to (1) your classes and the interfaces they support, (2) public properties, and even (3) the elements you choose to serialize.

Let's examine why you need to consider support for these nongeneric interfaces, and let's look at how to support these classic interfaces while still encouraging the users of your class to use the newer generic versions. Let's start with a simple implementation of a `Name` class that stores the names of people in an application:

```
public class Name :
    IComparable<Name>,
    IEquatable<Name>
{
    public string First { get; set; }
    public string Last { get; set; }
    public string Middle { get; set; }

    //  IComparable<Name> Members
    public int CompareTo(Name other)
    {
        if (Object.ReferenceEquals(this, other))
            return 0;
        if (Object.ReferenceEquals(other, null))
            return 1; // Any non-null object > null.
        int rVal = Comparer<string>.Default.Compare
            (Last, other.Last);
        if (rVal != 0)
            return rVal;
        rVal = Comparer<string>.Default.Compare
            (First, other.First);
        if (rVal != 0)
            return rVal;
        return Comparer<string>.Default.Compare(Middle,
            other.Middle);
    }

    // IEquatable<Name> Members
    public bool Equals(Name other)
    {
        if (Object.ReferenceEquals(this, other))
            return true;
        if (Object.ReferenceEquals(other, null))
            return false;
        // Semantically equivalent to using
        // EqualityComparer<string>.Default
```

```
        return Last == other.Last &&
            First == other.First &&
            Middle == other.Middle;
    }


    // other details elided
}
```

All the core capabilities of the equality and ordering are implemented in terms of the generic (and type-safe) versions. Also, you can see that I've deferred the null checks in `CompareTo()` to the default string comparer. That saves quite a bit of code and provides the same semantics.

There is more work to do for a fully robust system. You may need to integrate types from various systems that represent the same logical type. Suppose you purchase an e-commerce system from one vendor and a fulfillment system from a different vendor. Both systems have the concept of an order: `Store.Order` and `Shipping.Order`. You need an equality relationship between those two types. Generics don't do that very well. You'll need a cross-type comparer. Furthermore, you may need to store both types of `Order` in a single collection. Again, a generic type won't do.

Instead, you need a method that checks for equality using `System .Object`, perhaps something like this:

```
public static bool CheckEquality(object left, object right)
{
    if (left == null)
        return right == null;
    return left.Equals(right);
}
```

Calling the `CheckEquality()` method using two `person` objects would yield unexpected results. Instead of calling the `IEquatable<Name>.Equals()` method, `CheckEquality()` would call `System.Object.Equals()`! You'll get the wrong answer, because `System.Object.Equals()` will use reference semantics, and you've overridden `IEquatable<T>.Equals` to follow value semantics.

If the `CheckEquality()` method is in your code, you can create a generic version of `CheckEquality` that calls the correct method:

```
public static bool CheckEquality<T>(T left, T right)
    where T : IEquatable<T>
```

```
{
    if (left == null)
        return right == null;

    return left.Equals(right);
}
```

Of course, that solution isn't available to you if `CheckEquality()` isn't in your codebase but is in a third-party library or even the .NET BCL. You must override the classic `Equals` method to call the `IEquatable<T>`.`Equals` method you've written:

```
public override bool Equals(object obj)
{
    if (obj.GetType() == typeof(Name))
        return this.Equals(obj as Name);
    else return false;
}
```

After this modification, almost any method that checks for equality on `Name` types works correctly. Notice that I'm checking the type of the `obj` parameter against the type of `Name` before using the `as` operator to convert to a `Name`. You might think that this check is redundant, because the `as` operator returns `null` if `obj` is not a type that's convertible to `Name`. That assumption misses some conditions: If `obj` is an instance of a class derived from `Name`, the `as` operator will return a `Name` reference to the object. The objects aren't equal, even if their `Name` portions are.

Next, overriding `Equals` means overriding `GetHashCode`:

```
public override int GetHashCode()
{
    int hashCode = 0;
    if (Last != null)
        hashCode ^= Last.GetHashCode();
    if (First != null)
        hashCode ^= First.GetHashCode();
    if (Middle != null)
        hashCode ^= Middle.GetHashCode();
    return hashCode;
}
```

Again, this simply expands the public API to ensure that your type plays well with version 1.x code.

If you want to completely ensure that you have covered all your bases, you need to handle a few operators. Implementing IEquality<T> means implementing operator ==, and that also means implementing operator !=:

```
public static bool operator ==(Name left, Name right)
{
    if (left == null)
        return right == null;
    return left.Equals(right);
}
public static bool operator !=(Name left, Name right)
{
    if (left == null)
        return right != null;
    return !left.Equals(right);
}
```

That's enough of equality. The Name class also implements IComparable<T>. You're going to run into the same conditions with ordering relations as you do with equality relations. There's a lot of code out there that expects you to implement the class IComparable interface. You've already written the algorithm, so you should just go ahead and add the IComparable interface to the list of implemented interfaces and create the proper method:

```
public class Name :
    IComparable<Name>,
    IEquatable<Name>,
    IComparable
{
    // IComparable Members
    int IComparable.CompareTo(object obj)
    {
        if (obj.GetType() != typeof(Name))
            throw new ArgumentException(
                "Argument is not a Name object");
        return this.CompareTo(obj as Name);
    }
    // other details elided
}
```

Notice that the classic interface is defined using explicit interface implementation. This practice ensures that no one accidentally gets the classic interface instead of the preferred generic interface. In normal use, the compiler will choose the generic method over the explicit interface method. Only when the called method has been typed to the classic interface (`IComparable`) will the compiler generate a call to that interface member.

Of course, implementing `IComparable<T>` implies that there is an ordering relation. You should implement the less-than (<) and greater-than (>) operators:

```
public static bool operator <(Name left, Name right)
{
    if (left == null)
        return right != null;
    return left.CompareTo(right) < 0;
}
public static bool operator >(Name left, Name right)
{
    if (left == null)
        return false;
    return left.CompareTo(right) < 0;
}
```

In the case of the `Name` type, because it both defines an ordering relation and defines equality, you should implement the "<=" and ">=" operators:

```
public static bool operator <=(Name left, Name right)
{
    if (left == null)
        return true;
    return left.CompareTo(right) <= 0;
}
public static bool operator >=(Name left, Name right)
{
    if (left == null)
        return right == null;
    return left.CompareTo(right) >= 0;
}
```

You must understand that the ordering relations are independent of the equality relations. You can define types in which equality is defined but ordering relations are not defined. And you can define types that implement an ordering relation and do not define equality relations.

The preceding code more or less implements the semantics provided by the `Equatable<T>` and `Comparer<T>`. The `Default` property of each of those classes contains code that determines whether the type parameter, `T`, implements a type-specific equality or comparison test. If it does, those type-specific versions are used. If it does not, the `System.Object` overrides are used.

I've concentrated on the comparison and ordering relations to demonstrate the incompatibilities between the old and the new (generic) style of interfaces. These incompatibilities can catch you in other ways, too. `IEnumerable<T>` inherits from `IEnumerable`. But full-featured collection interfaces do not: `ICollection<T>` does not inherit from `ICollection`, and `IList<T>` does not inherit from `IList`. However, because both `IList<T>` and `ICollection<T>` inherit from `IEnumerable<T>`, both of those interfaces include classic `IEnumerable` support.

In most cases, adding classic interface support is a simple matter of adding methods having the correct signature to your class. As with `IComparable<T>` and `IComparable`, you should explicitly implement the classic interface `IComparable` to encourage calling code to use the new versions. Visual Studio and other tools provide wizards that create stubs for the interface methods.

It would be great if we lived in a world where generics were implemented in .NET Framework 1.0. We don't, and there is a lot of code that was written before generics. Even now, our new code must work with that existing code. You should continue to support the analogous classic interfaces, although you should implement them using explicit interface implementation to avoid accidental misuse.

Item 27: Augment Minimal Interface Contracts with Extension Methods

Extension methods provide a mechanism for C# developers to define behavior in interfaces. You can define an interface with minimal capabilities and then create a set of extension methods defined on that interface to extend its capabilities. In particular, you can add behavior instead of just defining an API.

The `System.Linq.Enumerable` class provides a great example of this technique. `System.Enumerable` contains more than 50 extension methods defined on `IEnumerable<T>`. Those methods range from `Where` to `OrderBy` to `ThenBy` to `GroupInto`. Defining these as extension methods to `IEnumerable<T>` provides great advantages. First, none of these capabilities requires modifications to any class that already implements `IEnumerable<T>`. No new responsibilities have been added for classes that implement `IEnumerable<T>`. Implementers still need to define only `GetEnumerator()`, and `IEnumerator<T>` still needs to define only `Current`, `MoveNext()`, and `Reset()`. Yet by creating extension methods, the C# compiler ensures that all collections now support query operations.

You can follow the same pattern yourself. `IComparable<T>` follows a pattern from the days of C. If `left < right`, then `left.CompareTo(right)` returns a value less than 0. If `left > right`, then `left.CompareTo(right)` returns a value greater than 0. When `left` and `right` are equivalent, `left.CompareTo(right)` returns 0. This pattern has been used so often that many of us have it memorized, but that doesn't make it very approachable. It would be much more readable to write something like `left.LessThan(right)` or `left.GreaterThanEqual(right)`. That's easy to do with extension methods. Here's an implementation:

```
public static class Comparable
{
    public static bool LessThan<T>(this T left, T right)
        where T : IComparable<T> => left.CompareTo(right) < 0;

    public static bool GreaterThan<T>(this T left, T right)
        where T : IComparable<T> => left.CompareTo(right) < 0;

    public static bool LessThanEqual<T>(this T left, T right)
        where T : IComparable<T> => left.CompareTo(right) <= 0;

    public static bool GreaterThanEqual<T>(this T left,
        T right)
        where T : IComparable<T> => left.CompareTo(right) <= 0;
}
```

Every class that implements `IComparable<T>` now appears to include these additional methods if the proper `using` declaration is in scope. Implementers still need only create one method (`CompareTo`), and the client code can use other, easier-to-read signatures.

You should also follow the same pattern with interfaces you've created in your applications. Rather than define rich interfaces, use the interface to define the minimal functionality necessary to satisfy the requirements. Any convenience methods that can be built on that minimal interface should be created using extension methods. Compared with richer interface contracts, using extension methods enables implementers to write fewer methods and still provide a richer interface to client code.

By using interfaces and extension methods in this way, you can provide a default implementation for methods that are part of an interface. This practice provides a way for classes to reuse implementations based on an interface definition. Whenever you define an interface, consider methods that could be implemented using existing interface members. Those methods are candidates to be defined as extension methods that can be reused by all interface implementers.

Be aware that you could cause strange behavior by defining extension methods on an interface when some classes may want to define their own implementation of that extension method. Although the rules of method resolution mean that the class method will be called in favor of an extension method, that is a compile-time resolution. Any code that is typed to use the interface will call the extension method rather than the method defined on its type.

Let's look at a small, rather contrived example. Here's a simple interface that keeps a marker on an object:

```
public interface IFoo
{
    int Marker { get; set; }
}
```

You could write an extension method to increment the marker:

```
public static class FooExtensions
{
    public static void NextMarker(this IFoo thing)
    {
        thing.Marker += 1;
    }
}
```

Throughout your code, you use this extension method:

```
public static void NextMarker(this IFoo thing) =>
    thing.Marker += 1;

public class MyType : IFoo
{
    public int Marker { get; set; }

    // Elided
    public void NextMarker() => Marker += 5;
}


// elsewhere:
MyType t = new MyType();
UpdateMarker(t); // t.Marker == 1
```

Time passes, and one of your developers creates a new version of a type and introduces that type's own (semantically different) version of NextMarker. It's important to note that MyType has a different implementation of NextMarker:

```
// MyType version 2
public class MyType : IFoo
{
    public int Marker { get; set; }

    public void NextMarker() => Marker += 5;
}
```

That introduces a breaking change in the application. This code snippet sets the value of Marker to 5:

```
MyType t = new MyType();
UpdateMarker(t); // t.Marker == 5
```

You can't avoid this problem entirely, but you can minimize its effects. This sample was contrived to exhibit bad behavior. In production code, the behavior of the extension method should be semantically the same as that of the class method having the same signature. If you can create a better, more efficient algorithm in a class, you should do that. However, you must ensure that the behavior is the same. If you do that, this behavior won't affect program correctness.

When you find that your design calls for making an interface definition that many classes will be forced to implement, consider creating the smallest possible set of members defined in the interface. Then provide an implementation of convenience methods in the form of extension methods. In that way, class designers who implement your interface will have the least amount of work to do, and developers using your interface can get the greatest possible benefit.

Item 28: Consider Enhancing Constructed Types with Extension Methods

You'll probably use a number of constructed generic types in your application. You'll create specific collection types: List<int>, Dictionary<EmployeeID, Employee>, and many other collections. The purpose of creating these collections is that your application has a specific need for a collection of a certain type and you want to have specific behavior defined for those specific constructed types. To implement that functionality in a low-impact way, you can create a set of extension methods on specific constructed types.

You can see this pattern in the System.Linq.Enumerable class. Item 27 earlier in this chapter discusses the extension pattern used by Enumerable<T> to implement many common methods on sequences as extension methods on IEnumerable<T>. In addition, Enumerable contains a number of methods that are implemented specifically for particular constructed types that implement IEnumerable<T>. For example, several numeric methods are implemented on numeric sequences (IEnumerable<int>, IEnumerable<double>, IEnumerable<long>, and IEnumerable<float>). Here are a few of the extension methods implemented specifically for IEnumerable<int>:

```
public static class Enumerable
{
    public static int Average(this IEnumerable<int>
    sequence);
    public static int Max(this IEnumerable<int> sequence);
    public static int Min(this IEnumerable<int> sequence);
    public static int Sum(this IEnumerable<int> sequence);

    // other methods elided
}
```

Once you recognize the pattern, you can see many ways you could implement the same kind of extensions for the constructed types in your own domain. If you were writing an e-commerce application and you wanted to send email coupons to a set of customers, the method signature might look something like this:

```
public static void SendEmailCoupons(this
    IEnumerable<Customer> customers, Coupon specialOffer)
```

Similarly, you could find all customers with no orders in the past month:

```
public static IEnumerable<Customer> LostProspects(
    IEnumerable<Customer> targetList)
```

If you didn't have extension methods, you could achieve a similar effect by deriving a new type from the constructed generic type you used. For example, the `Customer` methods just shown could be implemented like this:

```
public class CustomerList : List<Customer>
{
    public void SendEmailCoupons(Coupon specialOffer)
    public static IEnumerable<Customer> LostProspects()
}
```

It works, but it is actually much more limiting than extension methods on `IEnumerable<Customer>` to the users of this list of customers. The difference in the method signatures provides part of the reason. The extension methods use `IEnumerable<Customer>` as the parameter, but the methods added to the derived class are based on `List<Customer>`. They mandate a particular storage model. For that reason, they can't be composed as a set of iterator methods (see Item 31). You've placed unnecessary design constraints on the users of these methods. That's a misuse of inheritance.

Another reason to prefer the extension methods as a way to implement this functionality has to do with the way queries are composed. The `LostProspects()` method probably would be implemented something like this:

```
public static IEnumerable<Customer> LostProspects(
    IEnumerable<Customer> targetList)
```

```
{
    IEnumerable<Customer> answer =
        from c in targetList
        where DateTime.Now - c.LastOrderDate > TimeSpan.
            FromDays(30)
        select c;
    return answer;
}
```

Implementing these features as extension methods means that they provide a reusable query expressed as a lambda expression. You can reuse the entire query rather than try to reuse the predicate of the `where` clause.

If you examine the object model for any application or library you are writing, you'll likely find many constructed types used for the storage model. You should look at these constructed types and decide what methods logically would be added to each of them. It's best to create the implementation for those methods as extension methods by using either the constructed type or a constructed interface implemented by the type. You'll turn a simple generic instantiation into a class having all the behavior you need. Furthermore, you'll create that implementation in a manner that decouples the storage model from the implementation to the greatest extent possible.

4 | Working with LINQ

The driving force behind the language enhancements to C# 3.0 was LINQ. The new features and the implementation of those features were driven by the need to support deferred queries, translate queries into SQL to support LINQ to SQL, and add a unifying syntax to query the various data stores. Chapter 4 shows you how those language features can be used for many development idioms in addition to data query. This chapter concentrates on using those features for querying data, regardless of source.

A goal of LINQ is that language elements perform the same work no matter what the data source is. However, even though the syntax works with all kinds of data sources, the query provider that connects your query to the actual data source is free to implement that behavior in different ways. If you understand the behaviors, it will be easier to work with various data sources transparently. If you need to, you can even create your own data provider.

Item 29: Prefer Iterator Methods to Returning Collections

Many of the methods you write will return a sequence of items rather than a single object. Whenever you create a method that returns a sequence, you should create an iterator method. You give the caller more options in terms of how to process the sequence.

An iterator method is a method that uses the `yield return` syntax to generate elements of the sequence as they are asked for. Here's a basic iterator method that generates a sequence containing the lowercase letters of the alphabet:

```
public static IEnumerable<char> GenerateAlphabet()
{
    var letter = 'a';
    while (letter <= 'z')
```

```
    {
        yield return letter;
        letter++;
    }
}
```

What makes iterator methods interesting is not the syntax you use to create them, but rather how the compiler translates them. The code above
generates a class that is similar to the following construct:

```
public class EmbeddedIterator : IEnumerable<char>
{
    public IEnumerator<char> GetEnumerator() =>
        new LetterEnumerator();

    IEnumerator IEnumerable.GetEnumerator() =>
        new LetterEnumerator();

    public static IEnumerable<char> GenerateAlphabet() =>
        new EmbeddedIterator();

    private class LetterEnumerator : IEnumerator<char>
    {
        private char letter = (char)('a' - 1);

        public bool MoveNext()
        {
            letter++;
            return letter <= 'z';
        }

        public char Current => letter;

        object IEnumerator.Current => letter;

        public void Reset() =>
            letter = (char)('a' -1);


        void IDisposable.Dispose() {}
    }
}
```

When the iterator method is called, an object of this compiler-generated class is created. That object then creates the sequence, but only when some calling code requests the items in the sequence. That has minimal impact on a small sequence such as this, but consider a method in the .NET Framework like `Enumerable.Range()`. It generates sequences of numbers and can be asked to generate every nonnegative value for the `int` type:

```
var allNumbers = Enumerable.Range(0, int.MaxValue);
```

This method generates objects that create the numbers in the sequence when requested. Callers don't pay for storing a huge collection, unless they specifically store the results of the iterator method in a collection. Callers can call `Enumerable.Range()` and produce a huge sequence but use only a small number of the result numbers. It's not as efficient as generating only the numbers needed, but it is better than generating and storing the set of all valid integers. And, in many scenarios, it may not be as easy to generate only the objects that are in use. Examples include reading data from an external sensor, processing network requests, and other scenarios where the data source already produces large amounts of data in a given time.

This generate-as-needed strategy highlights one other important idiom when writing iterator methods. Iterator methods create an object that knows how to generate the sequence. The code to generate the sequence executes only when a caller requests an item in the sequence. That means very little of the code executes when a generator method is called.

Let's examine another possible generator method, one that takes arguments to generate its sequence:

```
public static IEnumerable<char>
    GenerateAlphabetSubset(char first, char last)
{
    if (first < 'a')
        throw new ArgumentException(
        "first must be at least the letter a", nameof(first));
    if (first > 'z')
        throw new ArgumentException(
        "first must be no greater than z", nameof(first));
    if (last < first)
        throw new ArgumentException(
        "last must be at least as large as first",
```

```
            nameof(last));
    if (last > 'z')
        throw new ArgumentException(
        "last must not be past z", nameof(last));
    var letter = first;
    while (letter <= last)
    {
        yield return letter;
        letter++;

    }
}
```

The compiler creates an object with an implementation similar to the following:

```
public class EmbeddedSubsetIterator : IEnumerable<char>
{
    private readonly char first;
    private readonly char last;
    public EmbeddedSubsetIterator(char first, char last)
    {
        this.first = first;
        this.last = last;

    }
    public IEnumerator<char> GetEnumerator() =>
        new LetterEnumerator(first, last);

    IEnumerator IEnumerable.GetEnumerator() =>
        new LetterEnumerator(first, last);

    public static IEnumerable<char> GenerateAlphabetSubset(
        char first, char last) =>
            new EmbeddedSubsetIterator(first, last);
    private class LetterEnumerator : IEnumerator<char>
    {
        private readonly char first;
        private readonly char last;

        private bool isInitialized = false;

        public LetterEnumerator(char first, char last)
        {
```

```csharp
        this.first = first;
        this.last = last;
    }

    private char letter = (char)('a' - 1);

    public bool MoveNext()
    {
        if (!isInitialized)
        {
            if (first < 'a')
                throw new ArgumentException(
                "first must be at least the letter a",
                nameof(first));
            if (first > 'z')
                throw new ArgumentException(
                "first must be no greater than z",
                nameof(first));
            if (last < first)
                throw new ArgumentException(
                "last must be at least as large as first",
                nameof(last));
            if (last > 'z')
                throw new ArgumentException(
                "last must not be past z",
                nameof(last));
            letter = (char)(first -1 );

        }
        letter++;
        return letter <= last;
    }

    public char Current => letter;

    object IEnumerator.Current => letter;

    public void Reset() => isInitialized = false;

    void IDisposable.Dispose() {}
    }
}
```

Significantly, this code does not execute any of the argument checking until the first element is requested. That can make it much harder to diagnose and fix programming errors if another developer calls this method incorrectly. Instead of having an exception thrown at the point where you make the programming error, you see the error later, when you use the return value of the function. You can't change the compiler's algorithm, but you can rearrange your code to separate the initial argument checks from the generation of the sequence. In the previous example, you would separate the two like this:

```
public static IEnumerable<char> GenerateAlphabetSubset(
    char first, char last)
{
    if (first < 'a')
        throw new ArgumentException(
            "first must be at least the letter a",
            nameof(first));
    if (first > 'z')
        throw new ArgumentException(
            "first must be no greater than z",
            nameof(first));
    if (last < first)
        throw new ArgumentException(
            "last must be at least as large as first",
            nameof(last));
    if (last > 'z')
        throw new ArgumentException(
            "last must not be past z", nameof(last));
    return GenerateAlphabetSubsetImpl(first, last);
}

private static IEnumerable<char> GenerateAlphabetSubsetImpl(
    char first, char last)
{
    var letter = first;
    while (letter <= last)
    {
        yield return letter;
        letter++;
    }
}
```

Now, if you call this code incorrectly, for example with a null delegate, the public method throws an exception before entering the private generator method. This means callers would observe the exception immediately, not after trying to access the generated sequence. This enables callers to observe the error at the point where the mistake was made.

At this point, you may be wondering when generating sequences using iterator methods is not recommended. What if the sequence will be used repeatedly and can be cached? Leave that decision up to the code calling your generator method. You should not try to assume how callers will use the method you've created. Callers can make their own decisions and cache the results of your sequence-returning methods themselves. The extension methods `ToList()` and `ToArray()` create a stored collection from any sequence represented by `IEnumerable<T>`. Therefore, by creating sequence methods you can support both scenarios: those where storing a collection is more efficient, and those where generating the sequence is more efficient. If your public APIs generate the sequences, you can't support scenarios where generating the sequence is easier. Internally, you can still cache the results of an earlier generation if that design provides measurable advantages.

Methods can have different return types, and the cost of creating those different types varies. Methods that return sequences may have a high cost to create the entire sequence. That cost may involve both compute time and storage. While you can't anticipate the usage of every API you've created, you can make it easier for the developers using your APIs. You can give them the maximum flexibility in consuming your APIs. That's done by creating generator methods. The developers calling your method can eagerly generate the entire sequence using `ToList` or `ToArray`, or they can process each element as it's created, while your code generates each element only as it's needed.

Item 30: Prefer Query Syntax to Loops

There is no lack of support for different control structures in the C# language: `for`, `while`, `do/while`, and `foreach` are all part of the language. But there's often a much better way: query syntax.

Query syntax enables you to move your program logic from a more imperative model to a declarative model. Query syntax defines what the question is and defers the decision about how to create the answer to the particular implementation. You can get the same benefits from the method call syntax as you can from the query syntax as described in this item. The important point is that the query syntax, and by extension the method syntax that implements the query expression pattern, provides a cleaner expression of your intent than imperative looping constructs.

This code snippet shows an imperative method of filling an array and then printing its contents to the console:

```
var foo = new int[100];

for (var num = 0; num < foo.Length; num++)
    foo[num] = num * num;

foreach (int i in foo)
    Console.WriteLine(i.ToString());
```

Even this small example focuses too much on how actions are performed rather than on what actions are performed. Reworking this small example to use the query syntax creates more readable code and enables reuse of different building blocks.

As a first step, you can change the generation of the array to a query result:

```
var foo = (from n in Enumerable.Range(0, 100)
            select n * n).ToArray();
```

You can then do a similar change to the second loop, although you'll also need to write an extension method to perform some action on all the elements:

```
foo.ForAll((n) => Console.WriteLine(n.ToString()));
```

The .NET BCL has a ForAll implementation in List<T>. It's just as simple to create one for IEnumerable<T>:

```
public static class Extensions
{
    public static void ForAll<T>(this IEnumerable<T> sequence,
        Action<T> action)
    {
        foreach (T item in sequence)
            action(item);
    }
}
```

This is a small, simple operation, so you may think there's not much benefit. In fact, you're probably right. Let's look at some different problems.

Many operations require you to work through nested loops. Suppose you need to generate (X,Y) pairs for all integers from 0 through 99. It's obvious how you would do that with nested loops:

```
private static IEnumerable<Tuple<int, int>> ProduceIndices()
{
    for (var x = 0; x < 100; x++)
        for (var y = 0; y < 100; y++)
            yield return Tuple.Create(x, y);
}
```

Of course, you could produce the same objects with a query:

```
private static IEnumerable<Tuple<int, int>> QueryIndices()
{
    return from x in Enumerable.Range(0, 100)
            from y in Enumerable.Range(0, 100)
            select Tuple.Create(x, y);
}
```

They look similar, but the query syntax keeps its simplicity even as the problem description gets more difficult. Change the problem to generating only those pairs where the sum of X and Y is less than 100. Compare these two methods:

```
private static IEnumerable<Tuple<int, int>> ProduceIndices2()
{
    for (var x = 0; x < 100; x++)
        for (var y = 0; y < 100; y++)
            if (x + y < 100)
                yield return Tuple.Create(x, y);
}
private static IEnumerable<Tuple<int, int>> QueryIndices2()
{
    return from x in Enumerable.Range(0, 100)
            from y in Enumerable.Range(0, 100)
            where x + y < 100
            select Tuple.Create(x, y);
}
```

It's still close, but the imperative syntax starts to hide its meaning under the necessary syntax used to produce the result. So let's change the problem a bit again. Now, add that you must return the points in decreasing order based on their distance from the origin.

Here are two different methods that would produce the correct result:

```
private static IEnumerable<Tuple<int, int>> ProduceIndices3()
{
    var storage = new List<Tuple<int, int>>();

    for (var x = 0; x < 100; x++)
        for (var y = 0; y < 100; y++)
            if (x + y < 100)
                storage.Add(Tuple.Create(x, y));

    storage.Sort((point1, point2) =>
        (point2.Item1*point2.Item1 + point2.Item2 *
        point2.Item2).CompareTo(
        point1.Item1 * point1.Item1 + point1.Item2 *
        point1.Item2));
    return storage;
}


private static IEnumerable<Tuple<int, int>> QueryIndices3()
{
    return from x in Enumerable.Range(0, 100)
            from y in Enumerable.Range(0, 100)
            where x + y < 100
            orderby (x*x + y*y) descending
            select Tuple.Create(x, y);
}
```

Something has clearly changed. The imperative version is much more difficult to comprehend. If you looked quickly, you almost certainly did not notice that the arguments on the comparison function got reversed. That's to ensure that the sort is in descending order. Without comments or other supporting documentation, the imperative code is much more difficult to read.

Even if you did spot where the parameter order was reversed, did you think that it was an error? The imperative model places so much more emphasis on how actions are performed that it's easy to get lost in those actions and lose the original intent for what actions are being accomplished.

There's one more justification for using query syntax over looping constructs: Queries create a more composable API than looping constructs can provide. Query syntax naturally leads to constructing algorithms as small blocks of code that perform one operation on a sequence. The deferred execution model for queries enables developers to compose these single operations into multiple operations that can be accomplished in one enumeration of the sequence. Looping constructs cannot be similarly composed. You must either create interim storage for each step, or create methods for each combination of operations on a sequence.

That last example shows how this works. The operation combines a filter (the `where` clause) with a sort (the `orderby` clause) and a projection (the `select` clause). All of these are accomplished in one enumeration operation. The imperative version creates an interim storage model and separates the sort into a distinct operation.

I've discussed this as query syntax, though you should remember that every query has a corresponding method call syntax. Sometimes the query is more natural, and sometimes the method call syntax is more natural. In the example above, the query syntax is much more readable. Here's the equivalent method call syntax:

```
private static IEnumerable<Tuple<int, int>> MethodIndices3()
{
    return Enumerable.Range(0, 100).
        SelectMany(x => Enumerable.Range(0,100),
        (x,y) => Tuple.Create(x,y)).
        Where(pt => pt.Item1 + pt.Item2 < 100).
        OrderByDescending(pt =>
            pt.Item1* pt.Item1 + pt.Item2 * pt.Item2);
}
```

It's a matter of style whether the query or the method call syntax is more readable. In this instance, I'm convinced the query syntax is clearer. However, other examples may be different. Furthermore, some methods do not have equivalent query syntax. Methods such as `Take`, `TakeWhile`, `Skip`, `SkipWhile`, `Min`, and `Max` require you to use the method syntax at some level. Other languages, in particular VB.NET, did define query syntax for many of these keywords.

This is the part of any discussion where someone usually asserts that queries perform more slowly than other loops. While you can certainly create examples where a hand-coded loop will outperform a query, it's not a general rule. You do need to measure performance to determine if you have a specific case where the query constructs don't perform well enough. However, before completely rewriting an algorithm, consider the parallel extensions for LINQ. Another advantage to using query syntax is that you can execute those queries in parallel using the `.AsParallel()` method.

C# began as an imperative language. It continues to include all the features that are part of that heritage. It's natural to reach for the most familiar tools at your disposal. However, those tools might not be the best tools. When you find yourself writing any form of a looping construct, ask yourself if you can write that code as a query. If the query syntax does not work, consider using the method call syntax instead. In almost all cases, you'll find that you create cleaner code than you would using imperative looping constructs.

Item 31: Create Composable APIs for Sequences

You've probably written code that contains loops. In most programs, you tend to write algorithms that operate more often on a sequence of items than on a single item. It's common to use keywords such as `foreach`, `for` loops, `while`, and so on. As a result, you create methods that take a collection as input, examine or modify it or its items, and return a different collection as output.

The problem is that the strategy of operating on entire collections introduces a lot of inefficiencies. That's because it's rare that you have only one operation to perform. More likely, you'll perform several transformations between the source collection and the ultimate result. Along the way, you create collections (perhaps large ones) to store the interim results. You don't begin the next step, even on the first item, until the preceding step has completely finished. Furthermore, this strategy means iterating the collection once for every transformation. That increases the execution time for algorithms that contain many transformations of the elements.

Another alternative is to create one method that processes every transformation in one loop, producing the final collection in one iteration. That approach improves your application's performance by iterating the collection only once. It also lowers the application's memory footprint because it doesn't create collections of N elements for every step. However, this strategy sacrifices reusability. You're far more likely to reuse the algorithm for each individual transformation than you would for a multistep operation.

C# **iterators** enable you to create methods that operate on a sequence but process and return each element as it is requested. The `yield return` statement lets you create methods that return sequences. These iterator methods have a sequence as one input (expressed as `IEnumerable<T>`) and produce a sequence as output (another `IEnumerable<T>`). By leveraging the `yield return` statement, these iterator methods do not need to allocate storage for the entire sequence of elements. Instead, these methods ask for the next element on the input sequence only when needed, and they produce the next value on the output sequence only when the calling code asks for it.

It's a shift from your usual way of thinking to create input and output parameters from `IEnumerable<T>` or from a specific instance of `IEnumerable<T>`. That's why many developers don't do it. But making that shift provides many benefits. For example, you naturally create building blocks that can be combined in many ways, promoting reuse. Moreover, you can apply multiple operations while iterating a sequence only once, increasing runtime efficiency. Each iterator method executes the code to produce the *N*th element when that element is requested and not before. This **deferred execution model** (see Item 37) means that your algorithms use less storage space and compose better (see Item 40) than traditional imperative methods. And, as libraries evolve, you'll be able to assign different operations to different CPU cores, promoting even better performance. Furthermore, the bodies of these methods often do not make any assumptions about the types on which they operate. This means that you can turn these methods into generic methods to gain more reuse.

To see the benefits of writing iterator methods, let's take a simple example and examine the translation. The following method takes as its input an array of integers and writes all the unique values to the output console:

```
public static void Unique(IEnumerable<int> nums)
{
    var uniqueVals = new HashSet<int>();

    foreach (var num in nums)
    {
        if (!uniqueVals.Contains(num))
        {
            uniqueVals.Add(num);
```

```
            WriteLine(num);
        }
    }
}
```

It's a simple method, but you can't reuse any of the interesting parts. But chances are, this search for unique numbers would be useful in other places in your program.

Suppose that instead you wrote the routine this way:

```
public static IEnumerable<int> UniqueV2(IEnumerable<int> nums)
{
    var uniqueVals = new HashSet<int>();
    foreach (var num in nums)
    {
        if (!uniqueVals.Contains(num))
        {
            uniqueVals.Add(num);
            yield return num;
        }
    }
}
```

Unique returns a sequence that contains the unique numbers. Here's how you use it:

```
foreach (var num in Unique(nums))
    WriteLine(num);
```

It may look as if we haven't gained anything—or even as if the second version is much less efficient—but that's not the case. I added several tracing statements to the Unique method that will help you see how methods like Unique do their magic.

This is the updated Unique:

```
public static IEnumerable<int> Unique(IEnumerable<int> nums)
{
    var uniqueVals = new HashSet<int>();
    WriteLine("\tEntering Unique");
    foreach (var num in nums)
    {
        WriteLine("\tevaluating {0}", num);
        if (!uniqueVals.Contains(num))
```

```
        {
            WriteLine("\tAdding {0}", num);
            uniqueVals.Add(num);
            yield return num;
            WriteLine("\tRe-entering after yield return");
        }
    }
    WriteLine("\tExiting Unique ");
}
```

When you run this version, here's the output:

```
Entering Unique
evaluating 0
Adding 0
```
0
```
Reentering after yield return
evaluating 3
Adding 3
```
3
```
Reentering after yield return
evaluating 4
Adding 4
```
4
```
Reentering after yield return
evaluating 5
Adding 5
```
5
```
Reentering after yield return
evaluating 7
Adding 7
```
7
```
Reentering after yield return
evaluating 3
evaluating 2
Adding 2
```
2
```
Reentering after yield return
evaluating 7
evaluating 8
Adding 8
```

```
8

        Reentering after yield return
        evaluating 0
        evaluating 3
        evaluating 1
        Adding 1
1

        Reentering after yield return
        Exiting Unique
```

The `yield return` statement plays an interesting trick: It returns a value and retains information about its current location and the current state of its internal iteration. You've got a method that operates on an entire sequence: Both the input and the output are iterators. Internally, the iteration continues to return the next item in the output sequence while it keeps track of its current location in the input sequence. That's a continuable method. **Continuable methods** keep track of their state and resume execution at their current location when code enters them again.

The fact that `Unique()` is a continuation method provides two important benefits. First, that's what enables the deferred evaluation of each element. Second, and more important, the deferred execution provides a composability that would be difficult to achieve if each method had its `foreach` loop.

Notice that `Unique()` does not exploit the fact that the input sequence contains integers. It is an excellent candidate to be converted to a generic method:

```
public static IEnumerable<T> UniqueV3<T>(IEnumerable<T>
    sequence)
{
    var uniqueVals = new HashSet<T>();
    foreach (T item in sequence)
    {
        if (!uniqueVals.Contains(item))
        {
            uniqueVals.Add(item);
            yield return item;
        }
    }
}
```

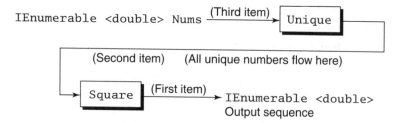

Figure 4.1 Items are pulled through a series of iterator methods. When each iterator method is ready for the next item, that item is pulled from the iterator method it uses for a source sequence. Only one element is at a given stage of the process at a given time.

The true power of an iterator method like this comes when you compose it into a many-step process. Suppose you want the final output to be a sequence containing the square of each of the unique numbers. `Square` as an iterator method is a simple set of code:

```
public static IEnumerable<int> Square(IEnumerable<int> nums)
{
    foreach (var num in nums)
        yield return num * num;
}
```

The call location is a simple nested call:

```
foreach (var num in Square(Unique(nums)))
    WriteLine("Number returned from Unique: {0}", num);
```

No matter how many different iterator methods you call, the iteration happens only once. In pseudocode, the algorithm proceeds as though it were written as shown in Figure 4.1.

The code in Figure 4.1 illustrates the composability of multiple iterator methods. These methods do their work in one enumeration of the entire sequence. In contrast, traditional implementation idioms would have a new iteration of the entire sequence for each action.

When you build iterator methods that take one sequence as input and produce one sequence as output, other ideas emerge. For example, you can combine two sequences to form a single sequence:

```
public static IEnumerable<string> Zip(IEnumerable<string> first,
    IEnumerable<string> second)
{
    using (var firstSequence = first.GetEnumerator())
```

```
    {
        using (var secondSequence =
            second.GetEnumerator())
        {
            while (firstSequence.MoveNext() &&
                secondSequence.MoveNext())
            {
                yield return string.Format("{0} {1}",
                    firstSequence.Current,
                    secondSequence.Current);
            }
        }
    }
}
```

As shown in Figure 4.2, `Zip` forms a single sequence that concatenates each pair of items in two different string sequences, returning a sequence of those concatenations. And yes, `Zip` is another possible generic method, although it's a bit more complicated than `Unique`. That's the subject of Item 18.

The `Square()` iterator method shows that iterator methods can modify the source elements, modifying the contents of the sequences as part of its processing. The `Unique()` iterator method shows how an iterator method can modify the sequence itself as part of its processing: Only the first copy of each value is returned by the `Unique()` iterator method. However, iterator methods do not mutate the source sequence. Instead, they produce a new sequence as output. If the sequence contains reference types, however, the items may be modified.

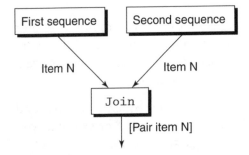

Figure 4.2 `Join` pulls individual items from two different source sequences. As each new output is requested, one element is pulled from each of the source sequences. Those two elements are combined into one output value, and that value is passed in the output sequence.

These iterator methods fit together like a child's marble chute toy—you know, the kind where you drop in marbles one at a time, and they proceed to roll through tubes and past obstacles, tripping various action features along the way. The marbles don't group at each obstacle; the first marbles may be several obstacles ahead of the last ones. Each iterator method performs one action on each element of the input sequence, adding the new object to the output sequence. Individually, iterator methods do very little. But because these methods are based on a single input and output stream, it's easy to combine them. If you create these small iterator methods, it is much simpler to create complicated algorithms that are a single pipeline of many small transformations.

Item 32: Decouple Iterations from Actions, Predicates, and Functions

I've just discussed using `yield return` to create methods that operate on sequences rather than individual data types. As you gain experience with these methods, you'll often find code that has two portions: a portion that modifies the iteration of a sequence, and a portion that performs an action on each element in the sequence. For example, you might want to iterate only those items in a list that match certain criteria, or you might want to sample every Nth element or skip groups of elements.

The latter enumerations are distinct from the actions you might perform on every element that matches the criteria. Maybe you're writing different reports with the data, or summing certain values, or even modifying the properties of the items in the collection. No matter what you are doing, the enumeration pattern is not related to the action performed, and the two things should be handled separately. Putting them together means tighter coupling and probably duplicated code.

The reason many developers combine various operations into one method is that the portion to be customized falls between the standard opening and closing parts. The only way to customize the inner portion of such an algorithm is to pass a method call or function object to the enclosing method. In C#, the way to do that is to use delegates to define the inner operation. In the following samples, I show the more concise lambda expression syntax.

There are two main idioms that you use with anonymous delegates: functions and actions. You'll also find references to a special case of function: a predicate. A **predicate** is a Boolean method that determines whether an element in a sequence matches some condition. An **action delegate** performs some action on an element in the collection. These method signatures are so common that the .NET library contains definitions for Action<T>, Func<T, TResult>, and Predicate<T>:

```
namespace System
{
    public delegate bool Predicate<T>(T obj);
    public delegate void Action<T>(T obj);
    public delegate TResult Func<T, TResult>(T arg);
}
```

For example, the List<T>.RemoveAll() method is a method with a predicate. The following invocation removes all instances of 5 from a list of integers:

```
myInts.RemoveAll(collectionMember => collectionMember == 5);
```

Internally, List<T>.RemoveAll() calls your delegate method (defined earlier anonymously) successively for every item in the list. Whenever the delegate returns true, that element is removed from the list. (It's a bit more complicated, because RemoveAll() actually creates new internal storage so that the original list isn't modified during the enumeration, but that's an implementation-specific detail.)

Action methods are called successively for every item in the collection. The List<T>.ForEach() method contains an example. The following invocation prints to the console every integer in the collection:

```
myInts.ForEach(collectionMember => WriteLine(collectionMember));
```

Sure, that's boring, but the concept can be extended to any action you might need performed. The anonymous delegate performs the action, and the ForEach method calls the anonymous method on each element in the collection.

With these two methods, you can see different ways to expand the techniques to execute complex operations on collections. Let's look again at other examples of operations wherein you can save code by using predicates and actions.

Filter methods use Predicate to perform their tests. Predicate defines which objects should be passed or blocked by the filter. Following the advice in Item 31 (earlier in this chapter), you can build a generic filter that returns a sequence of all items that meet some criterion:

```
public static IEnumerable<T> Where<T>
    (IEnumerable<T> sequence,
    Predicate<T> filterFunc)
{
    if (sequence == null)
        throw new ArgumentNullException(nameof(sequence),
            "sequence must not be null");
    if (filterFunc == null)
        throw new ArgumentNullException(
        "Predicate must not be null");
    foreach (T item in sequence)
        if (filterFunc(item))
            yield return item;
}
```

Each element in the input sequence is evaluated using the `Predicate` method. If the `Predicate` returns `true`, that element is returned as part of the output sequence. Any developer can write a method on a type that tests a condition, and the method will be compatible with this filter method.

You can also sample a sequence and return every *N*th element:

```
public static IEnumerable<T> EveryNthItem<T>(
    IEnumerable<T> sequence, int period)
{
    var count = 0;
    foreach (T item in sequence)
        if (++count % period == 0)
            yield return item;
}
```

You can apply that filter to any sequence you want, sampling only selected items.

A `Func` delegate can be used in combination with any enumeration pattern. Here, we create a transform method that builds a new sequence from an existing sequence by calling a method:

```
public static IEnumerable<T> Select<T>(
    IEnumerable<T> sequence, Func<T, T> method)
{
    // null checks on sequence and method elided.
    foreach (T element in sequence)
        yield return method(element);
}
```

Here's how you would call `Select` to convert a sequence of integers into a sequence containing the squares of those integers:

```
foreach (int i in Select(myInts, value => value * value))
    WriteLine(i);
```

The `Transform` method need not return the same type of element. You can modify the `Transform` method to support changes from one type to another:

```
public static IEnumerable<Tout> Select<Tin, Tout>(
    IEnumerable<Tin> sequence, Func<Tin, Tout> method)
{
    // null checks on sequence and method elided.
    foreach (Tin element in sequence)
        yield return method(element);
}
```

And you call this version as follows:

```
foreach (string s in Select(myInts, value => value.ToString()))
    WriteLine(s);
```

As you saw in Item 31, it isn't difficult to write or use any of these methods. The key is that you've separated two distinct operations: (1) iterating a sequence and (2) operating on the individual elements in the sequence. You've applied anonymous delegates or lambda expressions to create building blocks that you can use in various ways with various techniques. Any of these routines can be used as larger building blocks in your applications. You can implement many modifications to a sequence as a function (including the special case of predicates), and you can use an action delegate (or similar definition) to manipulate the items in a collection while enumerating a subset of the elements.

Item 33: Generate Sequence Items as Requested

Iterator methods do not necessarily need to take a sequence as an input parameter. An iterator method that uses the `yield return` approach can create a new sequence, essentially becoming a factory for a sequence of elements. Instead of creating the entire collection before proceeding with any operations, you create the values only as requested. This means that you avoid creating elements that aren't used by the consumers of the sequence.

Let's look at a simple example that generates a sequence of integral numbers. You might write it like this:

```
static IList<int> CreateSequence(int numberOfElements,
    int startAt, int stepBy)
{
    var collection =
        new List<int>(numberOfElements);
    for (int i = 0; i < numberOfElements; i++)
        collection.Add(startAt + i * stepBy);

    return collection;
}
```

It works, but it has many deficiencies compared with using `yield return` to create the sequence. First, this technique assumes that you're putting the results into a `List<double>`. If clients want to store the results in some other structure, such as `BindingList<double>`, they must convert it:

```
var data = new
    BindingList<int>(CreateSequence(100,0,5).ToList());
```

There may be a subtle bug lurking in that construct. The `BindingList<T>` constructor does not copy the elements of the list but instead uses the same storage location as the list given in the constructor. If the storage location used to initialize the `BindingList<T>` is reachable by other code, you could introduce data integrity errors. Multiple references are synonyms for the same storage location.

Moreover, creating the entire list doesn't give client code a chance to stop the generation function based on a specified condition. The `CreateSequence` method always generates a requested number of elements. As written, it can't be stopped if the user wants to stop the process—for paging or for any other reason.

Also, this method could be the first stage of several transformations on a sequence of data (see Item 31 earlier in this chapter). In that case, it would be a bottleneck in the pipeline: Every element would have to be created and added to the internal collection before the next step could continue.

You can remove all those limitations by making the generation function an iterator method:

```
static IEnumerable<int> CreateSequence(int numberOfElements,
    int startAt, int stepBy)
{
    for (var i = 0; i < numberOfElements; i++)
        yield return startAt + i * stepBy;
}
```

The core logic is still the same: It generates a sequence of numbers.

It is important to note that there is a change in the way this version executes. Each time code enumerates the sequence, it regenerates the sequence of numbers. Because the code always generates the same sequence of numbers, this change does not affect the behavior. This version does not make any assumptions about what the client code will do with that storage location. If the client code wants values as a List<double>, there's a constructor that takes an IEnumerable<double> as the initial collection:

```
var listStorage = new List<int>(CreateSequence(100, 0, 5));
```

That's necessary to ensure that only one sequence of numbers is generated. You would create a BindingList<double> collection this way:

```
var data = new
    BindingList<int>(CreateSequence(100,0,5).ToList());
```

This code might look a bit inefficient. The BindingList<T> class does not support a constructor that takes an IEnumerable<T>. It really isn't inefficient, though, because BindingList holds the reference to the existing list; it doesn't create another copy. ToList() creates one List object that contains all the elements in the sequence generated by CreateSequence. That List object is also held by BindingList<int>.

It's easy to stop the enumeration if you use the following method. You simply don't ask for the next element. The code works with both versions of CreateSequence(). However, if you use the first implementation of CreateSequence(), all 1,000 elements are generated, no matter where in the collection the caller wishes to stop enumerating the list. Using the enumerator version, the generation short-circuits as soon as the first nonconforming value is found. That can result in a significant performance improvement.

```
// Using an anonymous delegate
var sequence = CreateSequence(10000, 0, 7).
    TakeWhile(delegate (int num) { return num < 1000; });

// using lambda notation
var sequence = CreateSequence(10000, 0, 7).
    TakeWhile((num) => num < 1000);
```

Of course, any condition can be used to determine when the enumeration should stop. You can check to see whether the user wishes to continue, poll another thread for input, or do anything else needed by your application. The enumerator method provides a simple means of interrupting the enumeration anywhere in the sequence. This deferred execution means that only the elements requested are generated. Essentially, client code requests that an algorithm create a new element only when that element is actually used in the algorithm.

It's best to generate sequence items only when each item is requested by the consumer of the sequence. You'll avoid doing extra work when the consumer needs only a portion of the algorithm to perform its work. It may be a small savings, or the savings may be much greater if the cost of creating elements is large. In any case, the code that creates the sequence will be clearer when you generate the sequence items only as needed.

Item 34: Loosen Coupling by Using Function Parameters

Developers often reach for the most familiar language features to describe contracts between components. For most developers, that means defining a base class or an interface to declare the methods needed by a new class and then coding against those defined interfaces. Often that is the correct answer, but using function parameters can make it easier for other developers to create code that can work with your components and libraries. Using **function parameters** means that your component is not responsible for creating the concrete type of the classes it needs. Rather, your component uses any dependencies through an abstract definition.

You should be familiar with the separation of interfaces and classes. But sometimes even defining and implementing an interface are too cumbersome for a particular usage. Probably you'll most often use traditional object-oriented techniques, but these other techniques can make for a simpler API. You can create contracts by using delegates to minimize the requirements on client code.

The challenge for you is to isolate your work from these dependencies and from assumptions you implicitly make about the client developers who use your code. There are various reasons for this difficulty from both sides of your code. The more your code relies on other pieces, the harder it is to unit-test or use your code in other environments. From the other side, the more closely you rely on a particular implementation pattern from those developers who use your code, the more constraints you place on them.

You can use function parameters to decouple your components from the code that uses those components. However, each of those possible techniques comes with a cost. There is more work for you, and a little less clarity for your users, if you adopt techniques that loosen the coupling between sets of code that must work together. You need to balance the potential needs of client developers against the lack of understanding that decoupled techniques can provide. In addition, implementing looser coupling—by using delegates or other communication mechanisms—also means that you need to work around some of the checking that the compiler provides for you.

At one end of the spectrum, you have likely specified a base class for your client classes. Doing so is the simplest way for clients to develop code that works with your component. The contract is clear: Derive from this specified base class, implement these known abstract (or other virtual) methods, and it just works. In addition, you can implement any common functionality in the abstract base class. Users of your component do not need to reimplement any of that code.

From your component's perspective, this approach is also a little less work. You can assume that certain behavior has been implemented. The compiler won't allow someone to build a derived class without providing an implementation for all the abstract methods. Nothing can force a correct implementation, but you know that a proper method exists.

However, forcing client code to derive from a base class you define is the most restrictive way to demand certain behaviors from client code. Creating a component that demands a base class can be very limiting to all your users. You're mandating a certain class hierarchy. There's no other way to use it.

Creating interfaces and coding against them results in looser coupling than does relying on base classes. You've likely created an interface and forced client coders to implement that interface. This practice creates a relationship that's similar to the relationship you establish by using a base class. There are only two important differences: First, using an interface does not enforce any class hierarchy on your users. But second, you can't easily provide a default implementation for any of the behavior necessary for client code.

Often, either of those mechanisms will be too much work for your purpose. Do you really need to define an interface? Or will a more loosely coupled approach, such as defining a delegate signature, be better?

You have already seen an example of this in Item 32 earlier in this chapter. The `List.RemoveAll()` method signature takes a delegate of type `Predicate<T>`:

```
void List<T>.RemoveAll(Predicate<T> match);
```

The .NET Framework designers could have implemented this method by defining an interface:

```
// Improper extra coupling.
public interface IPredicate<T>
{
    bool Match(T soughtObject);
}
public class List<T>
{
    public void RemoveAll(IPredicate<T> match)
    {
        // elided
    }
    // Other apis elided
}
//The usage for this second version is quite a bit more work:
public class MyPredicate : IPredicate<int>
{
    public bool Match(int target) =>
        target < 100;
}
```

Look back at Item 31 to see how much easier it is to use the version that is defined for `List<T>`. Often, it is much easier on all the developers who use your class when you define your interfaces using delegates or other loose-coupling mechanisms.

The reason for using delegates instead of an interface is that the delegate is not a fundamental attribute of the type. It's not the number of methods.

Several interfaces in the .NET Framework contain only one method. `IComparable<T>` and `IEquatable<T>` are perfectly good interface definitions. Implementing those interfaces says something about your type: that it supports comparisons or equality. Implementing this hypothetical `IPredicate<T>` doesn't say anything interesting about a particular type. You really need only one method definition for one single API.

You often can use function parameters in conjunction with generic methods when you may have considered defining interfaces or creating base classes. Item 31 contains this version of a `Zip` method that merges two sequences:

```
public static IEnumerable<string> Zip(
    IEnumerable<string> first,
    IEnumerable<string> second)
{
    using (var firstSequence = first.GetEnumerator())
    {
        using (var secondSequence = second.GetEnumerator())
        {
            while (firstSequence.MoveNext() &&
                secondSequence.MoveNext())
            {
                yield return string.Format("{0} {1}",
                    firstSequence.Current,
                    secondSequence.Current);
            }
        }
    }
}
```

You can make a generic method and use function parameters to build the output sequence:

```
public static IEnumerable<TResult> Zip<T1, T2, TResult>(
    IEnumerable<T1> first,
    IEnumerable<T2> second, Func<T1, T2, TResult> zipper)
{
    using (var firstSequence = first.GetEnumerator())
    {
        using (var secondSequence =
            second.GetEnumerator())
        {
```

```
      while (firstSequence.MoveNext() &&
          secondSequence.MoveNext())
      {
          yield return zipper(firstSequence.Current,
              secondSequence.Current);
      }
    }
  }
}
```

The caller must now define the body of the `zipper`:

```
var result = Zip(first, second, (one, two) =>
    string.Format("{0} {1}", one, two));
```

That creates much looser coupling between the `Zip` method and its callers.

The `CreateSequence` method from Item 33 (earlier in this chapter) would benefit from the same kinds of changes. The version in Item 33 creates a sequence of integers. You can make that a generic method and use a function parameter to specify how that sequence should be generated:

```
public static IEnumerable<T> CreateSequence<T>(
    int numberOfElements,
    Func<T> generator)
{
    for (var i = 0; i < numberOfElements; i++)
        yield return generator();
}
```

A caller defines the original behavior this way:

```
var startAt = 0;
var nextValue = 5;
var sequence = CreateSequence(1000,
    () => startAt += nextValue);
```

At other times, you'll want to perform an algorithm on all the items in a sequence, returning a single scalar value. For example, this method creates the sum of a sequence of integers:

```
public static int Sum(IEnumerable<int> nums)
{
    var total = 0;
    foreach (int num in nums)
    {
```

```
        total += num;
    }
    return total;
}
```

You can make this method a general-purpose accumulator by factoring out the Sum algorithm and replacing it with a delegate definition:

```
public static T Sum<T>(IEnumerable<T> sequence, T total,
    Func<T, T, T> accumulator)
{
    foreach (T item in sequence)
    {
        total = accumulator(total, item);
    }
    return total;
}
```

You would call it this way:

```
var total = 0;
total = Sum(sequence, total, (sum, num) => sum + num);
```

The Sum method is still too limiting. As written, it must use the same type for the sequence, the return value, and the initial value. You'd like to use it with different types:

```
var peeps = new List<Employee>();
// All employees added elsewhere.
// Calculate the total salary:
var totalSalary = Sum(peeps, 0M, (person, sum) =>
    sum + person.Salary);
```

All you need is a bit of modification to the Sum method definition, allowing different parameter types for the sequence element and the accumulated sum. Let's also change the name to this more general method in the BCL, Fold:

```
public static TResult Fold<T, TResult>(
    IEnumerable<T> sequence,
    TResult total,
    Func<T, TResult, TResult> accumulator)
{

    foreach (T item in sequence)
    {
```

```
        total = accumulator(item, total);
    }
    return total;
}
```

Using functions as parameters does a great deal to separate algorithms from the specific data types on which they operate. However, as you loosen the coupling, you increase the amount of work you might need to do to ensure proper error handling when these decoupled components communicate. For example, suppose you've created code that defines events. You know that you must check that event member against `null` whenever you intend to raise that event. Client code may not have created the event handlers. You'll have the same work when you create interfaces using delegates. What is the correct behavior when your client passes a null delegate? Is it an exception, or is there a correct default behavior? What happens if client code delegates `throw` exceptions? Can you recover? If so, how?

Finally, when you switch from using inheritance to using delegates to define your expectations, you must understand that you have the same runtime coupling you would have by holding a reference to an object or an interface. If your object stores a copy of the delegate that it can call later, your object now controls the lifetime of the object to which that delegate refers. You may be extending the lifetime of those objects. This is no different from having your object hold a reference to an object (by storing a reference to an interface or a base class) that your object will invoke later. It's a little harder to see by reading the code, though.

The default choice is still to create interface contracts that mandate how your component will communicate with client code. Abstract base classes give you the extra ability to provide a default implementation of some of the work that otherwise would be done by client code. Defining delegates for the methods you expect gives you the most flexibility, but it also means you have less support from tools. You buy more work but gain greater flexibility.

Item 35: Never Overload Extension Methods

Earlier (Items 27 and 28) I discussed three reasons to create extension methods for interfaces or types: adding default implementation to interfaces, creating behaviors on closed generic types, and creating composable interfaces. However, extension methods are not always a good way to express your designs. In all those cases, you made some enhancements to an existing type definition, but those enhancements did not fundamentally change the behavior of the type.

Item 27 explains that you can create extension methods to provide a default implementation for common actions that can be built using a minimal interface definition. You may be tempted to use the same technique to enhance class types. You may even be tempted to create multiple versions of class extensions that you can substitute by changing the namespaces you are using. Don't do that. Extension methods give you a great way to provide a default implementation for types that implement interfaces. However, there are much better alternatives to extending class types. Overusing and misapplying extension methods quickly create a morass of conflicting methods that will increase maintenance costs.

Let's begin with an example that misuses extension methods. Suppose you have a simple `Person` class that was generated by some other library:

```
public sealed class Person
{
    public string FirstName
    {
        get;
        set;
    }
    public string LastName
    {
        get;
        set;
    }
}
```

You might consider writing an extension method to create a report of people's names to the console:

```
// Bad start.
// extending classes using extension methods
namespace ConsoleExtensions
{
    public static class ConsoleReport
    {
        public static string Format(this Person target) =>
```

```
                $"{target.LastName,20}, {target.FirstName,15}";
    }
}
```

Generating the console report is simple:

```
static void Main(string[] args)
{
    List<Person> somePresidents =
        new List<Person>{
    new Person{
        FirstName = "George",
        LastName = "Washington" },
    new Person{
        FirstName = "Thomas",
        LastName = "Jefferson" },
    new Person{
        FirstName = "Abe",
        LastName = "Lincoln" }
        };

    foreach (Person p in somePresidents)
        Console.WriteLine(p.Format());
}
```

That might seem harmless enough. But requirements change. Later you find that you need to create a report in XML format. Someone might think of writing this method:

```
// Even Worse.
// ambiguous extension methods
// in different namespaces
namespace XmlExtensions
{
    public static class XmlReport
    {
        public static string Format(this Person target) =>
            new XElement("Person",
                new XElement("LastName", target.LastName),
                new XElement("FirstName", target.FirstName)
                ).ToString();
    }
}
```

Switching a `using` statement in the source file changes the format of the report. This is a misuse of extension methods. It's a fragile way to extend a type. If a developer uses the wrong namespace, the program behavior changes. If she forgets to use any of the extension namespaces, the program won't compile. If she needs both namespaces in different methods, she must split the class definition into different files, based on which extension method she needs. Using both namespaces causes a compiler error on an ambiguous reference.

You clearly need a different way to implement this functionality. Extension methods force call dispatch based on the compile-time type of the object. Switching based on the namespace to determine which method is desired makes that strategy even more fragile.

This functionality isn't based on the type you're extending: Formatting a `Person` object for either XML or a console report is not part of the `Person` type but instead more closely belongs to the outside environment that uses the `Person` object.

Extension methods should be used to enhance a type with functionality that naturally extends a type. You should create extension methods only to add functionality that would logically be part of that type. Items 27 and 28 explain two techniques for augmenting interfaces and closed types. If you look at the examples in those items, you can see that all those extension methods create methods that feel like part of the type from the standpoint of consumers of that type.

Contrast that with the examples here. Instead of being part of the `Person` type, the `Format` methods are methods that use the `Person` type. They don't belong in the `Person` type from the standpoint of code that uses that type.

The methods themselves are valid, but they should be regular static methods in a class that can be used with `Person` objects. In fact, if possible, they should be placed in the same class, with different method names:

```
public static class PersonReports
{
    public static string FormatAsText(Person target)=>
        $"{target.LastName,20}, {target.FirstName,15}";
    public static string FormatAsXML(Person target) =>
        new XElement("Person",
            new XElement("LastName", target.LastName),
            new XElement("FirstName", target.FirstName)
            ).ToString();
}
```

This class contains both methods as static methods, and the different names clearly reflect each method's purpose. You have provided both methods to your class's users without introducing ambiguity in the public interface, or the perceived public interface, for the class. Any developer can use either method, should he need those methods. You have not created any ambiguity by introducing the same method signature in different namespaces. That's critical, because very few developers would assume that changing the list of `using` statements would change the runtime behavior of a program. They may assume that it would cause compile-time errors but not runtime errors.

Of course, once you've changed the method names so that they do not collide, you could make these methods into extension methods again. There isn't much to gain from these methods, which don't seem to be extending the type but rather are using the type. However, because the names don't collide, you can put both methods in the same namespace and the same class. That avoids the pitfalls of the earlier example.

You should view the set of extension methods for a type as a single global set. Extension methods should never be overloaded on namespaces. If at any time you find yourself needing to create multiple extension methods having the same signature, stop. Instead, change the method signature, and consider creating plain old static methods. That practice avoids the ambiguity caused when the compiler selects the overload based on `using` statements.

Item 36: Understand How Query Expressions Map to Method Calls

LINQ is built on two concepts: a query language, and a translation from that query language into a set of methods. The C# compiler converts query expressions written in that query language into method calls.

Every query expression has a mapping to a method call or calls. You should understand this mapping from two perspectives. From the perspective of a class user, you need to understand that your query expressions are nothing more than method calls. A `where` clause translates to a call to a method named `Where()`, with the proper set of parameters. As a class designer, you should evaluate the implementations of those methods provided by the base framework and determine whether you can create better implementations for your types. If not, you should simply defer to the base library versions. However, when you can create a better version, you must make sure that you fully understand the translation from query expressions into method calls. It's your responsibility to ensure that your method signatures correctly handle every translation case. For some of the query expressions, the correct path is rather obvious. However, it's a little more difficult to comprehend a couple of the more complicated expressions.

The full **query expression pattern** contains 11 methods. The following is the definition that first appeared in *The C# Programming Language, Third Edition*, by Anders Hejlsberg, Mads Torgersen, Scott Wiltamuth, and Peter Golde (Microsoft Corporation, 2009), §7.15.3 (reprinted with permission from Microsoft Corporation):

```
delegate R Func<T1, R>(T1 arg1);
delegate R Func<T1, T2, R>(T1 arg1, T2 arg2);
class C
{
    public C<T> Cast<T>();
}

class C<T> : C
{
    public C<T> Where(Func<T, bool> predicate);
    public C<U> Select<U>(Func<T, U> selector);
    public C<V> SelectMany<U, V>(Func<T, C<U>> selector,
        Func<T, U, V> resultSelector);
    public C<V> Join<U, K, V>(C<U> inner,
        Func<T, K> outerKeySelector,
        Func<U, K> innerKeySelector,
        Func<T, U, V> resultSelector);
    public C<V> GroupJoin<U, K, V>(C<U> inner,
        Func<T, K> outerKeySelector,
        Func<U, K> innerKeySelector,
        Func<T, C<U>, V> resultSelector);
    public O<T> OrderBy<K>(Func<T, K> keySelector);
    public O<T> OrderByDescending<K>(Func<T, K> keySelector);
    public C<G<K, T>> GroupBy<K>(Func<T, K> keySelector);
    public C<G<K, E>> GroupBy<K, E>(Func<T, K> keySelector,
        Func<T, E> elementSelector);
}

class O<T> : C<T>
{
    public O<T> ThenBy<K>(Func<T, K> keySelector);
```

```
        public O<T> ThenByDescending<K>(Func<T, K> keySelector);
}


class G<K, T> : C<T>
{
        public K Key { get; }
}
```

The .NET base library provides two general-purpose reference implementations of this pattern. `System.Linq.Enumerable` provides extension
methods on `IEnumerable<T>` that implement the query expression
pattern. `System.Linq.Queryable` provides a similar set of extension
methods on `IQueryable<T>` that support a query provider's ability to
translate queries into another format for execution. (For example, the
LINQ to SQL implementation converts query expressions into SQL queries
that are executed by the SQL database engine.) As a class user, you are
probably using one of those two reference implementations for most of
your queries.

Second, as a class author, you can create a data source that implements
`IEnumerable<T>` or `IQueryable<T>` (or a closed generic type from
`IEnumerable<T>` or `IQueryable<T>`), and in that case your type
already implements the query expression pattern. Your type has that
implementation because you're using the extension methods defined in
the base library.

Before we go further, you should understand that the C# language does
not enforce any execution semantics on the query expression pattern.
You can create a method that matches the signature of one of the query
methods and does anything internally. The compiler cannot verify that
your `Where` method satisfies the expectations of the query expression
pattern. All it can do is ensure that the syntactic contract is satisfied.
This behavior isn't any different from that of any interface method. For
example, you can create an interface method that does anything, whether
or not it meets users' expectations.

Of course, this doesn't mean that you should ever consider such a plan. If
you implement any of the query expression pattern methods, you should
ensure that its behavior is consistent with the reference implementations,
both syntactically and semantically. Except for performance differences,
callers should not be able to determine whether your method is being
used or the reference implementations are being used.

Translating from query expressions to method invocations is a complicated iterative process. The compiler repeatedly translates expressions
to methods until all expressions have been translated. Furthermore, the
compiler has a specified order in which it performs these translations,
although I'm not explaining them in that order. The compiler order is
easy for the compiler and is documented in the C# specification. I chose
an order that makes it easier to explain to humans. For our purposes,
I discuss some of the translations in smaller, simpler examples.

In the following query, let's examine the `where`, `select`, and `range`
variables:

```
var numbers = { 0, 1, 2, 3, 4, 5, 6, 7, 8, 9 };
var smallNumbers = from n in numbers
                   where n < 5
                   select n;
```

The expression `from n in numbers` binds the range variable n to each value
in `numbers`. The `where` clause defines a filter that will be translated into
a `where` method. The expression `where n < 5` translates to the following:

```
numbers.Where(n => n < 5);
```

`Where` is nothing more than a filter. The output of `Where` is a subset of
the input sequence containing only those elements that satisfy the predicate. The input and output sequences must contain the same type, and a
correct `Where` method must not modify the items in the input sequence.
(User-defined predicates may modify items, but that's not the responsibility of the query expression pattern.)

That `where` method can be implemented either as an instance method
accessible to `numbers` or as an extension method matching the type of
`numbers`. In the example, `numbers` is an array of `int`. Therefore, n in the
method call must be an integer.

`Where` is the simplest of the translations from query expression to method
call. Before we go on, let's dig a little deeper into how this works and
what that means for the translations. The compiler completes its translation from query expression to method call before any overload resolution or type binding. The compiler does not know whether there are any
candidate methods when the compiler translates the query expression
to a method call. It doesn't examine the type, and it doesn't look for any
candidate extension methods. It simply translates the query expression
into the method call. After all queries have been translated into method

call syntax, the compiler performs the work of searching for candidate methods and then determining the best match.

Next, you can extend that simple example to include the `select` expression in the query. The `select` clauses are translated into `Select` methods. However, in certain special cases the `Select` method can be optimized away. The sample query is a **degenerate select**, selecting the `range` variable. Degenerate select queries can be optimized away, because the output sequence is not equal to the input sequence. The sample query has a `where` clause, which breaks that identity relationship between the input sequence and the output sequence. Therefore, the final method call version of the query is this:

```
var smallNumbers = numbers.Where(n => n < 5);
```

The `select` clause is removed because it is redundant. That's safe because the `select` operates on an immediate result from another query expression (in this example, `where`).

When the `select` does not operate on the immediate result of another expression, it cannot be optimized away. Consider this query:

```
var allNumbers = from n in numbers select n;
```

It will be translated into this method call:

```
var allNumbers = numbers.Select(n => n);
```

While we're on this subject, note that `select` is often used to transform or project one input element into a different element or into a different type. The following query modifies the value of the result:

```
var numbers = { 0, 1, 2, 3, 4, 5, 6, 7, 8, 9 };
var smallNumbers = from n in numbers
                   where n < 5
                   select n * n;
```

Or you could transform the input sequence into a different type as follows:

```
var numbers = { 0, 1, 2, 3, 4, 5, 6, 7, 8, 9 };
var squares = from n in numbers
              select new { Number = n, Square = n * n };
```

The `select` clause maps to a `Select` method that matches the signature in the query expression pattern:

```
var squares = numbers.Select(n =>
    new { Number = n, Square = n * n });
```

`Select` transforms the input type into the output type. A proper `select` method must produce exactly one output element for each input element. Also, a proper implementation of `Select` must not modify the items in the input sequence.

That's the end of the simpler query expressions. Now we discuss some of the less obvious transformations.

Ordering relations map to the `OrderBy` and `ThenBy` methods, or `OrderByDescending` and `ThenByDescending`. Consider this query:

```
var people = from e in employees
             where e.Age > 30
             orderby e.LastName, e.FirstName, e.Age
             select e;
```

It translates into this:

```
var people = employees.Where(e => e.Age > 30).
    OrderBy(e => e.LastName).
    ThenBy(e => e.FirstName).
    ThenBy(e => e.Age);
```

Notice in the definition of the query expression pattern that `ThenBy` operates on a sequence returned by `OrderBy` or `ThenBy`. Those sequences can contain markers that enable `ThenBy` to operate on the sorted subranges when the sort keys are equal.

This transformation is not the same if the `orderby` clauses are expressed as different clauses. The following query sorts the sequence entirely by `LastName`, then sorts the entire sequence again by `FirstName`, and then sorts again by `Age`:

```
// Not correct. Sorts the entire sequence three times.
var people = from e in employees
             where e.Age > 30
             orderby e.LastName
             orderby e.FirstName
             orderby e.Age
             select e;
```

As separate queries, you could specify that any of the `orderby` clauses use descending order:

```
var people = from e in employees
             where e.Age > 30
```

```
orderby e.LastName descending, e.FirstName, e.Age
select e;
```

The `OrderBy` method creates a different sequence type as its output so that `thenby` clauses can be more efficient and so that the types are correct for the overall query. `ThenBy` cannot operate on an unordered sequence, only on a sorted sequence (typed as `O<T>` in the sample). Subranges are already sorted and marked. If you create your own `Orderby` and `Thenby` methods for a type, you must adhere to this rule. You'll need to add an identifier to each sorted subrange so that any subsequent `ThenBy` clause can work properly. `ThenBy` methods need to be typed to take the output of an `OrderBy` or `ThenBy` method and then sort each subrange correctly.

Everything I've said about `OrderBy` and `ThenBy` also applies to `OrderByDescending` and `ThenByDescending`. In fact, if your type has a custom version of any of those methods, you should always implement all four of them.

The remaining expression translations involve multiple steps. Those queries involve either groupings or multiple `from` clauses that introduce continuations. Query expressions that contain continuations are translated into nested queries. Then those nested queries are translated into methods. Following is a simple query with a continuation:

```
var results = from e in employees
              group e by e.Department into d
              select new
              {
                  Department = d.Key,
                  Size = d.Count()
              };
```

Before any other translations are performed, the continuation is translated into a nested query:

```
var results = from d in
              from e in employees group e by e.Department
              select new { Department = d.Key,
              Size = d.Count()};
```

Once the nested query is created, the methods translate into the following:

```
var results = employees.GroupBy(e => e.Department).
    Select(d => new { Department = d.Key,
    Size = d.Count() });
```

The foregoing query shows a GroupBy that returns a single sequence. The other GroupBy method in the query expression pattern returns a sequence of groups in which each group contains a key and a list of values:

```
var results = from e in employees
              group e by e.Department into d
              select new
              {
                  Department = d.Key,
                  Employees = d.AsEnumerable()
              };
```

That query maps to the following method calls:

```
var results2 = employees.GroupBy(e => e.Department).
    Select(d => new {
        Department = d.Key,
        Employees = d.AsEnumerable()
    });
```

GroupBy methods produce a sequence of key/value list pairs; the keys are the group selectors, and the values are the sequence of items in the group. The query select clause may create new objects for the values in each group. However, the output should always be a sequence of key/value pairs in which the value contains some element created by each item in the input sequence that belongs to that particular group.

The final methods to understand are SelectMany, Join, and GroupJoin. These three methods are complicated, because they work with multiple input sequences. The methods that implement these translations perform the enumerations across multiple sequences and then flatten the resulting sequences into a single output sequence. SelectMany produces the Cartesian product on the two source sequences. For example, consider this query:

```
int[] odds = { 1, 3, 5, 7 };
int[] evens = { 2, 4, 6, 8 };
var pairs = from oddNumber in odds
            from evenNumber in evens
            select new
            {
                oddNumber,
                evenNumber,
                Sum = oddNumber + evenNumber
            };
```

It produces a sequence having 16 elements:

```
1,2, 3
1,4, 5
1,6, 7
1,8, 9
3,2, 5
3,4, 7
3,6, 9
3,8, 11
5,2, 7
5,4, 9
5,6, 11
5,8, 13
7,2, 9
7,4, 11
7,6, 13
7,8, 15
```

Query expressions that contain multiple `select` clauses are translated into a `SelectMany` method call. The sample query would be translated into the following `SelectMany` call:

```
int[] odds = { 1, 3, 5, 7 };
int[] evens = { 2, 4, 6, 8 };
var values = odds.SelectMany(oddNumber => evens,
    (oddNumber, evenNumber) =>
    new {
        oddNumber,
        evenNumber,
        Sum = oddNumber + evenNumber
    });
```

The first parameter to `SelectMany` is a function that maps each element in the first source sequence to the sequence of elements in the second source sequence. The second parameter (the output selector) creates the projections from the pairs of items in both sequences.

`SelectMany()` iterates the first sequence. For each value in the first sequence, it iterates the second sequence, producing the result value from the pair of input values. The output selected is called for each element in a flattened sequence of every combination of values from both sequences. One possible implementation of `SelectMany` is as follows:

```
static IEnumerable<TOutput> SelectMany<T1, T2, TOutput>(
    this IEnumerable<T1> src,
    Func<T1, IEnumerable<T2>> inputSelector,
    Func<T1, T2, TOutput> resultSelector)
{
    foreach (T1 first in src)
    {
        foreach (T2 second in inputSelector(first))
            yield return resultSelector(first, second);
    }
}
```

The first input sequence is iterated. Then the second input sequence is iterated using the current value on the input sequence. That's important, because the input selector on the second sequence may depend on the current value in the first sequence. Then, as each pair of elements is generated, the result selector is called on each pair.

If your query has more expressions and if `SelectMany` does not create the final result, then `SelectMany` creates a tuple that contains one item from each input sequence. Sequences of that tuple are the input sequence for later expressions. For example, consider this modified version of the original query:

```
int[] odds = { 1, 3, 5, 7 };
int[] evens = { 2, 4, 6, 8 };
var values = from oddNumber in odds
             from evenNumber in evens
             where oddNumber > evenNumber
             select new
             {
                 oddNumber,
                 evenNumber,
                 Sum = oddNumber + evenNumber
             };
```

It produces this `SelectMany` method call:

```
odds.SelectMany(oddNumber => evens,
    (oddNumber, evenNumber) =>
    new { oddNumber, evenNumber });
```

The full query is then translated into this statement:

```
var values = odds.SelectMany(oddNumber => evens,
    (oddNumber, evenNumber) =>
    new { oddNumber, evenNumber }).
    Where(pair => pair.oddNumber > pair.evenNumber).
    Select(pair => new {
        pair.oddNumber,
        pair.evenNumber,
        Sum = pair.oddNumber + pair.evenNumber
    });
```

You can see another interesting property in the way `SelectMany` gets treated when the compiler translates multiple `from` clauses into `SelectMany` method calls. `SelectMany` composes well. More than two `from` clauses will produce more than one `SelectMany()` method call. The resulting pair from the first `SelectMany()` call will be fed into the second `SelectMany()`, which will produce a triple. The triple will contain all combinations of all three sequences. Consider this query:

```
var triples = from n in new int[] { 1, 2, 3 }
              from s in new string[] { "one", "two",
              "three" }
              from r in new string[] { "I", "II", "III" }
              select new { Arabic = n, Word = s, Roman = r };
```

It will be translated into the following method calls:

```
var numbers = new int[] { 1, 2, 3 };
var words = new string[] { "one", "two", "three" };
var romanNumerals = new string[] { "I", "II", "III" };
var triples = numbers.SelectMany(n => words,
    (n, s) => new { n, s }).
    SelectMany(pair => romanNumerals,
    (pair, n) =>
        new { Arabic = pair.n, Word = pair.s, Roman = n });
```

As you can see, you can extend from three to any arbitrary number of input sequences by applying more `SelectMany()` calls. These later examples also demonstrate how `SelectMany` can introduce anonymous types into your queries. The sequence returned from `SelectMany()` is a sequence of some anonymous type.

Now let's look at the two other translations you need to understand: `Join` and `GroupJoin`. Both are applied on join expressions. `GroupJoin` is always used when the join expression contains an `into` clause. `Join` is used when the join expression does not contain an `into` clause.

A join without an `into` looks like this:

```
var numbers = new int[] { 0, 1, 2, 3, 4, 5, 6, 7, 8, 9 };
var labels = new string[] { "0", "1", "2", "3", "4", "5" };
var query = from num in numbers
            join label in labels on num.ToString() equals label
            select new { num, label };
```

It translates into the following:

```
var query = numbers.Join(labels, num => num.ToString(),
    label => label, (num, label) => new { num, label });
```

The `into` clause creates a list of subdivided results:

```
var groups = from p in projects
             join t in tasks on p equals t.Parent
             into projTasks
             select new { Project = p, projTasks };
```

That translates into a `GroupJoin`:

```
var groups = projects.GroupJoin(tasks,
    p => p, t => t.Parent, (p, projTasks) =>
        new { Project = p, TaskList = projTasks });
```

The entire process of converting all expressions into method calls is complicated and often takes several steps.

The good news is that for the most part, you can happily go about your work secure in the knowledge that the compiler does the correct translation. And because your type implements `IEnumerable<T>`, users of your type are getting the correct behavior.

But you may have that nagging urge to create your own version of one or more of the methods that implement the query expression pattern. Maybe your collection type is always sorted on a certain key, and you can short-circuit the `OrderBy` method. Maybe your type exposes lists of lists, and this means that you may find that `GroupBy` and `GroupJoin` can be implemented more efficiently.

More ambitiously, maybe you intend to create your own provider and you'll implement the entire pattern. That being the case, you need to understand the behavior of each query method and know what should go into your implementation. Refer to the examples, and make sure you understand the expected behavior of each query method before you embark on creating your own implementations.

Many of the custom types you define model some kind of collection. The developers who use your types will expect to use your collections in the same way that they use every other collection type, with the built-in query syntax. As long as you support the IEnumerable<T> interface for any type that models a collection, you'll meet that expectation. However, your types may be able to improve on the default implementation by using the internal specifics in your type. When you choose to do that, ensure that your type matches the contract from the query pattern in all forms.

Item 37: Prefer Lazy Evaluation to Eager Evaluation in Queries

When you define a query, you don't actually get the data and populate a sequence. You are actually defining only the set of steps that you will execute when you choose to iterate that query. This means that each time you execute a query, you perform the entire recipe from first principles. That's usually the right behavior. Each new enumeration produces new results, in what is called **lazy evaluation**. However, often that's not what you want. When you grab a set of variables, you want to retrieve them once and retrieve them now, in what is called **eager evaluation**.

Every time you write a query that you plan to enumerate more than once, you need to consider which behavior you want. Do you want a snapshot of your data, or do you want to create a description of the code you will execute in order to create the sequence of values?

This concept is a major change in the way you are likely accustomed to working. You probably view code as something that is executed immediately. However, with LINQ queries, you're treating code as data. The lambda expression arguments will be invoked at a later time. More than that, if the provider uses expression trees instead of delegates, those expression trees can be combined later by combining new expressions into the same expression tree.

Let's start with an example to explain the difference between lazy and eager evaluation. The following bit of code generates a sequence and then iterates that sequence three times, with a pause between iterations:

```
private static IEnumerable<TResult>
    Generate<TResult>(int number, Func<TResult> generator)
{
    for (var i = 0; i < number; i++)
        yield return generator();
}


private static void LazyEvaluation()
{
    WriteLine($"Start time for Test One: {DateTime.Now:T}");
    var sequence = Generate(10, () => DateTime.Now);

    WriteLine("Waiting....\tPress Return");
    ReadLine();

    WriteLine("Iterating...");
    foreach (var value in sequence)
        WriteLine($"{value:T}");

    WriteLine("Waiting....\tPress Return");
    ReadLine();
    WriteLine("Iterating...");
    foreach (var value in sequence)
        WriteLine($"{value:T}");
}
```

Here's one sample output:

```
Start time for Test One: 6:43:23 PM
Waiting....    Press Return

Iterating...
6:43:31 PM
...
6:43:31 PM
Waiting....    Press Return

Iterating...
6:43:42 PM
...
6:43:42 PM
```

In this example of lazy evaluation, notice that the sequence is generated each time it is iterated, as evidenced by the different time stamps. The sequence variable does not hold the elements created. Rather, it holds the expression tree that can create the sequence. You should run this code yourself, stepping into each query to see exactly when the expressions are evaluated. It's the most instructive way to learn how LINQ queries are evaluated.

You can use this capability to compose queries from existing queries. Instead of retrieving the results from the first query and processing them as a separate step, you can compose queries in different steps and then execute the composed query only once. For example, suppose I modify the query to return times in universal format:

```
var sequence1 = Generate(10, () => DateTime.Now);
var sequence2 = from value in sequence1
                select value.ToUniversalTime();
```

Sequence 1 and sequence 2 share functional composition, not data. Sequence 2 is not built by enumerating the values in sequence 1 and modifying each value. Rather, it is created by executing the code that produces sequence 1, followed by the code that produces sequence 2. If you iterate the two sequences at different times, you'll see unrelated sequences. Sequence 2 will not contain the converted values from sequence 1. Instead, it will contain totally new values. It doesn't generate a sequence of dates and then convert the entire sequence into universal time. Instead, each line of code generates one set of values using universal time.

Query expressions may, in theory, operate on infinite sequences. They can do so because they are lazy. If written correctly, they examine the first portion of the sequence and then terminate when an answer is found. On the other hand, some query expressions must retrieve the entire sequence before they can proceed to create their answer. Understanding when these bottlenecks might occur will help you create queries that are natural without incurring performance penalties. In addition, this understanding will help you avoid those times when the full sequence is required and will create a bottleneck.

Consider this small program:

```
static void Main(string[] args)
{
    var answers = from number in AllNumbers()
                  select number;
```

```
    var smallNumbers = answers.Take(10);
    foreach (var num in smallNumbers)
        Console.WriteLine(num);
}

static IEnumerable<int> AllNumbers()
{
    var number = 0;
    while (number < int.MaxValue)
    {
        yield return number++;
    }
}
```

This sample illustrates what I mean about a method that does not need the full sequence. The output from this method is the sequence of numbers 0,1,2,3,4,5,6,7,8,9. That's the case even though the AllNumbers() method could generate an infinite sequence. (Yes, it eventually has an overflow, but you'll lose patience long before then.)

The reason this works as quickly as it does is that the entire sequence is not needed. The Take() method returns the first *N* objects from the sequence, so nothing else matters.

However, if you rewrite this query as follows, your program will run forever:

```
class Program
{
    static void Main(string[] args)
    {
        var answers = from number in AllNumbers()
                      where number < 10
                      select number;

        foreach (var num in answers)
            Console.WriteLine(num);
    }
}
```

It runs forever (or up to int.MaxValue) because the query must examine every single number to determine which methods match. This version of the same logic requires the entire sequence.

There are a number of query operators that must have the entire sequence in order to operate correctly. `Where` uses the entire sequence. `Where` examines each element in turn and may produce another infinite sequence. `OrderBy` needs the entire sequence to perform the sort operation. `Max` and `Min` need the entire sequence in a manner similar to `Where`. There's no way to perform these operations without examining every element in the sequence. When you need these capabilities, you'll use these methods.

You need to think about the consequences of using methods that require access to the entire sequence. As you've seen, you need to avoid any methods that require the entire sequence if the sequence might be infinite. Second, even if the sequence is not infinite, any query methods that filter the sequence should be front-loaded in the query. If the first steps in your query remove some of the elements from the collection, that will have a positive effect on the performance of the rest of the query.

For example, the following two queries produce the same result. However, the second query may execute faster. Sophisticated providers will optimize the query, and both queries will have the same performance metrics. However, in the LINQ to Objects implementation (provided by `System.Linq.Enumerable`), all products are read and sorted. Then the product sequence is filtered.

```
// Order before filter.
var sortedProductsSlow =
    from p in products
    orderby p.UnitsInStock descending
    where p.UnitsInStock > 100
    select p;
```

```
// Filter before order.
var sortedProductsFast =
    from p in products
    where p.UnitsInStock > 100
    orderby p.UnitsInStock descending
    select p;
```

Notice that the first query sorts the entire series and then throws away any products whose total in stock is less than 100. The second query filters the sequence first, resulting in a sort on what may be a much smaller sequence. At times, knowing whether the full sequence is needed for a method is the difference between an algorithm that never finishes and one that finishes quickly. You need to understand which methods require the full sequence, and try to execute those last in your query expression.

So far, I've given you quite a few reasons to use lazy evaluation in your queries. In most cases, that's the best approach. At other times, though, you do want a snapshot of the values taken at a point in time. There are two methods you can use to generate the sequence immediately and store the results in a container: `ToList()` and `ToArray()`. Both methods perform the query and store the results in a `List<T>` or an `Array`, respectively.

These methods are useful for a couple of purposes. By forcing the query to execute immediately, these methods capture a snapshot of the data right now. You force the execution to happen immediately, rather than later when you decide to enumerate the sequence. Also, you can use `ToList()` or `ToArray()` to generate a snapshot of query results that is not likely to change before you need it again. You can cache the results and use the saved version later.

In almost all cases, lazy evaluation saves work and is more versatile than eager evaluation. In the rare cases when you do need eager evaluation, you can force it by running the query and storing the sequence results using `ToList()` or `ToArray()`. But unless there is a clear need to use eager evaluation, it's better to use lazy evaluation.

Item 38: Prefer Lambda Expressions to Methods

This recommendation may appear counterintuitive. Coding with lambda expressions can lead to repeated code in the body of lambdas. You often find yourself repeating small bits of logic. The following code snippet has the same logic repeated several times:

```
var allEmployees = FindAllEmployees();

// Find the first employees:
var earlyFolks = from e in allEmployees
                 where e.Classification ==
                 EmployeeType.Salary
                 where e.YearsOfService > 20
                 where e.MonthlySalary < 4000
                 select e;
```

```
// find the newest people:
var newest = from e in allEmployees
             where e.Classification == EmployeeType.Salary
             where e.YearsOfService < 20
             where e.MonthlySalary < 4000
             select e;
```

You could replace the multiple calls to `Where` with a single `Where` clause that has both conditions. There isn't any noticeable difference between the two representations. Because queries compose (see Item 31) and because simple `where` predicates will likely be inlined, the performance will be the same.

You may be tempted to factor repeated lambda expressions into methods that can be reused. You'd end up with code that looks like this:

```
// factor out method:
private static bool LowPaidSalaried(Employee e) =>
    e.MonthlySalary < 4000 && e.Classification ==
    EmployeeType.Salary;


// elsewhere
var allEmployees = FindAllEmployees();
var earlyFolks = from e in allEmployees
             where LowPaidSalaried(e) &&
             e.YearsOfService > 20
             select e;


// find the newest people:
var newest = from e in allEmployees
             where LowPaidSalaried(e) && e.YearsOfService < 2
             select e;
```

It's a small example, so there's not much change here. But already it feels better. Now if the employee classifications change or if the low threshold changes, you're changing the logic in only one location.

Unfortunately, this method of refactoring your code makes it less reusable. The first version, as written, is actually more reusable than the second version. That's because of the way lambda expressions are evaluated, parsed, and eventually executed. If you're like most developers, you see code that has been copied as pure evil and something to be eradicated at all costs. The version with a single method is simpler. It has only one copy of the code to be modified later if needs change. It's just plain good software engineering.

Unfortunately, it's also wrong. Some code will convert the lambda expressions into a delegate to execute the code in your query expression. Other classes will create an expression tree from the lambda expression, parse that expression, and execute it in another environment. LINQ to Objects does the former, and LINQ to SQL does the latter.

LINQ to Objects performs queries on local data stores, usually stored in a generic collection. The implementation creates an anonymous delegate that contains the logic in the lambda expression and executes that code. The LINQ to Objects extension methods use `IEnumerable<T>` as the input sequence.

LINQ to SQL, on the other hand, uses the expression tree contained in the query. That expression tree contains the logical representation of your query. LINQ to SQL parses the tree and uses the expression tree to create the proper T-SQL query, which can be executed directly against the database. Then, the query string (as T-SQL) is sent to the database engine and is executed there.

This processing requires that the LINQ to SQL engine parse the expression tree and replace every logical operation with equivalent SQL. All method calls are replaced with an `Expression.MethodCall` node. The LINQ to SQL engine cannot translate any arbitrary method call into a SQL expression. Instead, it throws an exception. The LINQ to SQL engine fails rather than try to execute multiple queries, bring multiple data to the client side of the application boundary, and then process it there.

If you are building any kind of reusable library for which the data source could be anything, you must anticipate this situation. You must structure the code so that it will work correctly with any data source. This means that you need to keep lambda expressions separate, and as inline code, for your library to function correctly.

Of course, this doesn't mean that you should be copying code all over the library. It means only that you need to create different building blocks for your applications when query expressions and lambdas are involved. From our simple example, you can create larger reusable blocks this way:

```
private static IQueryable<Employee> LowPaidSalariedFilter
    (this IQueryable<Employee> sequence) =>
        from s in sequence
        where s.Classification == EmployeeType.Salary &&
        s.MonthlySalary < 4000
        select s;
```

```
// elsewhere:
var allEmployees = FindAllEmployees();

// Find the first employees:
var salaried = allEmployees.LowPaidSalariedFilter();

var earlyFolks = salaried.Where(e => e.YearsOfService > 20);

// find the newest people:
var newest = salaried.Where(e => e.YearsOfService < 2);
```

Of course, not every query is that simple to update. You need to move up the call chain a bit to find the reusable list-processing logic so that you need to express the same lambda expression only once. Recall from Item 31 earlier in this chapter that enumerator methods do not execute until you begin to traverse the items in the collection. Remembering that fact, you can create small methods that construct each portion of your query and contain commonly used lambda expressions. Each of those methods must take the sequence as input and must return the sequence using the `yield return` keyword.

Following that same pattern, you can compose `IQueryable` enumerators by building new expression trees that can be executed remotely. Here, the expression tree for finding sets of employees can be composed as a query before it is executed. The `IQueryProvider` object (such as the LINQ to SQL data source) processes the full query rather than pull out parts that must be executed locally.

You then put together those small methods to build the larger queries you will use in your application. The advantage of this technique is that you avoid the code-copying issues that we all dislike in the first sample in this item. You also have structured the code so that it creates an expression tree for execution when you have composed your completed query and begin to execute it.

One of the most efficient ways to reuse lambda expressions in complicated queries is to create extension methods for those queries on closed generic types. You can see that the method for finding the lower-paid salaried employees is such a method. It takes a sequence of employees and returns a filtered sequence of employees. In production code, you should create a second overload that uses `IEnumerable<Employee>` as the parameter type. In that way, you support both the LINQ-to-SQL-style implementations and the LINQ to Objects implementation.

You can build exactly the queries you need by composing the smaller building blocks from those methods that take lambda expressions and are sequence methods. You gain the advantage of creating code that works with `IEnumerable<T>` and `IQueryable<T>`. Furthermore, you haven't broken the possible evaluation of the queryable expression trees.

Item 39: Avoid Throwing Exceptions in Functions and Actions

When you create code that executes over a sequence of values and the code throws an exception somewhere in that sequence processing, you'll have problems recovering state. You don't know how many elements were processed, if any. You don't know what needs to be rolled back. You can't restore the program state at all.

Consider this snippet of code, which gives everyone a 5 percent raise:

```
var allEmployees = FindAllEmployees();
allEmployees.ForEach(e => e.MonthlySalary *= 1.05M);
```

One day, this routine runs and throws an exception. Chances are that the exception was not thrown on the first or last employee. Some employees got raises, but others didn't. It will be very difficult for your program to recover the previous state. Can you return the data to a consistent state? Once you lose knowledge of program state, you can't regain it without human examination of all the data.

This problem occurs because the code snippet modifies elements of a sequence in place. It doesn't follow the strong exception guarantee. In the face of errors, you can't know what happened and what didn't.

You fix this situation by guaranteeing that whenever the method does not complete, the observable program state does not change. You can implement this in various ways, each with its own benefits and risks.

Before talking about the risks, let's examine the reason for concern in a bit more detail. Not every method exhibits this problem. Many methods examine a sequence but do not modify it. The following method examines everyone's salary and returns the result:

```
var total = allEmployees.Aggregate(0M,
    (sum, emp) => sum + emp.MonthlySalary);
```

You don't need to carefully modify methods like this that do not modify any data in the sequence. In many applications, you'll find that most of your methods do not modify the sequence. Let's return again to our first method, giving every employee a 5 percent raise. What actions can you take to rework this method to ensure that the strong exception guarantee is satisfied?

The first and easiest approach is to rework the action so that you can ensure that the action method, expressed earlier in the lambda expression, never throws an exception. In many cases, it is possible to test any failure conditions before modifying each element in the sequence. You need to define the functions and predicates so that the method's contract can be satisfied in all cases, even error conditions. This strategy works if doing nothing is the right behavior for elements that caused the exception. In the example of granting raises, imagine that all exceptions are caused by employee records that are stale and include people who no longer work for the company but are still in persistent storage. That would make it correct behavior to skip them. This modification would work:

```
allEmployees.FindAll(
    e => e.Classification == EmployeeType.Active).
    ForEach(e => e.MonthlySalary *= 1.05M);
```

Fixing the problem in this way is the simplest path to avoiding inconsistencies in your algorithms. Whenever you can write your action methods to ensure that no exceptions leave a lambda expression or action method, that's the most efficient technique to use.

However, sometimes you may not be able to guarantee that those expressions never throw an exception. Now you must take more-expensive defensive measures. You need to rework the algorithm to take into account the possibility of an exception. That means doing all the work on a copy and then replacing the original sequence with the copy only if the operation completes successfully. If you felt you could not avoid the possibility of an exception, you could rewrite our earlier algorithm:

```
var updates = (from e in allEmployees
               select new Employee
               {
                   EmployeeID = e.EmployeeID,
                   Classification = e.Classification,
                   YearsOfService = e.YearsOfService,
                   MonthlySalary = e.MonthlySalary *= 1.05M
               }).ToList();
allEmployees = updates;
```

You can see the cost of those changes here. First, there's quite a bit more code than in the earlier versions. That's more work—more code to maintain and more to understand. But you've also changed the performance metrics for the application. This newer version creates a second copy of all the employee records and then swaps the reference to the new list of employees with the reference to the old list. If the employee list is large, that could cause a big performance bottleneck. You have created duplicates of all employees in the list before swapping references. The contract for the action now might throw an exception when the `Employee` object is invalid. The code outside the query now handles those conditions.

And there's still another issue with this particular fix: Whether or not it makes sense depends on how it's used. This new version limits your ability to compose operations using multiple functions. This code snippet caches the full list. This means that its modifications aren't composed along with other transformations in a single enumeration of the list. Each transformation becomes an imperative operation. In practice, you can work around this issue by creating one query statement that performs all the transformations. You cache the list and swap the entire sequence as one final step for all the transformations. Using that technique, you preserve the composability and still provide the strong exception guarantee.

In practice that means writing query expressions to return a new sequence rather than modifying each element of a sequence in place. Each composed query should be able to swap the list unless any exceptions are generated during the processing of any of the steps in the sequence.

Composing queries changes the way you write exception-safe code. If your actions or functions throw an exception, you may have no way to ensure that the data is not in an inconsistent state. You don't know how many elements were processed. You don't know what actions must be taken to restore the original state. However, returning new elements (rather than modifying the elements in place) gives you a better chance of ensuring that operations either complete or don't modify any program state.

This is the same advice for all mutable methods when exceptions may be thrown. It also applies in multithreaded environments. The problem can be harder to spot when you use lambda expressions and the code inside them may throw the exception. With the final operation, you should swap the entire sequence after you are sure that none of the operations has generated an exception.

Item 40: Distinguish Early from Deferred Execution

Declarative code is expository: It defines what gets done. **Imperative code** details step-by-step instructions that explain how something gets done. Both are valid and can be used to create working programs. However, mixing the two causes unpredictable behavior in an application.

All the imperative code you execute today will calculate any needed parameters and then call the method. This line of code describes an imperative set of steps to create the answer:

```
var answer = DoStuff(Method1(),
    Method2(),
    Method3());
```

At runtime, it does the following:

1. It calls `Method1` to generate the first parameter to `DoStuff()`.
2. It calls `Method2` to generate the second parameter to `DoStuff()`.
3. It calls `Method3` to generate the third parameter to `DoStuff()`.
4. It calls `DoStuff` with the three calculated parameters.

That should be a familiar style of code to you. All parameters are calculated, and the data is sent to any method. The algorithms you write are a descriptive set of steps that must be followed to produce the results.

Deferred execution, in which you use lambdas and query expressions, completely changes this process and may pull the rug out from under you. The following line of code seems to do the same thing as the foregoing example, but you'll soon see that there are important differences:

```
var answer = DoStuff(() => Method1(),
    () => Method2(),
    () => Method3());
```

At runtime, it does the following:

1. It calls `DoStuff()`, passing the lambda expressions that could call `Method1`, `Method2`, and `Method3`.
2. Inside `DoStuff`, if and only if the result of `Method1` is needed, `Method1` is called.
3. Inside `DoStuff`, if and only if the result of `Method2` is needed, `Method2` is called.

4. Inside `DoStuff`, if and only if the result of `Method3` is needed, `Method3` is called.

5. `Method1`, `Method2`, and `Method3` may be called in any order, as many times (including zero) as needed.

None of those methods will be called unless the results are needed. This difference is significant, and you will cause yourself major problems if you mix the two idioms.

From the outside, any method can be replaced by its return value, and vice versa, as long as that method does not produce any side effects. In our example, the `DoStuff()` method does not see any difference between the two strategies. The same value is returned, and either strategy is correct. If the method always returns the same value for the same inputs, then the method return value can always be replaced by a call to the method, and vice versa.

However, looking at the program as a whole, there may be significant differences between the two lines of code. The imperative model always calls all three methods. Any side effects from any of those methods always occur exactly once. In contrast, the declarative model may or may not execute all or any of the methods. The declarative version may execute any of the methods more than once. This is the difference between (1) calling a method and passing the results to a method and (2) passing a delegate to the method and letting the method call the delegate. You may get different results from different runs of the application, depending on what actions take place in those methods.

The addition of lambda expressions, type inference, and enumerators makes it much easier to use functional programming concepts in your classes. You can build higher-order functions that take functions as parameters or that return functions to their callers. In one way, this is not a big change: A pure function and its return value are always inter-changeable. In practice, a function may have side effects, and this means that different rules apply.

If data and methods are interchangeable, which should you choose? And, more importantly, when should you choose which? The most important difference is that data must be evaluated before being used, whereas a method can be lazy-evaluated. When you must evaluate data early, you must preevaluate the method and use the result as the data, rather than take a functional approach and substitute the method.

The most important criterion for deciding which to use is the possibility of side effects, both in the body of the function and in the mutability of its return value. Item 37 (earlier in this chapter) shows a query whose results are based on the current time. Its return value changes depending on whether you execute it and cache the results or you use the query as a function parameter. If the function itself produces side effects, the behavior of the program depends on when you execute the function.

There are techniques you can use to minimize the contrast between early and late evaluation. Pure immutable types cannot be changed, and they don't change other program states; therefore, they are not subject to side effects. In the brief example earlier, if `Method1`, `Method2`, and `Method3` are members of an immutable type, then the observable behavior of the early and the late evaluation statements should be exactly the same.

My example does not take any parameters, but if any of those late evaluation methods took parameters, those parameters would need to be immutable to ensure that the early and late binding results were the same.

Therefore, the most important point in deciding between early and late evaluation is the semantics that you want to achieve. If (and only if) the objects and methods are immutable, then the correctness of the program is the same when you replace a value with the function that calculates it, and vice versa. ("Immutable methods" in this case means that the methods cannot modify any global state, such as performing I/O operations, updating global variables, or communicating with other processes.) If the objects and methods are not immutable, you risk changing the program's behavior by changing from early to late evaluation and vice versa. The rest of this item assumes that the observable behavior won't change between early and late evaluation. We look at other reasons to favor one or the other strategy.

One decision point is the size of the input and output space versus the cost of computing the output. For example, programs would still work if `Math.PI` calculated pi when called. The value and the computation are interchangeable from the outside. However, programs would be slower because calculating pi takes time. On the other hand, a method `CalculatePrimeFactors(int)` could be replaced with a lookup table containing all factors of all integers. In that case, the cost of the data table in memory would likely be much greater than the cost in time of calculating the values when needed.

Your real-world problems probably fall somewhere between those two extremes. The right solution won't be as obvious, nor will it be as clear-cut.

In addition to analyzing the computational cost versus the storage cost, you need to consider how you will use the results of any given method. You will find that in some situations, early evaluation of certain queries will make sense. In other cases, you'll use interim results only infrequently. If you ensure that the code does not produce side effects and that either early or deferred evaluation produces the correct answer, then you can make the decision based on the measured performance metrics of both solutions. You can try both ways, measure the difference, and use the better result.

Finally, in some cases you may find that a mixture of the two strategies will work the best. You may find that caching sometimes provides the most efficiency. In those cases, you can create a delegate that returns the cached value:

```
var cache = Method1();
var answer = DoStuff(() => cache,
    () => Method2(),
    () => Method3());
```

The final decision point is whether the method can execute on a remote data store. This factor has quite a bearing on how LINQ to SQL processes queries. Every LINQ to SQL query starts as a deferred query: The methods, and not the data, are used as parameters. Some of the methods may involve work that can be done inside the database engine, and some of the work represents local methods that must be processed before the partially processed query is submitted to the database engine. LINQ to SQL parses the expression tree. Before submitting the query to the database engine, it replaces any local method calls with the result from those method calls. It can do this processing only if a method call does not rely on any individual items in the input sequence being processed (see Items 37 and 38, both in this chapter).

Once LINQ to SQL has replaced any local method calls with the equivalent return values, it translates the query from expressions into SQL statements, which are sent to the database engine and executed there. The result is that by creating a query as a set of expressions, or code, the LINQ to SQL libraries can replace those methods with equivalent SQL. That provides improved performance and lower bandwidth usage. It also means that you as a C# developer can spend less time learning T-SQL. Other providers can do the same.

However, all this work is possible only because you can treat data as code, and vice versa, under the right circumstances. With LINQ to SQL, local methods can be replaced with the return values when the parameters to the method are constants that do not rely on the input sequence. Also, there is quite a bit of functionality in the LINQ to SQL libraries that translates expression trees to a logical structure that can then be translated into T-SQL.

As you create algorithms in C# now, you can determine whether using the data as a parameter or the function as a parameter causes any difference in behavior. Once you've determined that either would be correct, you must determine which would be the better strategy. When the input space is smaller, passing data might be better. However, in other cases, when the input or output space may be very large and you don't necessarily use the entire input data space, you may find that it's much wiser to use the algorithm itself as a parameter. If you're not sure, lean toward using the algorithm as a parameter, because the developer who implements the function can create that function to eagerly evaluate the output space and work with those data values instead.

Item 41: Avoid Capturing Expensive Resources

Closures create objects that contain bound variables. The length of the lives of those bound variables may surprise you, and not always in a good way. As developers we've grown accustomed to looking at the lifetimes of local variables in a very simple way: Variables come into scope when we declare them, and they are out of scope when the corresponding block closes. Local variables are eligible for garbage collection when they go out of scope. We use these assumptions to manage resource usage and object lifetimes.

Closures and captured variables change those rules. When you capture a variable in a closure, the object referenced by that variable can have its lifetime extended. It is not garbage until the last delegate referencing that captured variable becomes garbage. Under some circumstances it may last even longer. After closures and captured variables escape one method, they can be accessed by closures and delegates in client code. Those delegates and closures can be accessed by other code, and so on. Eventually the code accessing your delegate becomes an open-ended set of methods with no idea when your closure and delegates are no longer reachable. The implication is that you really don't know when local variables go out of scope if you return something that is represented by a delegate using a captured variable.

The good news is that often you don't need to be concerned about this behavior. Local variables that are managed types and don't hold onto expensive resources are garbage-collected at a later point, just as regular variables are. If the only thing used by local variables is memory, there's no concern at all.

But some variables hold onto expensive resources. They represent types that implement `IDisposable` and need to be explicitly cleaned up. You may prematurely clean up those resources before you've actually enumerated the collection. You may find that files or connections aren't being closed quickly enough, and you're not able to access files because they are still open.

Item 44 shows you how the C# compiler produces delegates and how variables are captured inside a closure. In this item, we look at how to recognize when you have captured variables that contain other resources. We examine how to manage those resources and how to avoid pitfalls that can occur when captured variables live longer than you'd like.

Consider this construct:

```
var counter = 0;
var numbers = Extensions.Generate(30, () => counter++);
```

It generates code that looks something like this:

```
private class Closure
{
    public int generatedCounter;
    public int generatorFunc() =>
        generatedCounter++;
}


// usage
var c = new Closure();
c.generatedCounter = 0;
var sequence = Extensions.Generate(30, new Func<int>(
    c.generatorFunc));
```

This can get very interesting. The hidden nested class members have been bound to delegates used by `Extensions.Generate`. That can affect the lifetime of the hidden object and therefore can affect when any of the members are eligible for garbage collection. Look at this example:

```
public IEnumerable<int> MakeSequence()
{
    var counter = 0;
    var numbers = Extensions.Generate(30, () => counter++);
    return numbers;
}
```

In this code, the returned object uses the delegate that is bound by the closure. Because the return value needs the delegate, the delegate's lifetime extends beyond the activation of the method. The lifetime of the object representing the bound variables is extended. The object is reachable because the delegate instance is reachable, and the delegate is still reachable because it's part of the returned object. And all members of the object are reachable because the object is reachable.

The C# compiler generates code that looks like this:

```
public static IEnumerable<int> MakeSequence()
{
    var c = new Closure();
    c.generatedCounter = 0;
    var sequence = Extensions.Generate(30,
        new Func<int>(c.generatorFunc));
    return sequence;
}
```

Notice that this sequence contains a delegate reference to a method bound to c, the local object instantiating the closure. The local variable c lives beyond the end of the method.

Often, this situation does not cause much concern. But there are two cases in which it can cause confusion. The first involves IDisposable. Consider the following code. It reads numbers from a CSV input stream and returns the values as a sequence of sequences of numbers. Each inner sequence contains the numbers on that line. It uses some of the extension methods shown in Item 27.

```
public static IEnumerable<string> ReadLines(
    this TextReader reader)
{
    var txt = reader.ReadLine();
    while (txt != null)
```

```
    {
        yield return txt;
        txt = reader.ReadLine();
    }
}

public static int DefaultParse(this string input,
    int defaultValue)
{
    int answer;
    return (int.TryParse(input, out answer))
        ? answer : defaultValue;
}

public static IEnumerable<IEnumerable<int>>
    ReadNumbersFromStream(TextReader t)
{
    var allLines = from line in t.ReadLines()
                    select line.Split(',');
    var matrixOfValues = from line in allLines
                        select from item in line
                                select item.DefaultParse(0);
    return matrixOfValues;
}
```

You would use it like this:

```
var t = new StreamReader(File.OpenRead("TestFile.txt"));
var rowsOfNumbers = ReadNumbersFromStream(t);
```

Remember that queries generate the next value only when that value is accessed. The `ReadNumbersFromStream()` method does not put all the data in memory, but rather it loads values from the stream as needed. The two statements that follow don't actually read the file. It's only later when you start enumerating the values in `rowsOfNumbers` that you open the file and begin reading the values.

Later, in a code review, someone—say, that pedantic Alexander—points out that you never explicitly close the test file. Maybe he found it because there was a resource leak, or he found some error because the file was open when he tried to read it again. You make a change to fix that problem. Unfortunately, it doesn't address the root concerns.

```
IEnumerable<IEnumerable<int>> rowOfNumbers;
using (TextReader t = new
    StreamReader(File.OpenRead("TestFile.txt")))
    rowOfNumbers = ReadNumbersFromStream(t);
```

You happily start your tests, expecting success, but your program throws an exception a couple of lines later:

```
IEnumerable<IEnumerable<int>> rowOfNumbers;
using (TextReader t = new StreamReader(File.OpenRead(
    "TestFile.txt")))
    rowOfNumbers = ReadNumbersFromStream(t);


foreach (var line in rowOfNumbers)
{
    foreach (int num in line)
        Write("{0}, ", num);
    WriteLine();
}
```

What happened? You tried to read from the file after you closed it. The iteration throws an `ObjectDisposedException`. The C# compiler bound `TextReader` to the delegate that reads and parses items from the file. That set of code is represented by the variable `arrayOfNums`. Nothing has really happened yet. The stream has not been read, and nothing has been parsed. That's one of the issues that arise when you move the resource management back up to the callers. If those callers misunderstand the lifetimes of resources, they will introduce problems that range from resource leaks to broken code.

The specific fix is straightforward. You move the code around so that you use the array of numbers before you close the file:

```
using (TextReader t = new
    StreamReader(File.OpenRead("TestFile.txt")))
{
    var arrayOfNums = ReadNumbersFromStream(t);

    foreach (var line in arrayOfNums)
    {
        foreach (var num in line)
            Write("{0}, ", num);
        WriteLine();
    }
}
```

That's great, but not all your problems are that simple. This strategy will lead to lots of duplicated code, and we're always trying to avoid that. So let's look at this solution for some hints about what can lead to a more general answer. The foregoing piece of code works because it uses the array of numbers before the file is closed.

You've structured the code in such a way that it's almost impossible to find the right location to close the file. You've created an API wherein the file must be opened in one location but cannot be closed until a later point. Suppose the original usage pattern were more like this:

```
using (TextReader t = new
    StreamReader(File.OpenRead("TestFile.txt")))
    return ReadNumbersFromFile(t);
```

Now you're stuck with no possible way to close the file. It's opened in one routine, but somewhere up the call stack the file needs to be closed. Where? You can't be sure, but it's not in your code. It's somewhere up the call stack, outside your control, and you're left with no idea even what the file name is and no stream handle to examine what to close.

One obvious solution is to create one method that opens the file, reads the sequence, and returns the sequence. Here's a possible implementation:

```
public static IEnumerable<string> ParseFile(string path)
{
    using (var r = new StreamReader(File.OpenRead(path)))
    {
        var line = r.ReadLine();
        while (line != null)
        {
            yield return line;
            line = r.ReadLine();
        }
    }
}
```

This method uses the same deferred execution model I showed you in Item 31 earlier in this chapter. What's important here is that the `StreamReader` object is disposed of only after all elements have been read, whether that happens early or later. The file object will be closed, but only after the sequence has been enumerated. Here's a smaller contrived example to show what I mean:

```
class Generator : IDisposable
{
    private int count;
    public int GetNextNumber() => count++;

    public void Dispose()
    {
        WriteLine("Disposing now ");
    }
}
```

The `Generator` class implements `IDisposable`, but only to show you what happens when you capture a variable of a type that implements `IDisposable`. Here's one sample usage:

```
var query = (from n in SomeFunction()
             select n).Take(5);

foreach (var s in query)
    Console.WriteLine(s);


WriteLine("Again");
foreach (var s in query)
    WriteLine(s);
```

Here's the output from this code fragment:

```
0
1
2
3
4
Disposing now
Again
0
1
2
3
4
Disposing now
```

The `Generator` object is disposed of when you would hope: after you have completed the iteration for the first time. `Generator` is disposed of whether you complete the iteration sequence or you stop the iteration early, as this query does.

However, there is a problem here. Notice that "Disposing now" is printed twice. Because the code fragment iterated the sequence twice, the code fragment caused `Generator` to be disposed of twice. That's not a problem in the `Generator` class, because that's only a marker. But the file example throws an exception when you enumerate the sequence for the second time. The first enumeration finishes, and `StreamReader` gets disposed of. Then the second enumeration tries to access a stream reader that's been disposed of. It won't work.

If your application will likely perform multiple enumerations on a disposable resource, you need to find a different solution. You may find that your application reads multiple values, processing them in different ways during the course of an algorithm. It may be wiser to use delegates to pass the algorithm, or multiple algorithms, into the routine that reads and processes the records from the file.

You need a generic version of this method that will let you capture the use of those values and then use those values inside an expression before you finally dispose of the file. The same action would look like this:

```
// Usage pattern: parameters are the file
// and the action you want taken for each line in the file.
ProcessFile("testFile.txt",
    (arrayOfNums) =>
    {
        foreach (var line in arrayOfNums)
        {
            foreach (int num in line)
                Write("{0}, ", num);
            WriteLine();
        }
        // Make the compiler happy by returning something:
        return 0;
    }
);


// declare a delegate type
public delegate TResult ProcessElementsFromFile<TResult>(
    IEnumerable<IEnumerable<int>> values);
```

```
// Method that reads files, processing each line
// using the delegate
public static TResult ProcessFile<TResult>(string filePath,
    ProcessElementsFromFile<TResult> action)
{
    using (TextReader t = new StreamReader(File.Open(filePath)))
    {
        var allLines = from line in t.ReadLines()
                       select line.Split(',');

        var matrixOfValues = from line in allLines
                             select from item in line
                             select item.
                             DefaultParse(0);
        return action(matrixOfValues);
    }
}
```

This looks a bit complicated, but it is helpful if you find yourself using this data source in many ways. Suppose you need to find the global maximum in the file:

```
var maximum = ProcessFile("testFile.txt",
    (arrayOfNums) =>
        (from line in arrayOfNums
        select line.Max()).Max());
```

Here, the use of the file stream is completely encapsulated inside `ProcessFile`. The answer you seek is a value, and it gets returned from the lambda expression. By changing the code so that the expensive resource (here, the file stream) gets allocated and released inside the function, you don't have expensive members being added to your closures.

The other problem with expensive resources captured in closures is less severe, but it can affect your application's performance metrics. Consider this method:

```
IEnumerable<int> ExpensiveSequence()
{
    int counter = 0;
    var numbers = Extensions.Generate(30,
        () => counter++);
```

```
        Console.WriteLine("counter: {0}", counter);

        var hog = new ResourceHog();
        numbers = numbers.Union(
            hog.SequenceGeneratedFromResourceHog(
            (val) => val < counter));
        return numbers;
}
```

Like the other closures I've shown, this algorithm produces code that
will be executed later, using the deferred execution model. This means
that `ResourceHog` lives beyond the end of this method to whenever
client code enumerates the sequence. Furthermore, if `ResourceHog` is
not disposable, it will live on until all roots to it are unreachable and the
garbage collector frees it.

If this is a bottleneck, you can restructure the query so that the numbers
generated from `ResourceHog` get evaluated eagerly, and thus `ResourceHog`
can be cleaned up immediately:

```
IEnumerable<int> ExpensiveSequence()
{
    var counter = 0;
    var numbers = Extensions.Generate(30,
        () => counter++);

    WriteLine("counter: {0}", counter);

    var hog = new ResourceHog();
    var mergeSequence = hog.SequenceGeneratedFromResourceHog(
        (val) => val < counter).ToList();

    numbers = numbers.Union(mergeSequence);
    return numbers;
}
```

This sample is pretty clear, because the code isn't very complicated. If
you have more-complicated algorithms, it can be quite a bit more difficult to separate the inexpensive resources from the expensive resources.
Depending on how complicated your algorithms are in methods that
create closures, it may be quite a bit more difficult to unwind different
resources that are captured inside bound variables of the closure. The following method uses three different local variables captured in a closure:

```
private static IEnumerable<int> LeakingClosure(int mod)
{
    var filter = new ResourceHogFilter();
    var source = new CheapNumberGenerator();
    var results = new CheapNumberGenerator();

    var importantStatistic = (from num in
                                source.GetNumbers(50)
                                where filter.PassesFilter(num)
                                select num).Average();

    return from num in results.GetNumbers(100)
           where num > importantStatistic
           select num;
}
```

At first examination, it appears fine. `ResourceHog` generates the important statistic. It's scoped to the method, and it becomes garbage as soon as the method exits.

Unfortunately, this method is not as fine as it appears to be.

Here's why. The C# compiler creates one nested class per scope to implement a closure. The final query statement—which returns the numbers that are greater than the important statistic—needs a closure to contain the bound variable, the important statistic. Earlier in the method, the filter needs to be used in a closure to create the important statistic. This means that the filter gets copied into the nested class that implements the closure. The return statement returns a type that uses an instance of the nested class to implement the `where` clause. The instance of the nested class implementing the closure has leaked out of this method. Normally you wouldn't care. But if `ResourceHogFilter` really uses expensive resources, this would be a drain on your application.

To fix this problem, you need to split the method into two parts and get the compiler to create two closure classes:

```
private static IEnumerable<int> NotLeakingClosure(int mod)
{
    var importantStatistic = GenerateImportantStatistic();

    var results = new CheapNumberGenerator();
    return from num in results.GetNumbers(100)
```

```
                 where num > importantStatistic
                 select num;
}

private static double GenerateImportantStatistic()
{
    var filter = new ResourceHogFilter();
    var source = new CheapNumberGenerator();

    return (from num in source.GetNumbers(50)
            where filter.PassesFilter(num)
            select num).Average();
}
```

"But wait," you say. "That return statement in GenerateImportantStatistic contains the query that generates the statistic. The closure still leaks." No, it doesn't. The Average method requires the entire sequence (see Item 40 earlier in this chapter). The enumeration happens inside the scope of GenerateImportantStatistic, and the average value is returned. The closure containing the ResourceHogFilter object can be garbage-collected as soon as this method returns.

I chose to rework the method in this way because even more issues arise when you write methods that have multiple logical closures. Even though you think that the compiler should create multiple closures, it generally creates only one closure, which handles all the underlying lambdas bound in that method. You care in cases when one of the expressions can be returned from your method, and you think that the other expression doesn't really matter. But it does matter. Because the compiler creates one class to handle all the closures created by a single scope, all members used in any closures are injected into that class. Examine this short method:

```
public IEnumerable<int> MakeAnotherSequence()
{
    var counter = 0;

    var interim = Extensions.Generate(30,
        () => counter++);
    var gen = new Random();

    var numbers = from n in interim
                  select gen.Next() - n;
    return numbers;
}
```

`MakeAnotherSequence()` contains two queries. The first one generates a sequence of integers from 0 through 29. The second modifies that sequence using a random number generator. The C# compiler generates one private class to implement the closure that contains both `counter` and `gen`. The code that calls `MakeAnotherSequence()` will access an instance of the generated class containing both local variables. The compiler does not create two nested classes, only one. The instances of that one nested class will be passed to callers.

There's one final issue relating to when operations happen inside a closure. Here's a sample:

```
private static void SomeMethod(ref int i)
{
    //...
}
private static void DoSomethingInBackground()
{
    var i = 0;
    var thread = new Thread(delegate ()
    { SomeMethod(ref i); });
    thread.Start();
}
```

In this sample, you've captured a variable and examined it in two threads. Furthermore, you've structured it such that both threads are accessing it by reference. I'd explain more as to what happens to the value of `i` when you run this sample, but the truth is that it's not possible to know what's going to happen. Both threads can examine or modify the value of `i`, but, depending on which thread works faster, either thread could change the value at any time.

When you use query expressions in your algorithms, the compiler creates a single closure for all expressions in the entire method. An object of that type may be returned from your method, possibly as a member of the type implementing the enumeration. That object will live in the system until all users of it have been removed. That may create many issues. If any of the fields copied into the closure implements `IDisposable`, it can cause problems with correctness. If any of the fields is expensive to carry, it can cause performance problems. Either way, you need to understand that when objects created by a closure are returned from methods, the closure contains all the variables used to perform the calculations. You must ensure that you need those variables or, if you can't do that, ensure that the closure can clean them up for you.

Item 42: Distinguish between `IEnumerable` and `IQueryable` Data Sources

`IQueryable<T>` and `IEnumerable<T>` have very similar API signatures. `IQueryable<T>` derives from `IEnumerable<T>`. You might think that these two interfaces are interchangeable. In many cases they are, and that's by design. In contrast, a sequence is a sequence, but sequences are not always interchangeable. Their behaviors are different, and their performance metrics can be very, very different. The following two query statements are quite different:

```
var q =
        from c in dbContext.Customers
        where c.City == "London"
        select c;
var finalAnswer = from c in q
                  orderby c.Name
                  select c;
// Code to iterate the final Answer sequence elided


var q =
    (from c in dbContext.Customers
     where c.City == "London"
     select c).AsEnumerable();
var finalAnswer = from c in q
                  orderby c.Name
                  select c;


// Code to iterate final Answer elided.
```

These queries return the same result, but they do their work in very different ways. The first query uses the normal LINQ to SQL version that is built on `IQueryable` functionality. The second version forces the database objects into `IEnumerable` sequences and does more of its work locally. It's a combination of lazy evaluation and `IQueryable<T>` support in LINQ to SQL.

When the results of a query are executed, the LINQ to SQL libraries compose the results from all the query statements. In the example, this means that one call is made to the database. It also means that one SQL query performs both the `where` clause and the `orderby` clause.

In the second case, returning the first query as an `IEnumerable<T>` sequence means that subsequent operations use the LINQ to Objects implementation and are executed using delegates. The first statement causes a call to the database to retrieve all customers in London. The second orders the set returned by the first call by name. That sort operation occurs locally.

You should care about the differences because many queries work quite a bit more efficiently if you use `IQueryable` functionality than if you use `IEnumerable` functionality. Furthermore, because of the differences in how `IQueryable` and `IEnumerable` process query expressions, you'll find that sometimes queries that work in one environment do not work in the other.

The processing is different at every step of the way. That's because the types used are different. `Enumerable<T>` extension methods use delegates for the lambda expressions as well as the function parameters whenever they appear in query expressions. `Queryable<T>`, on the other hand, uses expression trees to process those same function elements. An **expression tree** is a data structure that holds all the logic that makes up the actions in the query. The `Enumerable<T>` version must execute locally. The lambda expressions have been compiled into methods, and they must execute now on the local machine. This means that you need to pull all the data into the local application space from wherever it resides. You'll transfer much more data, and you'll throw away whatever isn't necessary.

In contrast, the `Queryable` version parses the expression tree. After examining the expression tree, this version translates that logic into a format appropriate for the provider and then executes that logic where it is closest to the data location. The result is much less data transfer and better overall system performance. However, there are some restrictions on the code that goes into query expressions when you use the `IQueryable` interface and rely on the `Queryable<T>` implementation of your sequence.

As I showed earlier in this chapter in Item 37, `IQueryable` providers don't parse any arbitrary method. That would be an unbounded set of logic. Instead, they understand a set of operators, and possibly a defined set of methods, that are implemented in the .NET Framework. If your queries contain other method calls, you may need to force the query to use the `Enumerable` implementation.

```
private bool isValidProduct(Product p) =>
    p.ProductName.LastIndexOf('C') == 0;
```

```
// This works:
var q1 =
    from p in dbContext.Products.AsEnumerable()
    where isValidProduct(p)
    select p;
// This throws an exception when you enumerate the collection.
var q2 =
    from p in dbContext.Products
    where isValidProduct(p)
    select p;
```

The first query works, because LINQ to Objects uses delegates to implement queries as method calls. The AsEnumerable() call forces the query into the local client space, and the where clause executes using LINQ to Objects. The second query throws an exception. The reason is that LINQ to SQL uses an IQueryable<T> implementation. LINQ to SQL contains an IQueryProvider that translates your queries into T-SQL. That T-SQL then gets remoted to the database engine, and the database engine executes the SQL statements in that context (see Item 38 earlier in this chapter). That approach can give you an advantage, because far less data gets transferred across tiers and possibly across layers.

In a typical tradeoff of performance versus robustness, you can avoid the exception by translating the query result explicitly to an IEnumerable<T>. The downside of that solution is that the LINQ to SQL engine now returns the entire set of dbContext.Products from the database. Furthermore, the remainder of the query is executed locally. Because IQueryable<T> inherits from IEnumerable<T>, this method can be called using either source.

That sounds good, and it can be a simple approach. But it forces any code that uses your method to fall back to the IEnumerable<T> sequence. If your client developer is using a source that supports IQueryable<T>, you have forced her to pull all the source elements into this process's address space, then process all those elements here, and finally return the results.

Even though normally you would be correct to write that method once, and write it to the lowest common class or interface, that's not the case with IEnumerable<T> and IQueryable<T>. Even though they have almost the same external capabilities, the differences in their respective implementations mean that you should use the implementation that matches your data source. In practice, you'll know whether the data source implements `IQueryable<T>` or only `IEnumerable<T>`. When your source implements `IQueryable`, you should make sure that your code uses that type.

However, you may occasionally find that a class must support queries on `IEnumerable<T>` and `IQueryable<T>` for the same `T`:

```
public static IEnumerable<Product>
    ValidProducts(this IEnumerable<Product> products) =>
    from p in products
    where p.ProductName.LastIndexOf('C') == 0
    select p;


// OK, because string.LastIndexOf() is supported
// by LINQ to SQL provider
public static IQueryable<Product>
    ValidProducts(this IQueryable<Product> products) =>
    from p in products
    where p.ProductName.LastIndexOf('C') == 0
    select p;
```

Of course, this code reeks of duplicated effort. You can avoid the duplication by using `AsQueryable()` to convert any `IEnumerable<T>` to an `IQueryable<T>`:

```
public static IEnumerable<Product>
    ValidProducts(this IEnumerable<Product> products) =>
    from p in products.AsQueryable()
    where p.ProductName.LastIndexOf('C') == 0
    select p;
```

`AsQueryable()` looks at the runtime type of the sequence. If the sequence is an `IQueryable`, it returns the sequence as an `IQueryable`. In contrast, if the runtime type of the sequence is an `IEnumerable`, then `AsQueryable()` creates a wrapper that implements `IQueryable` using the LINQ to Objects implementation, and it returns that wrapper. You get the `Enumerable` implementation, but it's wrapped in an `IQueryable` reference.

Using `AsQueryable()` gives you the maximum benefit. Sequences that already implement `IQueryable` will use that implementation, and sequences that support only `IEnumerable` will still work. When client code hands you an `IQueryable` sequence, your code will properly use the `Queryable<T>` methods and will support expression trees and foreign execution. And if you are working with a sequence that supports only `IEnumerable<T>`, then the runtime implementation will use the `IEnumerable` implementation.

Notice that this version still uses a method call: `string.LastIndexOf()`. That is one of the methods that is parsed correctly by the LINQ to SQL libraries, and therefore you can use it in your LINQ to SQL queries. However, every provider has unique capabilities, so you should not consider that method available in every `IQueryProvider` implementation.

`IQueryable<T>` and `IEnumerable<T>` might seem to provide the same functionality. All the difference lies in how each implements the query pattern. Make sure to declare query results using the type that matches your data source. Query methods are statically bound, and declaring the proper type of query variables means that you get the correct behavior.

Item 43: Use `Single()` and `First()` to Enforce Semantic Expectations on Queries

A quick perusal of the LINQ libraries might lead you to believe that they were designed to work exclusively with sequences. But there are methods that escape out of a query and return a single element. Each of these methods behaves differently from the others, and those differences help you express your intention and expectations for the results of a query that returns a scalar result.

`Single()` returns exactly one element. If no elements exist, or if multiple elements exist, then `Single()` throws an exception. That's a rather strong statement about your expectations. However, if your assumptions are proven false, you probably want to find out immediately. When you write a query that is supposed to return exactly one element, you should use `Single()`. This method expresses your assumptions most clearly: You expect exactly one element back from the query. Yes, it fails if your assumptions are wrong, but it fails quickly and in a way that doesn't cause any data corruption. That immediate failure helps you make a quick diagnosis and correct the problem. Furthermore, your application data doesn't get corrupted by executing later program logic using faulty data. The query fails immediately, because the assumptions are wrong.

```
var somePeople = new List<Person>{
    new Person { FirstName = "Bill", LastName = "Gates"},
    new Person { FirstName = "Bill", LastName = "Wagner"},
    new Person { FirstName = "Bill", LastName = "Johnson"}};
```

```
// Will throw an exception because more than one
// element is in the sequence
var answer = (from p in somePeople
                where p.FirstName == "Bill"
                select p).Single();
```

Furthermore, unlike many of the other queries I've shown you, this one throws an exception even before you examine the result. `Single()` immediately evaluates the query and returns the single element. The following query fails with the same exception (although a different message):

```
var answer = (from p in somePeople
                where p.FirstName == "Larry"
                select p).Single();
```

Again, your code assumes that exactly one result exists. When that assumption is wrong, `Single()` always throws an `InvalidOperationException`.

If your query can return zero or one element, you can use `SingleOrDefault()`. However, remember that `SingleOrDefault()` still throws an exception when more than one value is returned. You are still expecting no more than one value to be returned from your query expression.

```
var answer = (from p in somePeople
                where p.FirstName == "Larry"
                select p).SingleOrDefault();
```

This query returns `null` (the default value for a reference type) to indicate that there were no values that matched the query.

Of course, there are times when you expect to get more than one value but you want a specific one. The best choice is `First()` or `FirstOrDefault()`. Both methods return the first element in the returned sequence. If the sequence is empty, the default is returned. The following query finds the forward who scored the most goals, but it returns `null` if none of the forwards has scored any goals:

```
// Works. Returns null
var answer = (from p in Forwards
                where p.GoalsScored > 0
                orderby p.GoalsScored
                select p).FirstOrDefault();
```

```
// throws an exception if there are no values in the sequence:
var answer2 = (from p in Forwards
               where p.GoalsScored > 0
               orderby p.GoalsScored
               select p).First();
```

Of course, sometimes you don't want the first element. There are quite a few ways to solve this problem. You could reorder the elements so that you do get the correct first element. (You could put them in the other order and grab the last element, but that would take somewhat longer.)

If you know exactly where in the sequence to look, you can use `Skip` and `First` to retrieve the one sought element. Here, we find the third-best goal-scoring forward:

```
var answer = (from p in Forwards
              where p.GoalsScored > 0
              orderby p.GoalsScored
              select p).Skip(2).First();
```

I chose `First()` rather than `Take()` to emphasize that I wanted exactly one element, and not a sequence containing one element. Note that because I use `First()` instead of `FirstOrDefault()`, the compiler assumes that at least three forwards have scored goals.

However, once you start looking for an element in a specific position, it's likely that there is a better way to construct the query. Are there different properties you should be looking for? Should you look to see whether your sequence supports `IList<T>` and supports index operations? Should you rework the algorithm to find exactly the one item? You may find that other methods of finding results will give you much clearer code.

Many of your queries are designed to return one scalar value. Whenever you query for a single value, it's best to write your query to return a scalar value rather than a sequence of one element. Using `Single()` means that you expect to always find exactly one item. `SingleOrDefault()` means zero or one item. `First` and `Last` mean that you are pulling one item out of a sequence. Using any other method of finding one item likely means that you haven't written your query as well as you should have. It won't be as clear for developers using your code or maintaining it later.

Item 44: Avoid Modifying Bound Variables

The following small code snippet illustrates what can happen when you capture variables in a closure and then modify those variables:

```
var index = 0;
Func<IEnumerable<int>> sequence =
    () => Utilities.Generate(30, () => index++);

index = 20;
foreach (int n in sequence())
    WriteLine(n);
WriteLine("Done");
index = 100;
foreach (var n in sequence())
    WriteLine(n);
```

This snippet prints the numbers from 20 through 50, followed by the numbers 100 through 130. That result may surprise you. During the rest of this item, I discuss the code the compiler produces that creates this result. The behavior makes sense, and you'll learn to use it to your advantage.

The C# compiler does quite a bit of work in translating your query expressions into executable code. Even though there are a great many new features in the C# language, all those new constructs compile down to IL that is compatible with the 2.0 version of the .NET CLR. Query syntax depends on new assemblies but not on any new CLR features. The C# compiler converts your queries and lambda expressions into static delegates, instance delegates, or closures. It chooses which one to create based on the code inside the lambda. Which path the compiler takes depends on the body of the lambda. That may sound like so much language trivia, but it has important implications for your code. Which construct the compiler uses does change some subtle behaviors of your code.

Not all lambda expressions create the same code. The simplest work for the compiler is to generate the delegate for this style of code:

```
int[] someNumbers = { 0, 1, 2, 3, 4, 5, 6, 7, 8, 9, 10 };
var answers = from n in someNumbers
              select n * n;
```

The compiler implements the lambda expression `select  n  *  n` using a static delegate definition. The compiler writes code as though you had written it:

```
private static int HiddenFunc(int n) => (n * n);

private static Func<int, int> HiddenDelegateDefinition;

// usage:
int[] someNumbers = new int[] { 0, 1, 2, 3, 4, 5,
    6, 7, 8, 9, 10 };
if (HiddenDelegateDefinition == null)
{
    HiddenDelegateDefinition  = new
        Func<int, int>(HiddenFunc);
}
var answers = someNumbers
    .Select<int, int>(HiddenDelegateDefinition);
```

The body of the lambda expression does not access any instance variables or local variables. The lambda expression accesses only its parameters. Therefore, the C# compiler creates a static method for the target of the delegate. That's the simplest path the compiler can take. The compiler generates a private static method and corresponding delegate definition whenever the expression to be enclosed can be implemented in a private static method. That includes simple expressions such as the example here or a method that accesses any static class variables.

The sample lambda expression is only concise syntax for a method call wrapped in a delegate. Simple as can be. The next-simplest version is a lambda expression that requires access to instance variables but not to any local variables:

```
public class ModFilter
{
    private readonly int modulus;

    public ModFilter(int mod)
    {
        modulus = mod;
    }

    public IEnumerable<int> FindValues(
        IEnumerable<int> sequence)
```

```
        {
            return from n in sequence
                   where n % modulus == 0 // New expression
                   select n * n; // previous example
        }
}
```

Here the compiler creates an instance method to wrap the delegate for the new expression. It's the same basic concept as before but now uses an instance method so that the delegate can read and modify the object's state. As with the static delegate sample, here the compiler converts the lambda expression to code that you are already familiar with. It's a combination of delegate definitions and method calls:

```
// Equivalent pre-LINQ version
public class ModFilter
{
    private readonly int modulus;

    // New method
    private bool WhereClause(int n) =>
        ((n % this.modulus) == 0);

    // original method
    private static int SelectClause(int n) =>
        (n * n);

    // original delegate
    private static Func<int, int> SelectDelegate;

    public IEnumerable<int> FindValues(
        IEnumerable<int> sequence)
    {
        if (SelectDelegate == null)
        {
            SelectDelegate = new Func<int, int>(SelectClause);
        }
        return sequence.Where<int>(
            new Func<int, bool>(this.WhereClause)).
            Select<int, int>(SelectClause);
    }
    // Other methods elided.
}
```

Whenever the code inside your lambda expression accesses member variables for your object instances, the compiler generates an instance method representing the code in your lambda expression. There's nothing magical going on here. The compiler saves you some typing, but that's all you gain. It's just plain old method calls.

However, the compiler does quite a bit more work if any of the code in your lambda expressions accesses local variables or accesses parameters to methods. Here, you need a closure. The compiler generates a private nested class to implement the closure for your local variables. The local variable must be passed to the delegate that implements the body of the lambda expression. In addition, any changes to that local variable performed by the lambda expression must be visible in the outer scope. *The C# Programming Language, Third Edition* (and later), by Anders Hejlsberg, Mads Torgersen, Scott Wiltamuth, and Peter Golde (Microsoft Corporation, 2009), §7.14.4.1, describes this behavior. Of course, you may have more than one variable in both the inner and outer scopes. You also may have more than one query expression.

Let's make a small change to the sample method so that it accesses a local variable:

```
public class ModFilter
{
    private readonly int modulus;

    public ModFilter(int mod)
    {
        modulus = mod;
    }

    public IEnumerable<int> FindValues(
        IEnumerable<int> sequence)
    {
        int numValues = 0;
        return from n in sequence
                where n % modulus == 0 // New expression
                // Select clause accesses local variable:
                select n * n / ++numValues;
    }
    // other methods elided
}
```

Notice that the `select` clause needs to access the local variable, `numValues`. To create the closure, the compiler creates a nested class to implement the behavior you need. Here's a version of the code that matches what the compiler generates:

```
// Pre-LINQ version of a simple closure
public class ModFilter
{
    private sealed class Closure
    {
        public ModFilter outer;
        public int numValues;

        public int SelectClause(int n) =>
            ((n * n) / ++this.numValues);
    }

    private readonly int modulus;

    public ModFilter(int mod)
    {
        this.modulus = mod;
    }

    private bool WhereClause(int n) =>
        ((n % this.modulus) == 0);

    public IEnumerable<int> FindValues
        (IEnumerable<int> sequence)
    {
        var c = new Closure();
        c.outer = this;
        c.numValues = 0;
        return sequence.Where<int>
            (new Func<int, bool>(this.WhereClause))
            .Select<int, int>(
                new Func<int, int>(c.SelectClause));
    }
}
```

In this version, the compiler creates a nested class to contain all the variables that are accessed or modified inside the lambda expression. In fact, those local variables are completely replaced by fields of that nested class. Both the code inside the lambda expression and the code outside the lambda (but in the local method) access that same field. The logic inside the lambda expression has been compiled into a method in the inner class.

The compiler treats method parameters used in lambda expressions in exactly the same way that it treats local variables: It copies those parameters into the nested class representing the closure.

Let's reexamine that initial example. Now it's clear why the behavior is strange. The variable `incrementBy` is modified after it has been placed in the closure but before the query has been executed. You modified the internal structure and then expected it to move back in time and use its previous version.

Modifying the bound variables between queries can introduce errors caused by the interaction of deferred execution and the way the compiler implements closures. Therefore, you should avoid modifying bound variables that have been captured by a closure.

5 | Exception Practices

Errors happen. Despite our best efforts, our programs encounter situations we didn't anticipate. Throughout the .NET Framework, methods either succeed, or they indicate their failure by throwing an exception. The libraries and applications you write will be easier to use and extend if you follow this same practice. Making your code robust when exceptions are thrown is a key skill for every C# developer.

Your code will call methods that throw exceptions. Your code must behave in a well-known manner when it calls a method that throws an exception.

Your code may also throw exceptions directly. The .NET Framework Design Guidelines recommend throwing exceptions in all cases when your method does not do what was asked. You must provide all the information necessary to diagnose, and possibly correct, the root cause of the failure. You must also ensure that the application is in a known state in case recovery is possible.

The items in this chapter explain ways to communicate failures through exceptions in a clear and accurate way. You'll also learn how to manage program state to increase the chances of recovery.

Item 45: Use Exceptions to Report Method Contract Failures

Any method that cannot perform its stated actions should report that failure by throwing an exception. Error codes can be easily ignored, and the code to check or propagate error codes pollutes the normal flow of execution, obscuring the core logic. But exceptions should not be used as a general flow-control mechanism. This means that you must provide other public methods that enable your library's users to minimize the chances that exceptions will be thrown under an application's normal operating conditions. Exceptions are costly at runtime, and writing exception-proof code is difficult. Provide APIs for developers to test conditions without writing try/catch blocks everywhere.

Exceptions are the preferred failure-reporting mechanism because they have many advantages over return codes as an error-reporting mechanism. Return codes are part of a method's signature, and they often convey information other than error reporting. Whereas return codes are often the result of a computation, exceptions have one purpose only: to report failures. Because exceptions are class types and you can derive your own exception types, you can use exceptions to convey rich information about the failure.

Error return codes must be processed by the method caller. In contrast, thrown exceptions propagate up the call stack until a suitable catch clause is found. That gives developers the freedom to isolate error handling from error generation by many levels in the call stack. No error information is lost in this separation because of the richness of your exception classes.

Finally, exceptions aren't easily ignored. If a program does not contain a suitable catch clause, then a thrown exception terminates the application. You can't continue running after an unnoticed failure, something that would cause data corruption.

Using exceptions to report contract failures does not mean that any method that cannot do what you want must exit by throwing an exception. This doesn't mean that every failure is an exception. File.Exists() returns true if a file exists and false if it doesn't. File.Open() throws an exception if the file does not exist. The difference is simple: File.Exists() satisfies its contract by telling whether or not a file exists. The method succeeds even when the file does not exist. In contrast, File.Open() succeeds only when the file exists, the current user can read the file, and the current process can open the file for read access. In the first case, the method succeeds even when it tells you an answer you don't desire. In the second case, the method fails, and your program can't continue. An undesired answer from a method is different from a failure. The method succeeds; it gives you the information you requested.

This is a distinction that has an important influence on how you name your methods. Methods that perform actions should be named to clearly state the action that must be performed. In contrast, methods that test particular actions should be named to indicate the test action. What's more, you should provide test methods to minimize the need to use the exceptions as a flow-control mechanism. Processing exceptions takes more time than normal method calls. You should strive to create methods in your classes that enable users to test possible failure conditions before performing work. This practice lets them program more defensively, and you can still throw exceptions if developers choose not to test conditions before calling methods.

Whenever you write methods that may throw exceptions, you should also provide methods that test for the conditions that would cause those exceptions. Internally, you can use those test methods to check for any prerequisites before you continue, throwing the exception in those cases when it fails.

Suppose you have a worker class that fails when certain widgets aren't in place. If your API includes only the worker methods but does not provide an alternative path through the code, you'll encourage developers to write code like this:

```
// Don't promote this:
DoesWorkThatMightFail worker = new DoesWorkThatMightFail();
try
{
    worker.DoWork();
}
catch (WorkerException e)
{
    ReportErrorToUser(
        "Test Conditions Failed. Please check widgets");
}
```

Instead, you should add public methods that enable developers to explicitly check conditions before doing the work:

```
public class DoesWorkThatMightFail
{
    public bool TryDoWork()
    {
        if (!TestConditions())
            return false;
        Work(); // may throw on failures, but unlikely
        return true;
    }

    // Called only when failure means a catastrophic
    // problem.
```

```
public void DoWork()
{
    Work(); // will throw on failures.
}

private bool TestConditions()
{
    // body elided
    // Test conditions here
    return true;
}

private void Work()
{
    // elided
    // Do the work here
}
}
```

This pattern requires you to write four methods: two public methods and two private methods. The `TryDoWork()` method validates all input parameters and any internal object state necessary to perform the work. Then it calls the `Work()` method to perform the task. `DoWork()` simply calls the `Work()` method and lets any failures generate exceptions. This idiom is used in .NET because there are performance implications involved in throwing exceptions, and developers may wish to avoid those costs by testing conditions before allowing methods to fail.

Now, after adding the foregoing extra code, developers who wish to test conditions before performing the work can do so in a much cleaner way:

```
if (!worker.TryDoWork())
{
    ReportErrorToUser
        ("Test Conditions Failed. Please check widgets");
}
```

In practice, testing the preconditions enables more checking, such as parameter checking and internal state. You use this idiom most often when your worker class processes some form of untrusted input, such as user input, file input, or parameters from unknown code. Those failures have application-defined recovery scenarios and are rather common occurrences. You need to support them by using a control mechanism that does not involve exceptions. Notice that I have not made any claims that Work() won't throw any exceptions. Other, more unexpected failures may occur even after normal parameter checking. Those failures would be reported using exceptions, even if the user calls TryDoWork().

It is your responsibility to throw an exception whenever your method cannot complete its contract. Contract failures are always reported by throwing exceptions. Because exceptions should not be used as a general flow-control mechanism, you should also provide an alternative set of methods that enable developers to test for possible invalid conditions before calling methods that might throw exceptions.

Item 46: Utilize using and try/finally for Resource Cleanup

Types that use unmanaged system resources should be explicitly released using the Dispose() method of the IDisposable interface. The rules of the .NET environment make that the responsibility of the code that uses the type, not the responsibility of the type or the system. Therefore, anytime you use types that have a Dispose() method, it's your responsibility to release those resources by calling Dispose(). The best way to ensure that Dispose() always gets called is to utilize the using statement or a try/finally block.

All types that own unmanaged resources implement the IDisposable interface. In addition, they defensively create a finalizer for those times when you forget to dispose properly. If you forget to dispose of those items, those nonmemory resources are freed later, when finalizers get their chance to execute. All those objects then stay in memory that much longer, and your application becomes a slowly executing resource hog.

Luckily for you, the C# language designers knew that explicitly releasing resources would be a common task. They added keywords to the language that make it easy.

Suppose you wrote this code:

```
public void ExecuteCommand(string connString,
  string commandString)
```

```
{
    SqlConnection myConnection = new SqlConnection(
        connString);
    var mySqlCommand = new SqlCommand(commandString,
        myConnection);

    myConnection.Open();
    mySqlCommand.ExecuteNonQuery();
}
```

Two disposable objects are not properly cleaned up in this example: SqlConnection and SqlCommand. Both of these objects remain in memory until their finalizers are called. (Both of these classes inherit their finalizer from System.ComponentModel.Component.)

You fix this problem by calling Dispose when you are finished with the command and the connection:

```
public void ExecuteCommand(string connString,
    string commandString)
{
    var myConnection = new SqlConnection(
        connString);
    var mySqlCommand = new SqlCommand(commandString,
        myConnection);

    myConnection.Open();
    mySqlCommand.ExecuteNonQuery();

    mySqlCommand.Dispose();
    myConnection.Dispose();
}
```

That's fine, unless any exceptions get thrown while the SQL command executes. In that case, your calls to Dispose() never happen. The using statement ensures that Dispose() is called. You allocate an object inside a using statement, and the C# compiler generates a try/finally block around each object:

```
public void ExecuteCommand(string connString,
    string commandString)
{
    using (SqlConnection myConnection = new
        SqlConnection(connString))
```

```
    {
        using (SqlCommand mySqlCommand = new
            SqlCommand(commandString,
            myConnection))
        {
            myConnection.Open();
            mySqlCommand.ExecuteNonQuery();
        }
    }
}
```

Whenever you use one `Disposable` object in a function, the `using` clause is the simplest method to use to ensure that objects get disposed of properly. The `using` statement generates a `try/finally` block around the object being allocated. These two blocks generate exactly the same IL:

```
SqlConnection myConnection = null;

// Example Using clause:
using (myConnection = new SqlConnection(connString))
{
    myConnection.Open();
}


// example Try / Catch block:
try
{
    myConnection = new SqlConnection(connString);
    myConnection.Open();
}
finally
{
    myConnection.Dispose();
}
```

If you use the `using` statement with a variable of a type that does not support the `IDisposable` interface, the C# compiler generates an error. For example:

```
// Does not compile:
// String is sealed, and does not support IDisposable.
using (string msg = "This is a message")
    Console.WriteLine(msg);
```

The using statement works only if the compile-time type supports the IDisposable interface. You cannot use it with arbitrary objects:

```
// Does not compile.
// Object does not support IDisposable.
using (object obj = Factory.CreateResource())
    Console.WriteLine(obj.ToString());
```

A quick defensive as clause is all you need to safely dispose of objects that might or might not implement IDisposable:

```
// The correct fix.
// Object may or may not support IDisposable.
object obj = Factory.CreateResource();
using (obj as IDisposable)
    Console.WriteLine(obj.ToString());
```

If obj implements IDisposable, the using statement generates the cleanup code. If not, the using statement degenerates to using(null), which is safe but doesn't do anything. If you're not sure whether you should wrap an object in a using block, err on the side of safety: Assume that it does and wrap it in the using clause shown earlier.

That covers the simple case: Whenever you use one disposable object that is local to a method, wrap that one object in a using statement. Now you can look at a few more-complicated usages. Two different objects need to be disposed of in that first example: the connection and the command. My example creates two different using statements, one wrapping each of the two objects that need to be disposed of. Each using statement generates a different try/finally block. In effect, you have written this construct:

```
public void ExecuteCommand(string connString,
    string commandString)
{
    SqlConnection myConnection = null;
    SqlCommand mySqlCommand = null;
    try
    {
        myConnection = new SqlConnection(connString);
        try
        {
            mySqlCommand = new SqlCommand
                (commandString, myConnection);
```

```
            myConnection.Open();
            mySqlCommand.ExecuteNonQuery();
        }
        finally
        {
            if (mySqlCommand != null)
                mySqlCommand.Dispose();
        }
    }
    finally
    {
        if (myConnection != null)
            myConnection.Dispose();
    }
}
```

Every `using` statement creates a new nested `try/finally` block. Thankfully, it's rare that you'll allocate two different objects that both implement `IDisposable` in one method. That being the case, it's fine to leave it as is, because it does work. However, I find that an ugly construct, so when I allocate multiple objects that implement `IDisposable`, I prefer to write my own `try/finally` blocks:

```
public void ExecuteCommand(string connString,
    string commandString)
{
    SqlConnection myConnection = null;
    SqlCommand mySqlCommand = null;
    try
    {
        myConnection = new SqlConnection(connString);
        mySqlCommand = new SqlCommand(commandString,
            myConnection);

        myConnection.Open();
        mySqlCommand.ExecuteNonQuery();
    }
    finally
    {
        if (mySqlCommand != null)
            mySqlCommand.Dispose();
```

```
        if (myConnection != null)
            myConnection.Dispose();
    }
}
```

One reason to just leave well enough alone is that you can easily get too cute and try to build one `using` clause with `as` statements:

```
public void ExecuteCommand(string connString,
  string commandString)
{
    // Bad idea. Potential resource leak lurks!
    SqlConnection myConnection =
      new SqlConnection(connString);
    SqlCommand mySqlCommand = new SqlCommand
        (commandString, myConnection);
    using (myConnection as IDisposable)
    using (mySqlCommand as IDisposable)
    {
        myConnection.Open();
        mySqlCommand.ExecuteNonQuery();
    }
}
```

It looks cleaner, but it has a subtle bug. The `SqlConnection` object never gets disposed of if the `SqlCommand()` constructor throws an exception. The object referenced by `myConnection` has already been created, but the code has not entered the `using` block when the `SqlCommand` constructor executes. Without the constructor inside the `using` block, the call to `Dispose` gets skipped. You must make sure that any objects that implement `IDisposable` are allocated inside the scope of a `using` block or a `try` block. Otherwise, resource leaks can occur.

So far, you've handled the two most obvious cases. Whenever you allocate one disposable object in a method, the `using` statement is the best way to ensure that the resources you've allocated are freed in all cases. When you allocate multiple objects in the same method, create multiple `using` blocks or write your own single `try/finally` block.

There is one more nuance to freeing disposable objects. Some types support both a `Dispose` method and a `Close` method to free resources. `SqlConnection` is one of those classes. You could close `SqlConnection` like this:

```
public void ExecuteCommand(string connString,
    string commandString)
{
    SqlConnection myConnection = null;
    try
    {
        myConnection = new SqlConnection(connString);
        SqlCommand mySqlCommand = new SqlCommand
            (commandString, myConnection);

        myConnection.Open();
        mySqlCommand.ExecuteNonQuery();
    }
    finally
    {
        if (myConnection != null)
            myConnection.Close();
    }
}
```

This version does close the connection, but that's not exactly the same as disposing of it. The Dispose method does more than free resources: It also notifies the garbage collector that the object no longer needs to be finalized. Dispose calls GC.SuppressFinalize(). Close typically does not. As a result, the object remains in the finalization queue, even though finalization is not needed. If you have the choice, Dispose() is better than Close(). You can read all the gory details in Item 17.

Dispose() does not remove objects from memory. It is a hook to let objects release unmanaged resources. That means you can get into trouble by disposing of objects that are still in use. The examples above use SQLConnection. The SQLConnection's Dispose() method closes the connection to the database. After you dispose of the connection, the SQLConnection object is still in memory, but it is no longer connected to a database. It's in memory, but it's not useful. Do not dispose of objects that are still being referenced elsewhere in your program.

In some ways, resource management can be more difficult in C# than it was in C++. You can't rely on deterministic finalization to clean up every resource you use. But a garbage-collected environment really is much simpler for you. The vast majority of the types you make use of do not implement IDisposable. A small percentage of the.NET Framework classes implement `IDisposable`. When you use the ones that do implement `IDisposable`, remember to dispose of them in all cases. You should wrap those objects in `using` clauses or `try/finally` blocks. Whichever you use, make sure that objects get disposed of properly all the time, every time.

Item 47: Create Complete Application-Specific Exception Classes

Exceptions are the mechanism of reporting errors that might be handled at a location far removed from the location where the error occurred. All the information about the error's cause must be contained in the exception object. Along the way, you might want to translate a low-level error to more of an application-specific error, without losing any information about the original error. You need to be very thoughtful when you create your own specific exception classes in your C# applications.

The first step is to understand when and why to create new exception classes, and how to construct informative exception hierarchies. When developers using your libraries write `catch` clauses, they differentiate actions based on the specific runtime type of the exception. Each different exception class can have a different set of actions taken:

```
try
{
    Foo();
    Bar();
}
catch (MyFirstApplicationException e1)
{
    FixProblem(e1);
}
catch (AnotherApplicationException e2)
{
    ReportErrorAndContinue(e2);
}
catch (YetAnotherApplicationException e3)
{
    ReportErrorAndShutdown(e3);
}
```

```
catch (Exception e)
{
    ReportGenericError(e);
    throw;
}
finally
{
    CleanupResources();
}
```

Different `catch` clauses can exist for different runtime types of exceptions. You, as an application author, must create or use different exception classes when `catch` clauses might take different actions. Note that every exception above is handled in a different way. Developers want to provide different `catch` clauses for different exception classes only when the handling is different. Otherwise, it's just extra work. Therefore, you should consider creating different exception classes only when you believe developers will take different actions for the problems that cause the exception. If you don't, your users are left with only unappealing options. You can punt and terminate the application whenever an exception gets thrown. That's certainly less work, but it won't win kudos from users. Or, they can reach into the exception to try to determine whether the error can be corrected:

```
private static void SampleTwo()
{
    try
    {
        Foo();
        Bar();
    }
    catch (Exception e)
    {
        switch (e.TargetSite.Name)
        {
            case "Foo":
                FixProblem(e);
                break;
            case "Bar":
                ReportErrorAndContinue(e);
                break;
```

```
        // some routine called by Foo or Bar:
        default:
            ReportErrorAndShutdown(e);
            throw;
    }
  }
  finally
  {
      CleanupResources();
  }
}
```

That's far less appealing than using multiple `catch` clauses. It's very brittle code: If you change the name of a routine, it's broken. If you move the error-generating calls into a shared utility function, it's broken. The deeper into the call stack an exception is generated, the more fragile this kind of construct becomes.

Before going any deeper into this topic, let me add two disclaimers. First, exceptions are not for every error condition you encounter. There are no firm guidelines, but I prefer throwing exceptions for error conditions that cause long-lasting problems if they are not handled or reported immediately. For example, data integrity errors in a database should generate an exception. The problem only gets bigger if it is ignored. Failure to correctly write the user's window location preferences is not likely to cause far-reaching consequences. A return code indicating the failure is sufficient.

Second, writing a `throw` statement does not mean it's time to create a new exception class. My recommendation to create more rather than fewer exception classes comes from normal human nature: People seem to gravitate to overusing `System.Exception` anytime they throw an exception. That provides the least amount of helpful information to the calling code. Instead, think through and create the necessary exception classes to enable calling code to understand the cause and provide the best chance of recovery.

I'll say it again: The reason for different exception classes—in fact, the only reason—is to make it easier to take different actions when developers using your API write `catch` handlers. Look for those error conditions that might be candidates for some kind of recovery action and create specific exception classes to handle those actions. Can your application recover from missing files and directories? Can it recover from inadequate security privileges? What about missing network resources? Create new exception classes when you encounter errors that might lead to different actions and recovery mechanisms.

So now you are creating your own exception classes. You do have very specific responsibilities when you create a new exception class. Your exception class must end in `Exception`. You should always derive your exception classes from the `System.Exception` class, or some other appropriate exception class. You will rarely add capabilities to this base class. The purpose of different exception classes is to have the capability to differentiate the causes of errors in `catch` clauses. Tools like Visual Studio or other editors contain templates that make it easy to create a new exception class.

But don't take anything away from the exception classes you create, either. The `Exception` class contains four constructors:

```
// Default constructor
public Exception();


// Create with a message.
public Exception(string);


// Create with a message and an inner exception.
public Exception(string, Exception);


// Create from an input stream.
protected Exception(
    SerializationInfo, StreamingContext);
```

When you create a new exception class, create all four of these constructors. Notice that the last constructor implies that your exception class must be serializable. Different situations call for different methods of constructing exceptions. (If you choose to derive from a different exception class, you should include all the appropriate constructors from that particular base class.) You delegate the work to the base class implementation:

```
[Serializable]
public class MyAssemblyException :
  Exception
{
    public MyAssemblyException() :
        base()
    {
    }
```

```
    public MyAssemblyException(string s) :
        base(s)
    {
    }

    public MyAssemblyException(string s,
      Exception e) :
        base(s, e)
    {
    }

    // May not be supported on all platforms in .NET Core
    protected MyAssemblyException(
      SerializationInfo info, StreamingContext cxt) :
        base(info, cxt)
    {
    }
}
```

The constructors that take an exception parameter deserve a bit more discussion. Sometimes, one of the libraries you use generates an exception. The code that called your library will get minimal information about the possible corrective actions when you simply pass on the exceptions from the utilities you use:

```
public double DoSomeWork()
{
    // This might throw an exception defined
    // in the third-party library:
    return ThirdPartyLibrary.ImportantRoutine();
}
```

You should provide your own library's information when you generate the exception. Throw your own specific exception and include the original exception as its InnerException property. You can provide as much extra information as you can generate:

```
public double DoSomeWork()
{
    try
    {
        // This might throw an exception defined
        // in the third-party library:
```

```
        return ThirdPartyLibrary.ImportantRoutine();
    }
    catch (ThirdPartyException e)
    {
        var msg =
         $"Problem with {ToString()} using library";
        throw new DoingSomeWorkException(msg, e);
    }
}
```

This new version creates more information at the point where the problem is generated. As long as you have created a proper ToString() method, you've created an exception that describes the complete state of the object that generated the problem. More than that, the inner exception shows the root cause of the problem: something in the third-party library you used.

This technique is called **exception translation**, translating a low-level exception into a higher-level exception that provides more context about the error. The more information you generate when an error occurs, the easier it will be for users to diagnose and possibly correct the error. By creating your own exception types, you can translate low-level generic problems into specific exceptions that contain all the application-specific information that you need to fully diagnose and possibly correct the problem.

Your application will throw exceptions—ideally not often, but it will happen. If you don't do anything specific, your application will generate the default .NET Framework exceptions whenever something goes wrong in the methods you call on the core framework. Providing more detailed information will go a long way toward enabling you and your users to diagnose and possibly correct errors in the field. You create different exception classes when different corrective actions are possible and only when different actions are possible. You create full-featured exception classes by providing all the constructors that the base exception class supports. You use the InnerException property to carry along all the error information generated by lower-level error conditions.

Item 48: Prefer the Strong Exception Guarantee

When you throw an exception, you've introduced a disruptive event into the application. Control flow has been compromised. Expected actions did not occur. Worse, you've left the cleanup operation to the programmer writing the code that eventually catches the exception. The actions available when you catch exceptions are directly related to how well you manage program state when an exception gets thrown. Thankfully, the C# community does not need to create its own strategies for exception safety; the C++ community did all the hard work for us. Starting with Tom Cargill's article "Exception Handling: A False Sense of Security," and continuing with writings by Dave Abrahams, Herb Sutter, Scott Meyers, Matt Austern, and Greg Colvin, the C++ community developed a series of best practices that we can adapt to C# applications. The discussions on exception handling occurred over the course of six years, from 1994 to 2000. They discussed, debated, and examined many twists on a difficult problem. We should leverage all that hard work in C#.

Dave Abrahams defined three exception-safe guarantees: the basic guarantee, the strong guarantee, and the no-throw guarantee. Herb Sutter discussed these guarantees in his book *Exceptional C++* (Addison-Wesley, 2000). The basic guarantee states that no resources are leaked and all objects are in a valid state after your exception leaves the function emitting it. That means after any `finally` clauses have run in the method that throws the exception. The strong exception guarantee builds on the basic guarantee and adds that if an exception occurs, the program state did not change. The no-throw guarantee states that an operation never fails, from which it follows that a method does not ever throw exceptions. The strong exception guarantee provides the best tradeoff between recovering from exceptions and simplifying exception handling.

You get some help on the basic guarantee from the .NET CLR. The environment handles memory management. The only way you can leak resources due to exceptions is to throw an exception while you own a resource that implements `IDisposable`. Item 17 explains how to avoid leaking resources in the face of exceptions. But that's only part of the story. You are still responsible for ensuring that your object's state is valid. Suppose your type caches the size of a collection, along with the collection. You'd need to ensure that the size matches the actual storage after an `Add()` operation throws an exception. There are countless actions your application may perform that if only partially completed would leave your application in an invalid state. These cases are harder to handle, because there are fewer standard idioms for automatic support. Many of these issues can best be solved by adhering to the strong guarantee.

The strong guarantee states that if an operation terminates because of an exception, program state remains unchanged. Either an operation completes or it does not modify program state; there is no middle ground. The advantage of the strong guarantee is that you can more easily continue execution after catching an exception when the strong guarantee is followed. Anytime you catch an exception, whatever operation was attempted did not occur. It did not start, and it did not make changes. The state of the program is as though you did not start the action.

Many of the recommendations I made earlier will help ensure that you meet the strong exception guarantee. Data elements that your program uses should be stored in immutable value types. You can also use the functional programming style, such as with LINQ queries. That programming style automatically follows the strong exception guarantee.

Sometimes, you can't use functional programming styles. If you combine those defensive copies with swap techniques, any modification to program state can easily take place after performing any operation that might throw an exception. The general guideline is to perform any data modifications in the following manner:

1. Make defensive copies of data that will be modified.
2. Perform any modifications to these defensive copies of the data. This includes any operations that might throw an exception.
3. Swap the temporary copies back to the original. This operation cannot throw an exception.

These guidelines are easier to follow when you create immutable data structures for your storage types.

As an example, the following code updates an employee's title and pay using defensive copy:

```csharp
public void PhysicalMove(string title, decimal newPay)
{
    // Payroll data is a struct:
    // ctor will throw if fields aren't valid.
    PayrollData d = new PayrollData(title, newPay,
        this.payrollData.DateOfHire);

    // if d was constructed properly, swap:
    this.payrollData = d;
}
```

Sometimes the strong guarantee is just too inefficient to support, and sometimes you cannot support the strong guarantee without introducing subtle bugs. The first and simplest case is looping constructs. When the code inside a loop modifies the state of the program and might throw an exception, you are faced with a tough choice: You can either create a defensive copy of all the objects used in the loop, or you can lower your expectations and support only the basic exception guarantee. There are no hard-and-fast rules, but copying heap-allocated objects in a managed environment is not as expensive as it was in native environments. A lot of time has been spent optimizing memory management in .NET. I prefer to support the strong exception guarantee whenever possible, even if it means copying a large container: The ability to recover from errors outweighs the small performance gain from avoiding the copy. In special cases, it doesn't make sense to create the copy. If any exceptions would result in terminating the program anyway, it makes no sense to worry about the strong exception guarantee. The larger concern is that swapping reference types can lead to program errors. Consider this example:

```
private List<PayrollData> data;
public IList<PayrollData> MyCollection
{
    get { return data; }
}

public void UpdateData()
{
    // Unreliable operation might fail:
    var temp = UnreliableOperation();

    // This operation will only happen if
    // UnreliableOperation does not throw an
    // exception.
    data = temp;
}
```

This looks like a great use of the defensive copy mechanism. You've created a copy of your data. Then you grab new data from somewhere to fill the temporary data. Finally, you swap the temporary storage back. It looks great. If anything goes wrong while trying to retrieve the data, you have not made any changes.

There's only one problem: It doesn't work. The MyCollection property returns a reference to the data object. All the clients of this class are left holding references to the original `List<>` after you call `UpdateData`. They are looking at the old view of the data. The swap trick does not work for reference types—it works only for value types. To fix this, you need to replace the data in the current reference object and ensure that you do it in such a way that it can never throw an exception. That is difficult, because it is two different atomic operations: removing all the existing objects in the collection and adding all the new objects. You might consider that the risk is small of removing and adding the new items:

```
private List<PayrollData> data;
public IList<PayrollData> MyCollection
{
    get
    {
        return data;
    }
}


public void UpdateData()
{
    // Unreliable operation might fail:
    var temp = UnreliableOperation();

    // These operations will only happen if
    // UnreliableOperation does not throw an
    // exception.
    data.Clear();
    foreach (var item in temp)
        data.Add(item);
}
```

That is a reasonable, but not a bulletproof, solution. I mention it because "reasonable" is often the bar you need. However, when you do need bulletproof, you need to do more work. The envelope-letter pattern will hide the internal swapping in an object that enables you to make the swap safely.

The envelope-letter pattern hides the implementation (letter) inside a wrapper (envelope) that you share with public clients of your code. In this example, you create a class that wraps the collection and implements the `IList<PayrollData>`. That class contains the `List<PayrollData>` and exposes all its methods to class clients.

Your class now works with the `Envelope` class to handle its internal data:

```
private Envelope data;
public IList<PayrollData> MyCollection
{
    get
    {
        return data;
    }
}


public void UpdateData()
{
    data.SafeUpdate(UnreliableOperation());
}
```

The `Envelope` class implements the `IList` by forwarding every request to the contained `List<PayrollData>`:

```
public class Envelope : IList<PayrollData>
{
    private List<PayrollData> data = new List<PayrollData>();

    public void SafeUpdate(IEnumerable<PayrollData> sourceList)
    {
        // make the copy:
        List<PayrollData> updates =
            new List<PayrollData>(sourceList.ToList());

        // swap:
        data = updates;
    }

    public PayrollData this[int index]
    {
        get { return data[index]; }
        set { data[index] = value; }
    }

    public int Count => data.Count;

    public bool IsReadOnly =>
        ((IList<PayrollData>)data).IsReadOnly;
```

```csharp
public void Add(PayrollData item) => data.Add(item);

public void Clear() => data.Clear();

public bool Contains(PayrollData item) =>
    data.Contains(item);

public void CopyTo(PayrollData[] array, int arrayIndex) =>
    data.CopyTo(array, arrayIndex);

public IEnumerator<PayrollData> GetEnumerator() =>
    data.GetEnumerator();

public int IndexOf(PayrollData item) =>
    data.IndexOf(item);

public void Insert(int index, PayrollData item) =>
    data.Insert(index, item);

public bool Remove(PayrollData item)
{
    return ((IList<PayrollData>)data).Remove(item);
}

public void RemoveAt(int index)
{
    ((IList<PayrollData>)data).RemoveAt(index);
}

IEnumerator IEnumerable.GetEnumerator() =>
    data.GetEnumerator();
}
```

There is a lot of boilerplate code to examine, and much of it is straightforward. However, there are a few important parts that you should examine with a bit more care. First, notice that a number of the members of the ILIst interface are implemented explicitly by the List<T> class. That is the reason for the casts included throughout many of the methods. Also, I've coded this based on the PayrollData type being a value type. If PayrollData were a reference type, this code would be a bit simpler. I made PayrollData a value type to demonstrate those differences. The type checks are based on PayrollData being a value type.

Of course, the point of this exercise was to create and implement the SafeUpdate method. Notice that it does essentially the same work that you did in place before. That guarantees that this code is safe, even in multithreaded applications. The swap cannot be interrupted.

In the general case, you cannot fix the problem of swapping reference types while still ensuring that all clients have the current copy of the object. Swapping works for value types only. That should be sufficient.

Last, and most stringent, is the no-throw guarantee. The no-throw guarantee is pretty much what it sounds like: A method satisfies the no-throw guarantee if it is guaranteed to always run to completion and never let an exception leave a method. This just isn't practical for all routines in large programs. However, in a few locations, methods must enforce the no-throw guarantee. Finalizers and Dispose methods must not throw exceptions. In both cases, throwing an exception can cause more problems than any alternative. In the case of a finalizer, throwing an exception terminates the program without further cleanup. Wrapping a large method in a try/catch block and swallowing all exceptions is how you achieve this no-throw guarantee. Most methods that must satisfy the no-throw guarantee, such as Dispose() and Finalize(), have limited responsibilities. Therefore, you should be able to write these methods so that they satisfy the no-throw guarantee by writing defensive code.

In the case of a Dispose method throwing an exception, the system might now have two exceptions running through the system. The .NET environment loses the first exception and throws the new exception. You can't catch the initial exception anywhere in your program; it was eaten by the system. This greatly complicates your error handling. How can you recover from an error you don't see?

You should never throw in the when clause of an exception filter. The new exception becomes the active exception, and any information about the original exception cannot be retrieved.

The last location for the no-throw guarantee is in delegate targets. When a delegate target throws an exception, none of the other delegate targets gets called from the same multicast delegate. The only way around this is to ensure that you do not throw any exceptions from a delegate target. Let's state that again: Delegate targets (including event handlers) should not throw exceptions. Doing so means that the code raising the event cannot participate in the strong exception guarantee. But here I'm going to modify that advice. Item 7 showed how you can invoke delegates so that you can recover from exceptions. Not everyone does, though, so you should avoid throwing exceptions in delegate handlers. Just because you don't throw exceptions in delegates does not mean that others follow that advice; do not rely on the no-throw guarantee for your own delegate invocations. It's that defensive programming: You should do the best you can because other programmers might do the worst they can.

Exceptions introduce serious changes to the control flow of an application. In the worst case, anything could have happened—or not happened. The only way to know what has and hasn't changed when an exception is thrown is to enforce the strong exception guarantee. Then an operation either completes or does not make any changes. Finalizers, `Dispose()`, when clauses, and delegate targets are special cases and should complete without allowing exceptions to escape under any circumstances. As a last word, watch carefully when swapping reference types; it can introduce numerous subtle bugs.

Item 49: Prefer Exception Filters to `catch` and `re-throw`

In a standard `catch` clause, you catch exceptions based on the type of the exception. Nothing else matters. Any logic that applies to program state, object state, or properties of the exception must be handled in the `catch` clause. Those limitations can result in code that catches an exception and then, after further analysis, re-throws the same exception.

That habit makes later analysis more difficult. It also imposes additional runtime costs on your application. You can better support later analysis and avoid those costs by using exception filters as a means of managing how you catch and process exceptions. For those reasons, you should develop the habit of using exception filters rather than conditional logic in `catch` clauses.

The differences in the compiler-generated code are the greatest justification for building the habit of using exception filters instead of catch and re-throw. An exception filter is an expression on your `catch` clause, following the when keyword, that limits when the `catch` clause handles an exception of a given type:

```
var retryCount = 0;
var dataString = default(String);

while (dataString == null)
{
    try
```

```
    {
        dataString = MakeWebRequest();
    }
    catch (TimeoutException e) when(retryCount++ < 3)
    {
        WriteLine("Operation timed out. Trying again");
        // pause before trying again.
        Task.Delay(1000 * retryCount);
    }
}
```

The compiler generates code that evaluates the exception filter before any stack unwinding occurs. The original exception location is known. All information on the call stack, including the value of any local variables, is still known. If the expression evaluates to `false`, the runtime continues to search up the call stack for a matching `catch` expression that can process the exception. As the runtime continues to search up the call stack, none of the program state is disturbed.

Contrast that processing with the processing when you catch an exception, then determine that you can't address the problem and re-throw the exception:

```
var retryCount = 0;
var dataString = default(String);

while (dataString == null)
{
    try
    {
        dataString = MakeWebRequest();
    }
    catch (TimeoutException e)
    {
        if (retryCount++ < 3)
        {
            WriteLine("Timed out. Trying again");
            // pause before trying again.
            Task.Delay(1000 * retryCount);
        }
        else
            throw;
    }
```

}

Using that code, the runtime finds a `catch` clause that can process the exception. As soon as the runtime finds that `catch` clause, it begins unwinding the stack. The majority of local variables that were declared in methods being unwound no longer have reachable roots. (Variables that have been closed over may be accessible if the closure is reachable.) Values important for diagnosing the root cause may no longer be valid. State has been lost.

Inside the `catch` clause, your code determines that you can't recover from this error. So, you re-throw the original exception. The code above uses the correct syntax to re-throw. Don't throw the exception explicitly; that creates a new exception object and creates a new origin of the throw point.

The differences between these two execution paths manifest themselves in very different diagnostic and debugging experiences. The second experience loses the values of all local variables. It also loses information about the course of execution at the time of the problem. Any diagnostic trace data created will contain all the program state information that can help you diagnose the original cause of the exception when you use exception filters. Some of that information will be lost when the stack is unwound when you use the first method. Examine these three methods where I've added comments on the reported call stack in the exception generated by calling `TreeOfErrors()`:

```
static void TreeOfErrors()
{
    try
    {
        SingleBadThing();
    }
    catch (RecoverableException e)
    {
        throw; // reported on Call Stack
    }
}
static void TreeOfErrorsTwo()
{
    try
    {
        SingleBadThing(); // reported on Call Stack
```

```
    }
    catch (RecoverableException e) when (false)
    {
        WriteLine("Can't happen");
    }
}
```

When you use the throw syntax, the call stack reports the location of throw as the location on the call stack. That's because execution entered the catch clause, and the exception is re-thrown. The line above in the try clause has been lost. However, when you use an exception filter, the call stack reports the location of the method call that resulted in an exception being thrown. I've trimmed the example code above to the smallest possible sample, so it's easy to determine where the exception was generated. In a larger application, it may be harder to determine where the exception was generated.

Using exception filters also has a positive effect on program performance. The .NET CLR has been optimized so that the presence of try/catch blocks where the catch clause is not entered have minimal effect on runtime performance. However, the stack unwinding and entering catch clauses does have a large runtime impact. Exception filters, which avoid stack unwinding and entering catch clauses when an exception cannot be processed, can improve performance. It certainly won't make performance worse.

There are a number of practices that you likely have adopted that should change. In some cases, you may find that some property of an exception dictates when you can or can't process an exception. One of the most common scenarios involves task-based asynchronous programming. A task enters the faulted state when some code it has executed has thrown an exception. A task may have started more than one child task, and therefore a task may fault due to multiple exceptions. To handle these cases consistently, the Exception property on the Task class is an AggregateException. You may need to look at the exception(s) that are stored in the InnerExceptions property to determine if your Task handling code can process the exception.

Another example would be the COMException class. It contains an HResult property that contains the COM HRESULT that was generated from an interop call. There may be HRESULT values where you can handle the exception, and others where you cannot. An exception filter can manage that logic without entering a catch clause.

As a final example, the HTTPException class has a GetHttpCode() method that returns the HTTP response code. You may be able to take corrective action for some error codes (such as a 301 redirect) but not others (such as a 404 not found). An exception filter can ensure that you process only those errors that you can correct.

The addition of exception filters means that you can structure your exception-handling code so that catch clauses are executed only when you can fully manage an exception. You'll save more information about any errors that occur. Your programs can run faster in some situations. When you need more information about an error than the type of the exception, add exception filters to determine if you can recover from an exception before entering a catch clause.

Item 50: Leverage Side Effects in Exception Filters

It may seem like an oxymoron to build an exception filter that always returns false, but there are good reasons to watch all exceptions as they are generated. As you read in Item 49 earlier in this chapter, exception filters execute as part of the stack walk while the runtime is searching for an applicable catch clause. That means they execute before the stack has been unwound.

Let's start with a canonical example. Production programs generally log all unhandled exceptions somewhere. They may send that information to a central location. They may log information locally. But one way or another, well-written programs create a record of anything that goes wrong.

For example, consider this method:

```
public static bool ConsoleLogException(Exception e)
{
    var oldColor = Console.ForegroundColor;
    Console.ForegroundColor = ConsoleColor.Red;
    WriteLine("Error: {0}", e);
    Console.ForegroundColor = oldColor;
    return false;
}
```

It writes out information about any exception to the console. This can be sprinkled anywhere in your code where you want to generate log information. Add a try/catch clause, and apply this false-returning exception filter:

```
try
{
```

```
        data = MakeWebRequest();
}
catch (Exception e) when(ConsoleLogException(e)) { }
catch (TimeoutException e) when(failures++ < 10)
{
        WriteLine("Timeout error: trying again");
}
```

There are a few important idioms to see in the example above. The exception filter must always return `false`. It can never return `true`, or your log method would stop any propagation of the exception. Second, notice that the `catch` clause catches all exceptions by catching the base `Exception` class. That enables logging of all exceptions. Even though it catches the base `Exception` class, this exception filter can be first in the list of `catch` clauses. This `catch` clause never processes the exception (remember that the filter always returns `false`), so the runtime continues to search for an applicable `catch` clause. This idiom is also one of very few locations where writing a `catch` clause to catch all exceptions is an acceptable practice.

Following those practices means that you can add this `catch` clause anywhere in your code without impacting execution. You can add new `try`/`catch` clauses anywhere. You can add a `catch (Exception e) when log(e) {}` at the beginning of any existing `catch` clause, or before a `try`/`finally` block.

You can consider specialized logging at different locations in your code. The examples shown log all exceptions, but you can apply the same technique to any more specific exception type. Because the logging exception filter always returns `false`, you can simply modify the exception type being logged.

Another option is to place the logging `catch` clause as the last `catch` clause. That would enable logging only those exceptions that are not processed in a given `catch` clause.

```
try
{
        data = MakeWebRequest();
}
catch (TimeoutException e) when(failures++ < 10)
{
        WriteLine("Timeout error: trying again");
}
catch (Exception e) when(ConsoleLogException(e)) { }
```

Another advantage to this method of logging items is that you can extend it to libraries and packages without modifying the flow of execution. In traditional scenarios, logging would be added only at the application level, and only in top-level methods. That would capture those exceptions that were not handled by any code at runtime. The other option is to create a log message at every point where an exception is about to be thrown in your application code. That enables logging when your code generates the exception but does not enable any messages when the exception is generated by underlying code. Neither of these strategies makes it easy to generate log information from libraries and packages. Catching and re-throwing exceptions makes the debugging cycle harder for your users (see Item 49). Library authors can use this idiom to log exceptions at each public API for the library. With this idiom, the stack information is not modified by the library log mechanism.

Logging isn't the only use for exception filters that aren't meant to handle any exceptions. You can also use an exception filter to ensure that a `catch` clause does not process any exceptions when you are running your application in a debugger session:

```
try
{
    data = MakeWebRequest();
}
catch (Exception e) when(ConsoleLogException(e)) { }
catch (TimeoutException e) when((failures++ < 10) &&
    (!System.Diagnostics.Debugger.IsAttached))
{
    WriteLine("Timeout error: trying again");
```

This exception filter prevents the `catch` clause from processing any exceptions when a debugger is attached. When you're not running under a debugger, the exception filter passes, and the exception clause executes.

Understand that this is affected by the runtime environment, not the build settings. The `Debugger.IsAttached` property returns `true` only when a debugger is attached to the process. It is not affected by a debug or a release build setting. The advantage of this setting is that when running under a debugger, your `catch` clauses will not be entered. If applied throughout your codebase, your application won't catch any exceptions when running under a debugger. If you set the debugger to stop on all unhandled exceptions, the program will break when running with a debugger attached whenever an exception is thrown. This idiom does not affect your application in any other environment. It is a great tool to find out the root cause of exceptions in a large codebase.

Exception filters with side effects are a great way to observe what's happening when exceptions are thrown somewhere in your code. In a large codebase, these tools can have a positive impact on finding the root cause of an exception being thrown by a misbehaving application. And once the source is found, fixing it is that much easier.

Index